™

References for the Rest of Us! ®

BESTSELLING BOOK SERIES

Are you intimidated and confused by computers? Do you find that traditional manuals are overloaded with technical details you'll never use? Do your friends and family always call you to fix simple problems on their PCs? Then the ...*For Dummies*® computer book series from IDG Books Worldwide is for you.

...*For Dummies* books are written for those frustrated computer users who know they aren't really dumb but find that PC hardware, software, and indeed the unique vocabulary of computing make them feel helpless. ...*For Dummies* books use a lighthearted approach, a down-to-earth style, and even cartoons and humorous icons to dispel computer novices' fears and build their confidence. Lighthearted but not lightweight, these books are a perfect survival guide for anyone forced to use a computer.

"I like my copy so much I told friends; now they bought copies."

— Irene C., Orwell, Ohio

"Quick, concise, nontechnical, and humorous."

— Jay A., Elburn, Illinois

"Thanks, I needed this book. Now I can sleep at night."

— Robin F., British Columbia, Canada

Already, millions of satisfied readers agree. They have made ...*For Dummies* books the #1 introductory level computer book series and have written asking for more. So, if you're looking for the most fun and easy way to learn about computers, look to ...*For Dummies* books to give you a helping hand.

IDG
BOOKS
WORLDWIDE

1/99

ACCESS 97 PROGRAMMING FOR WINDOWS® FOR DUMMIES®

by Rob Krumm

IDG Books Worldwide, Inc.
An International Data Group Company

Foster City, CA ♦ Chicago, IL ♦ Indianapolis, IN ♦ New York, NY

Access 97 Programming For Windows® For Dummies®

Published by
IDG Books Worldwide, Inc.
An International Data Group Company
919 E. Hillsdale Blvd.
Suite 400
Foster City, CA 94404
www.idgbooks.com (IDG Books Worldwide Web site)
www.dummies.com (Dummies Press Web site)

Library of Congress Catalog Card No.: 96-76243

ISBN: 1-56884-696-7

Printed in the United States of America

10 9 8 7 6 5 4 3

1B/QS/QU/ZZ/IN

Distributed in the United States by IDG Books Worldwide, Inc.

Distributed by CDG Books Canada Inc. for Canada; by Transworld Publishers Limited in the United Kingdom; by IDG Norge Books for Norway; by IDG Sweden Books for Sweden; by Woodslane Pty. Ltd. for Australia; by Woodslane (NZ) Ltd. for New Zealand; by TransQuest Publishers Pte Ltd. for Singapore, Malaysia, Thailand, Indonesia, and Hong Kong; by ICG Muse, Inc. for Japan; by Norma Comunicaciones S.A. for Colombia; by Intersoft for South Africa; by Le Monde en Tique for France; by International Thomson Publishing for Germany, Austria and Switzerland; by Distribuidora Cuspide for Argentina; by Livraria Cultura for Brazil; by Ediciones ZETA S.C.R. Ltda. for Peru; by WS Computer Publishing Corporation, Inc., for the Philippines; by Contemporanea de Ediciones for Venezuela; by Express Computer Distributors for the Caribbean and West Indies; by Micronesia Media Distributor, Inc. for Micronesia; by Grupo Editorial Norma S.A. for Guatemala; by Chips Computadoras S.A. de C.V. for Mexico; by Editorial Norma de Panama S.A. for Panama; by American Bookshops for Finland. Authorized Sales Agent: Anthony Rudkin Associates for the Middle East and North Africa.

For general information on IDG Books Worldwide's books in the U.S., please call our Consumer Customer Service department at 800-762-2974. For reseller information, including discounts and premium sales, please call our Reseller Customer Service department at 800-434-3422.

For information on where to purchase IDG Books Worldwide's books outside the U.S., please contact our International Sales department at 317-596-5530 or fax 317-596-5692.

For consumer information on foreign language translations, please contact our Customer Service department at 1-800-434-3422, fax 317-596-5692, or e-mail rights@idgbooks.com.

For information on licensing foreign or domestic rights, please phone +1-650-655-3109.

For sales inquiries and special prices for bulk quantities, please contact our Sales department at 650-655-3200 or write to the address above.

For information on using IDG Books Worldwide's books in the classroom or for ordering examination copies, please contact our Educational Sales department at 800-434-2086 or fax 317-596-5499.

For press review copies, author interviews, or other publicity information, please contact our Public Relations department at 650-655-3000 or fax 650-655-3299.

For authorization to photocopy items for corporate, personal, or educational use, please contact Copyright Clearance Center, 222 Rosewood Drive, Danvers, MA 01923, or fax 978-750-4470.

is a registered trademark or trademark under exclusive license to IDG Books Worldwide, Inc. from International Data Group, Inc. in the United States and/or other countries.

About the Author

Rob Krumm has been using personal computers since 1979, when he was working as a teacher in Philadelphia. In 1981 he founded his own school in Walnut Creek, California, designed to teach people how to use personal computers. In 1983 he published *Understanding and Using dBase II,* the first of 47 books he has written on computers and software. He has also contributed to publications such as the *San Francisco Chronicle, PC World,* and *InfoWorld.* He is a Microsoft Certified Professional specializing in Microsoft Office and SQL Server. Rob teaches Computer Science courses part-time in the Contra Costa Community College system in California. He is also an occasional consultant for the International Foundation for Election Systems.

Rob can be reached at `robkrumm@pacbell.net`.

ABOUT IDG BOOKS WORLDWIDE

Welcome to the world of IDG Books Worldwide.

IDG Books Worldwide, Inc., is a subsidiary of International Data Group, the world's largest publisher of computer-related information and the leading global provider of information services on information technology. IDG was founded more than 30 years ago by Patrick J. McGovern and now employs more than 9,000 people worldwide. IDG publishes more than 290 computer publications in over 75 countries. More than 90 million people read one or more IDG publications each month.

Launched in 1990, IDG Books Worldwide is today the #1 publisher of best-selling computer books in the United States. We are proud to have received eight awards from the Computer Press Association in recognition of editorial excellence and three from Computer Currents' First Annual Readers' Choice Awards. Our best-selling ...*For Dummies*® series has more than 50 million copies in print with translations in 31 languages. IDG Books Worldwide, through a joint venture with IDG's Hi-Tech Beijing, became the first U.S. publisher to publish a computer book in the People's Republic of China. In record time, IDG Books Worldwide has become the first choice for millions of readers around the world who want to learn how to better manage their businesses.

Our mission is simple: Every one of our books is designed to bring extra value and skill-building instructions to the reader. Our books are written by experts who understand and care about our readers. The knowledge base of our editorial staff comes from years of experience in publishing, education, and journalism — experience we use to produce books to carry us into the new millennium. In short, we care about books, so we attract the best people. We devote special attention to details such as audience, interior design, use of icons, and illustrations. And because we use an efficient process of authoring, editing, and desktop publishing our books electronically, we can spend more time ensuring superior content and less time on the technicalities of making books.

You can count on our commitment to deliver high-quality books at competitive prices on topics you want to read about. At IDG Books Worldwide, we continue in the IDG tradition of delivering quality for more than 30 years. You'll find no better book on a subject than one from IDG Books Worldwide.

John Kilcullen
Chairman and CEO
IDG Books Worldwide, Inc.

Steven Berkowitz
President and Publisher
IDG Books Worldwide, Inc.

Eighth Annual
Computer Press
Awards ≥ 1992

Ninth Annual
Computer Press
Awards ≥ 1993

Tenth Annual
Computer Press
Awards ≥ 1994

Eleventh Annual
Computer Press
Awards ≥ 1995

IDG is the world's leading IT media, research and exposition company. Founded in 1964, IDG had 1997 revenues of $2.05 billion and has more than 9,000 employees worldwide. IDG offers the widest range of media options that reach IT buyers in 75 countries representing 95% of worldwide IT spending. IDG's diverse product and services portfolio spans six key areas including print publishing, online publishing, expositions and conferences, market research, education and training, and global marketing services. More than 90 million people read one or more of IDG's 290 magazines and newspapers, including IDG's leading global brands — Computerworld, PC World, Network World, Macworld and the Channel World family of publications. IDG Books Worldwide is one of the fastest-growing computer book publishers in the world, with more than 700 titles in 36 languages. The "...For Dummies®" series alone has more than 50 million copies in print. IDG offers online users the largest network of technology-specific Web sites around the world through IDG.net (http://www.idg.net), which comprises more than 225 targeted Web sites in 55 countries worldwide. International Data Corporation (IDC) is the world's largest provider of information technology data, analysis and consulting, with research centers in over 41 countries and more than 400 research analysts worldwide. IDG World Expo is a leading producer of more than 168 globally branded conferences and expositions in 35 countries including E3 (Electronic Entertainment Expo), Macworld Expo, ComNet, Windows World Expo, ICE (Internet Commerce Expo), Agenda, DEMO, and Spotlight. IDG's training subsidiary, ExecuTrain, is the world's largest computer training company, with more than 230 locations worldwide and 785 training courses. IDG Marketing Services helps industry-leading IT companies build international brand recognition by developing global integrated marketing programs via IDG's print, online and exposition products worldwide. Further information about the company can be found at www.idg.com.

1/24/99

Dedication

For Michael Perlman

Life is beautiful. Let the future generations cleanse it of all evil, oppression, and violence and enjoy it to the full.

— From the *Last Testament of Leon Trotsky*

We crave only reality.

— H.D. Thoreau

Publisher's Acknowledgments

We're proud of this book; please register your comments through our IDG Books Worldwide Online Registration Form located at http://my2cents.dummies.com.

Some of the people who helped bring this book to market include the following:

Acquisitions, Development, and Editorial

Project Editors: Patricia Yuu Pan,
  Jennifer Ehrlich

Acquisitions Editor: Gareth Hancock

Media Development Manager: Joyce Pepple

Copy Editor: William A. Barton

Technical Editors: Publication Services, Inc.,
  Jim McCarter

Editorial Managers: Kristin A. Cocks,
  Mary C. Corder

Editorial Assistant: Chris H. Collins

Production

Project Coordinator: Debbie Stailey

Layout and Graphics: Cameron Booker,
  Linda M. Boyer, Dominique DeFelice,
  Angela F. Hunckler, Todd Klemme,
  Jane E. Martin, Mark C. Owens,
  Anna Rohrer, Brent Savage

Proofreaders: Christine D. Berman,
  Joel K. Draper, Rachel Garvey,
  Nancy Price, Robert Springer, Karen York

Indexer: Lori Lathrop

Special Help: Kevin Spencer,
  Associate Technical Editor

General and Administrative

IDG Books Worldwide, Inc.: John Kilcullen, CEO; Steven Berkowitz, President and Publisher

IDG Books Technology Publishing: Brenda McLaughlin, Senior Vice President and
  Group Publisher

Dummies Technology Press and Dummies Editorial: Diane Graves Steele, Vice President and
  Associate Publisher; Mary Bednarek, Director of Acquisitions and Product Development;
  Kristin A. Cocks, Editorial Director

Dummies Trade Press: Kathleen A. Welton, Vice President and Publisher; Kevin Thornton,
  Acquisitions Manager

IDG Books Production for Dummies Press: Michael R. Britton, Vice President of Production
  and Creative Services; Cindy L. Phipps, Manager of Project Coordination, Production Proofreading, and Indexing; Kathie S. Schutte, Supervisor of Page Layout; Shelley Lea, Supervisor
  of Graphics and Design; Debbie J. Gates, Production Systems Specialist; Robert Springer,
  Supervisor of Proofreading; Debbie Stailey, Special Projects Coordinator; Tony Augsburger,
  Supervisor of Reprints and Bluelines

Dummies Packaging and Book Design: Patty Page, Manager, Promotions Marketing

◆

The publisher would like to give special thanks to Patrick J. McGovern,
without whom this book would not have been possible.

◆

Contents at a Glance

Cartoons at a Glance

By Rich Tennant

page 107

page 285

page 217

page 353

page 335

page 9

Fax: 978-546-7747 • E-mail: the5wave@tiac.net

Table of Contents

Introduction

● ●

Access 97 is a pleasure to use, but many of the really powerful features lie below the surface. To transform Access from just another application into a custom-made tool you need to gain control of Access by writing Access programs.

Even though you may never have composed anything more elaborate than a formula that adds two numbers together, you will be well on your way to transforming Access 97 into your own custom-designed database application by the time you finish this book.

Who Needs This Book

Databases are different. Most PC applications (word processing, spreadsheet, graphics) are stand-alone applications designed for personal productivity. When you accumulate data into a database it's only natural to share that information with a group of people who work together in harmony (more or less) toward a common goal (despite appearances to the contrary). In fact, the real value of the data surfaces when many different people apply the data in different ways.

Access 97 provides Windows users with a powerful, simple-to-use tool for storing and sharing that data. This book explains how you can use the programming language built right into Access to make Access fit the needs and preferences of your organization, how to avoid tedious repetitive tasks, and how to make Access more intelligent.

There are two big reasons why you should take advantage of Access programming.

- ✔ It is easier to teach Access about your business than it is to teach your colleagues about Access.
- ✔ Since you have already paid for the programming language when you bought Access, you may as well get your money's worth.

Another reason is that you will get quite a kick out of watching other people use the programs you created. Take my word for it.

About This Book

The purpose of this book is to get you to exercise the power of Access programming as quickly as possible. If you've never done any programming, you can approach the subject in two ways:

- **Scholarly.** This approach begins with a chapter or two explaining the theory, terminology, philosophy, and conceptual framework of the programming language before you go on to actually doing something.

- **Total Immersion.** The other approach is to just jump in and start doing things and watch how the program reacts to your instructions. You pick up the theory, terminology, philosophy, and concepts along the way.

No big shock to say that in a ...*For Dummies* book the winner is Total Immersion. By the second chapter you will have already written your first program, and it will do a lot more than say "Hello World." The examples in this book deal with the same type of everyday information you find in any business, and the CD programs provide practical tools to process and organize that data. More about the CD later in this Introduction.

How This Book is Organized

This book is organized into six parts, and each part is divided into two or more chapters. Feel free to begin at Chapter 1 and then progress sequentially through the chapters, or just skip around and look for the juiciest tidbits. (Hey, it's *your* book.)

Part I: Building Blocks

Instead of an overview of Access or programming, the three chapters in this section get right to the heart of all Access programming, that is, the three building blocks: Objects, Statements, and SQL. This section provides all of the fundamental tools and techniques you need to use and understand Access programming.

Part II: Educating Access

Computers are very good at doing certain things — adding lots of numbers very quickly and very accurately. However, they don't know much about life on the planet Earth. What makes a good application is that it include some understanding of the work people are actually trying to do with the computer. The three chapters in this section look at how you can educate

Access by programming intelligent user interfaces. An intelligent interface combines standard Access forms and controls with Access programming code. The results are forms that are easy to use and intuitive to work with because the Access programming code logically connects the individual elements into a more intelligent whole.

Part III: Controlling the Dialog

This section expands on the concepts involved in making intelligent interfaces by explaining how to use forms and Access programming to create custom-designed dialog boxes. The three chapters in this section will show you how to create custom-designed dialog boxes that can be used for streamlining a variety of important tasks from data entry to printing reports.

Part IV: Active Controls and Objects

Inside of both Office 97 and Windows 95 is a set of technologies that Microsoft now refers to as ActiveX. ActiveX sounds like it's the secret ingredient in a new laundry detergent. As it turns out, ActiveX provides a way for a program like Access to interact with other programs or special applets that can be plugged into Access. The two chapters in this section look at some of the cool things that you can do in Access 97 with this secret ingredient.

Part V: The Part of Tens

Everybody likes lists. Here you will find some very handy items such as my favorite programming tips, my most often repeated programming boo-boos, and some Web sites where I turn to for guidance and free software.

Part VI: Appendixes

Who says the appendix is a useless organ? You haven't seen mine: Appendix A describes the key feature of the Office Developers Edition (ODE). ODE is a set of utilities that Microsoft sells as enhancements to the development tools included in Access 97. Appendix B tells you about all the good stuff you find on the CD that's included at the back of this book.

Conventions Used in This Book

In any technical book (and let's face it — computers are nothing if not technical) there is a need to distinguish different types of text or write about computer stuff, such as shortcut keys or menu commands. Here's what you need to know about those special items:

Programming code

This book is full of text that represents programs written in the Access Visual Basic language. Programmers refer to this text as *code*. This is the stuff you actually type into Access in order to create programs. You find code examples in this book styled as follows:

```
For k = 1 To 10
    Debug.Print "Number = " & k
Next
```

Syntax examples

A syntax example is a special type of code example used to illustrate the general form of a statement rather than a specific example. In the following code line the words *somenumber, start,* and *end* are in italics to indicate the location where you would enter some number, a start value, and an end value. I don't ask you to type in these examples. They are for reference purposes.

```
For somenumber = start To end
```

Sometimes I draw your attention to a particular segment of code by formatting the segment in boldface. This formatting has no purpose other than to grab your attention.

Literals

Programming languages allow you to insert words and phrases that don't mean anything to the program but are useful for humans who need to read the output of your programs. These phrases are called *literals*. Literals are always enclosed in punctuation marks called *delimiters*. In Access, text items can be enclosed in either double quotes (" ") or single quotes (' ') so long as you use the same punctuation at the beginning and the end of the literal.

```
"Walter Lafish" or 'Walter Lafish'
```

Access also supports literal dates. Dates are delimited with # characters as the following line of code shows.

```
#1/1/97#
```

Upper and lower

Access Visual Basic is not case-sensitive. This means that when you enter code it doesn't matter which of the letters is in upper- or lowercase. The three following lines have exactly the same meaning:

```
Orders.RecordCount
Orders.Recordcount
orders.recordcount
```

Having said that, the code in this book uses the upper- and lowercase conventions that appear in the official Access Visual Basic language guide from Microsoft. The guide uses uppercase letters in the middle of some words to make their meaning more clear. For example, the term RecordCount is shown with an uppercase C to indicate that it has something to do with the number of records.

```
Orders.RecordCount
```

If you type code, you really don't have to bother with uppercase letters at all if you don't want to. Access automatically changes the text to uppercase letters for you.

Line continuation

When you enter programming code into Access, you can type lines that are much wider than the width of the text that can be printed in this book. In order to write code that fits the pages of this book, I have inserted line-continuation characters. The following two lines actually represent one line of code because the end of the first line has a space followed by an _. This tells Access that the statement continues on the next line.

```
StandardListPrice = Cost * CustomerDiscount _
    * TaxRate
```

If you retype the code you are free to skip the line-continuation characters and enter the statement on a single line. If you choose to enter the line-continuation characters remember that you must include a space followed by an _. Don't forget the space!

Shortcut keys

When you need to enter a special key combination (such as pressing and holding down Ctrl and then pressing G), I write it as Ctrl+G.

Menu command

When you need to use a command on a menu, such as choosing the Open Database command from the File menu, I write it as File⇨Open Database.

Foolish Assumptions

Any book written in the *...For Dummies* style should avoid assuming too much about the potential reader. However, it's not possible to cover everything about Access in a single book. I assume that anyone reading about programming Access will be familiar with (not a master of) the following concepts:

- How to use the Database window
- How to create a table and define fields
- How to create a form or a report
- How to create a simple query using the Query form

Note that you don't need to know anything about macros in order to write programs. My own preference is to forget about macros altogether and simply work with Access Visual Basic.

On the CD

The CD attached to the back cover of this book includes all of the programs, plus the tables, queries, forms, and reports that support the programs. Before you get started, get the CD out (you can find installation instructions on the last page of this book), and read the appendix in this book called "About the CD." If you do this, you can work along with the examples in each chapter. The CD also includes additional data tables that you can use to practice writing your own program as well as a couple of bonus chapters that discuss debugging and Web publishing.

In order to use the CD, however, your system must have the following basic requirements:

- **Computer:** A 486-based (or higher) computer system with CD-ROM drive
- **Operating system:** Windows 95 or Windows NT 3.51 (or higher)
- **Application:** Access 97

ꞏ **Free hard disk space:** 32.3 megabytes

ꞏ **RAM:** 16 megabytes

Icons Used in This Book

 This icon flags useful information or suggestions that, while maybe not part of the current example, might come in handy later on.

 I have made my share of mistakes writing programs. A word to the wise will hopefully keep you out of some of these programming potholes.

 This data is included for those of you who wonder about why some odd-looking thing works or where some strange-sounding term got its name. You can program perfectly well without this information but some people find it comforting.

 This icon marks information that I may have given to you already, but I want to be sure that you remember (hence the name, right?).

 This icon marks a new feature added to Access 97 that wasn't included in earlier versions.

 This icon shows you where to find a table, query, form, report, or module on the CD. In general, each heading in this book contains one or more examples. The text tells you about the problem or task and the Access 97 technique you need to use. The explanation ends with the result followed by one of these icons which tells you where on the CD you can find the example.

Where to Go from Here

Now that you've got all of this preliminary stuff out of the way, you're ready to get started. Remember to check out the CD attached to the back cover of this book because it contains the files you need to duplicate the examples in the chapters.

Time to get started. Fire up Access and get started programming right now!

Part I
Building Blocks

The 5th Wave   By Rich Tennant

"FOR ADDITIONAL SOFTWARE SUPPORT, DIAL "9", "POUND," THE EXTENSION NUMBER DIVIDED BY YOUR ACCOUNT NUMBER, HIT "STAR", YOUR DOG, BLOW INTO THE RECEIVER TWICE, PUNCH IN YOUR HAT SIZE, PUNCH OUT YOUR LANDLORD,..."

In this part . . .

Even the Great Wall of China was built one brick at a time. As it turns out, programming is a lot like that. No matter how fancy the computer or hot or cool the language, the program is built one line at a time by someone — maybe you — writing those lines of computer code.

Access 97 programming has three basic building blocks which you use to create all of the other programming parts. The three chapters in Part I explain what these basic building blocks are and how you create Access programming code that can build programs out of these basic blocks.

Chapter 1

Objects and Names

· ·

In This Chapter

▶ Me? Programming?

▶ A name for everything

▶ Displaying object properties and methods

▶ Setting properties

▶ The DoCmd object

· ·

*T*he purpose of this book, to put things as simply as possible, is to help Access 97 users become Access 97 programmers. In this spirit, the term *programmer* doesn't refer to someone who necessarily makes a living writing computer applications. Here, the term refers to anyone who wants to move from simply clicking and typing through the Access interface to creating forms and reports that can automatically perform a range of operations that currently require manual implementation.

Me? Programming?

Programming is about building *intelligence* into Access. As do all generalized database applications, Access 97, as the program comes from the box (or should I say off the CD?), provides a set of information management tools that almost any business or organization can use, because, after all, *everyone* accumulates data. What programming adds to Access is the capability to embed a specific procedure that fits the work *you* need to do into a form, report, or even a single button. That specialized button or form you create wouldn't be of use to most people. In your business or activity, however, that button or form is critical.

By building intelligence into a form, report, or button, you accomplish several important goals:

▶ **Make the machine do the work.** While working with a program, you often find that you need to repeat the same series of actions over and over again to accomplish your goal — that is, you're trying to work like a *machine*.

All appearances to the contrary, you're not a machine. Attempts to behave like one always lead to errors because humans simply don't do well mechanically repeating a long series of operations. Such repetition also takes a lot of time — which you can use for tasks that actually actually require human intelligence!

Learning to program enables you to shift the burden of this mechanical work to the computer — where such work should have gone in the first place. You reduce errors and save time.

✔ **Ensure reliability if you go on vacation.** Suppose, for the moment, that you don't mind performing a lot of mindless mechanical work and that you seldom make any errors — at least, none that get you into trouble. You're still left with the problem that, if you're not present all the time, who's left at work who knows what to do to get your work done?

By programming your tasks into an Access 97 application, someone else at the office can keep things going even if you're not there to tell that person exactly what to do. In this case, you're transferring your *business knowledge* into a form that other people can work with fairly easily. So you don't need to wallpaper your cube with notes every time you want to take an afternoon off.

✔ **Make things work as they should.** One of the most important, but seldom appreciated, advantages of writing programs is that doing so forces you to think logically and in great detail about how a given job needs to be done. This process often yields insights about the program that eliminate a lot of problems that currently may fall through the cracks. As you write a program, you're actually trying to explain how to do a job to a very stupid machine — that is, the computer.

Although a computer can do many things very quickly, computers have an abysmal lack of knowledge about the planet Earth. Luckily, you've probably spent a good portion of your life on such a planet. If you gain an understanding of the computer's language, you can fill the thing in on how you do stuff around here.

Well, that's the story about programming in a nutshell — less than a page! The rest of this book describes how to explain to the computer what you want it to do. The programming language in this book is called *Visual Basic for Applications* (VBA). As you discover how to express ideas in that language, you're programming. Such a skill enables you to shape an Access 97 application that can perform the tasks you need the computer to do for you.

Another reason for knowing VBA is that Access is not the only program that speaks this language. All the programs in Office 97 (Word 97, Excel 97, PowerPoint 97, Outlook, and the Binder) also speak this language. You can add to that list many applications that are not part of the Office suite, such as Microsoft Project and even the Microsoft Internet Explorer, which uses a version called Visual Basic Script. If you want to go on to more professional style programming, you'll find that VBA is a good place to start because VBA and VB have a great deal in common.

A Name for Everything

You may wonder how a single language such as VBA can enable you to program in a wide variety of applications, from Word 97 to Excel 97 to Access 97. The trick is to separate the programming language into the following two parts:

- ✔ **Standard programming.** In any programming language, you must have commands to perform a core set of actions that all programs have in common. Because VBA is designed for Windows 95 (and its sister environment, Windows NT 4.0), the language includes basic operations common to all Windows programs. This core set of tasks doesn't change much from one application to another. Actions such as creating *variables,* evaluating *conditional expressions,* and executing *loops* are the stuff of which all programs consist. (In Chapter 2, you find out how to create and use these elements.)

- ✔ **Application-specific programming.** The other part of programming in Access 97 (or other Office 97 applications) is using the *objects* that the program provides for you. In Access 97, for example, objects include tables, queries, forms, and reports. If you program in Access 97, therefore, you don't need to create these things.They're already there for you to use. The same is true in Excel 97, except that there, the objects consist of worksheets, cells, and charts. What your Access programming does is manipulate Access 97 stuff that's already right there in the program. Each Office 97 application provides a set of objects that form the basic building blocks on which you build your programs.

The subject of this chapter is the set of objects that Access 97 provides. The key to understanding Access 97 programming and Access 97 objects is realizing that every element that Access 97 provides has a *name.* If you're just using the program by selecting from menus, clicking buttons, or filling in dialog boxes, you don't need to know the names of those items. You can simply point to and click different areas of the screen to indicate to the program what table, record, field, form, or control you want to manipulate.

But if you write a program to carry out a task, you no longer have the luxury of simply pointing at something to tell Access 97 what you want to work with. You must instead *write out* the name of the item in your program.

In Access 97 (and the other Office 97 applications), objects are the things that make up the program. The tables in which you store the data, for example, are table objects. The fields that make up a table are field objects. Forms, reports, and controls are also different types of objects.

The object model

To identify each object, Access 97 (as well as the other Office 97 applications) supports what's known as an *object model*. The object model reflects that each element in an application has specific relationships to all the other elements. Access 97, for example, has *database objects*. Within each database are one or more table objects. Within each table are one or more field objects. This series of interconnected relationships among the objects forms a *hierarchy*. A hierarchy is a sort of outline in which the objects in the model are arranged in sections and subsections. Figure 1-1 illustrates a portion of the Access 97 object-model hierarchy.

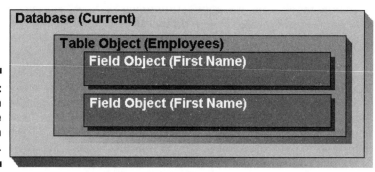

Figure 1-1: Application objects are organized in a hierarchy.

The object model indicates how Access 97 assigns names to each of the objects. At the top of the hierarchy lies the database object. Access 97 assigns the currently open database the name `Currentdb`. You find the table objects under the name `TableDefs`. Suppose that you want to refer to the Employees table in the current database. You can create a single phrase that indicates the database and table object by connecting the object names with the *dot operator*. The dot operator is simply a period inserted between the names. The names are written so that the larger objects precede the smaller ones. In this example, the name of the database object is then followed by the name of the smaller object, that is, the table.

```
Currentdb.TableDefs("employees")
```

You find the name of the Last Name field in the Employees table by adding a `Fields` object to the database and to `TableDefs`. Pay attention to the different way in which particular types of names are written. The general name for a class of objects, such as `TableDefs`, is written without quotation marks. On the other hand, the actual name that you assign to a specific object (the name that you see in the database window Tables tab) is enclosed in parentheses and surrounded by quotation marks. Access is not very fussy about case. You can refer to *Employees* using any combination of upper- or lowercase characters. Spaces in names (as in *Last Name*) are important. You can get away with *LAST name* or *last NAME* but not *LastName* when you enter the user given name of an object.

```
Currentdb.TableDefs("employees").Fields("Last Name")
```

Properties and methods

After you know how to refer to some part of the Access 97 object model, you can use the object names for the following two purposes:

- ✔ **Display/change properties.** A *property* is a quality or value that an object possesses. For example, Access 97 keeps track of the date on which you create each table. The creation date is known as the DateCreated property. To refer to this property, add the property name as a suffix to the object name, connected by a dot operator. The following example returns the creation date for the Employees table.

  ```
  Currentdb.TableDefs("employees").DateCreated
  ```

- ✔ **Execute methods.** A *method* is an operation that you can perform on an object. The TableDefs object can contain a number of individual tables. Applying the Count method causes Access 97 to actually count the number of tables in the database. The object referred to by the following phrase is a numeric value equal to the number of tables in the current database, such as 10 or 54.

  ```
  Currentdb.TableDefs.Count
  ```

Using Objects, Properties, and Methods

The CD-ROM at the back of this book contains MDB files for each chapter. These files provide all the tables, queries, forms, and other Access elements I discuss in each chapter. For this chapter, you need to open the following database:

> *Database Folder: Access Prog Dummies\Chapter 1*
> *Database File: OBJECTS.MDB*
> *Module: Object Examples*

For the purposes of this chapter, you don't do much more than enter one-line commands. I include all the commands shown in this chapter, however, on the CD for your convenience.

If you want to use the CD examples for this chapter, do the following:

1. **Open the database file OBJECT.MDB.**

2. **Click the Modules tab.**

   You see a module named *Object Examples* displayed in the window.

3. **Click the Design button to open the Object Examples module.**

   This module contains the 34 examples, named `Example1()` through `Example34()`, that appear in this chapter.

4. **To run an example, scroll down the screen until you position the cursor over the command you want to execute.**

5. **Press F5.**

   The command executes. If the command begins with `Debug.Print`, switch to the Debug window (by pressing Ctrl+G) to see the results because they will appear only in the Debug window.

Using the Debug window

You can discover how to explore the Access 97 object model directly by entering VBA commands into the *Debug window*. You primarily use the Debug window to help you locate and fix problems in your programs. But this window is also convenient for entering individual VBA commands into Access 97. In this case, you can see how the program's object-naming conventions enable you to manipulate parts of the Access 97 system by using *statements* instead of using the menu and dialog box interfaces. A statement is the programming equivalent of a sentence. In English, each sentence contains a complete thought. In programming, each statement contains a complete instruction.

The Debug window provides many useful tools for monitoring and analyzing how your programs operate and provides possible reasons why they're not operating exactly as you'd like.

You can access the Debug window at any time by pressing Ctrl+G. You find out more about the Debug window's special features in Chapter 13. After you press the key combination, Access 97 opens the Debug window, as shown in Figure 1-2. The window has two panes. The top pane divides into the *Locals tab* and the *Watch tab*. These tabs provide special displays that you use to track the value of various items while a program executes. The bottom pane is the *Immediate pane*. This pane contains a typing cursor so that you can enter and edit commands directly into the window.

You can use the Debug window, however, even before you find out how to write a single line of VBA programming code. The reason is that you can enter VBA commands in the *immediate pane* of the Debug window and see the results appear instantly right below your command.

The Immediate pane

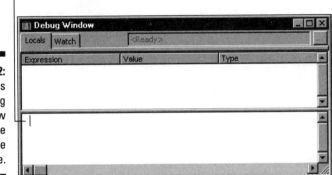

Figure 1-2:
The Access
97 Debug
window
and the
Immediate
pane.

One command that you can enter into the Immediate pane is the Print command. This command is one of the oldest in VBA, as well as one of the handiest. (The command works in VBA now just about the same as it did in versions of the BASIC language written in the 1970s.) Print outputs the specified information to the Immediate pane. Suppose, for example, that you want to see the name of the current database. If so, you actually want to Print the Name property of the Currentdb object (the current database object). You can put these elements together and create a command by following these steps:

1. **Type** Print Currentdb. **in the Immediate pane.**

   As soon as you type the period after the object name, Access 97 displays a drop-down list in the pane. This is the *Auto List Members* feature of Access 97. The list provides the names of objects, properties, and methods that you may want to select (and it can be a real timesaver). You can either keep typing or select something from the list and have Access insert that item into the code for you.

   If you continue typing, Access performs a speed search on the list to display the closest match to what you type.

2. **Type** n.

   Access locates the Name property in the Auto List Members drop-down list, as shown in Figure 1-3.

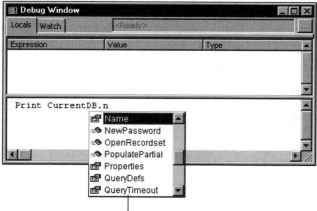

Figure 1-3:
Access 97
locates the
first name
in the list
that
matches
the
character
you enter.

Auto List Members drop-down list

You can either keep typing at this point (and the list keeps looking for a closer match, if any is available) or have Access complete the entry by pressing Tab.

3. Press Tab.

Access fills in the rest of the missing letters.

4. Press Enter to execute the command.

Access prints the name of the database on the next line of the Debug window.

Notice that the name of the database is the full path name of the OBJECTS.MDB file, as shown in the following example. The path that appears in this book may be different from what you see on-screen if you store your file on a different drive (for example, your C: drive).

```
Print Currentdb.Name
D:\Access Prog Dummies\Chapter 1\Objects.mdb
```

In addition to using the Auto List Members drop list, you can enter ? as a shortcut for the `Print` command. You enter this command as shown in the following example:

```
? Currentdb.Name
```

Using ? produces the same result as using the full `Print` command.

Another property of the database is `Version`, written as follows:

```
? Currentdb.Version
```

When the `Version` property command executes, Access 97 returns *3.0* indicating the version number of the currently open database. The version number does not refer to the version of Access (1.0, 1.1, 2.0, 7.0, or 8.0) but to the version of the *Jet Database Engine* (which Access 97 uses).

Access is actually one part of a complicated set of interrelated tools that integrate database functions within Windows and Microsoft Office 97. The part of Access that actually deals with tables and queries is the Jet Database Engine. The Jet Database Engine is a SQL-based database system that can function independently from Access. It is used to connect Excel, Word, and PowerPoint to databases without using the Access interface. I discuss SQL (Structured Query Language) in Chapter 3.

Table and field collections

In the preceding section, I discuss the `Print` command, which displays information about the database object. Tables are among the key elements contained in Access 97 databases.

All the tables in a given database make up a *collection.* A collection is a set of one or more objects of the same type contained within a larger object. The larger object is called the *container.*

The most obvious example of this type of relationship is the one between a database and its tables. The database is the container object. The database contains several collections, one of which is a collection of tables. Access 97 calls this collection `TableDefs` (which is short for *table definitions*). One property that every collection possesses is the `Count` property. This property returns the number of items in a collection. You put these elements together, as shown in the following example, to obtain the number of objects in a given collection.

```
container.collection.Count
```

The first line of the following example shows how you obtain the number of tables (in the `TableDefs` collection) in the current database. In this case, `Currentdb` is the container; `TableDefs` is the collection, and `Count` is the property. The number that Access 97 returns, 15, as shown in the second line of the example, indicates the total number of tables in the open database. (This number includes any hidden system tables.)

```
? Currentdb.TableDefs.Count
15
```

In addition to tables, databases can have other collections, such as QueryDefs (short for *query definitions*). The following example displays the number of queries in the current database. A QueryDefs object is the type of object you create when you create a Query form using the Access interface. Each of the items listed in the Queries tab of the database window is one QueryDef object. The entire list is the QueryDefs collection.

```
? Currentdb.QueryDefs.Count
 5
```

Object within a collection

The TableDefs and QueryDefs objects refer to the entire collection of tables or queries as a whole. You can, however, use these objects to refer to individual objects (tables, queries and so on) within the collection in either of the following two ways:

✔ **By name.** If you use Access 97 manually to create objects such as tables or queries, you must assign a unique name to each object. If you want to refer to a specific table or query within the TableDefs or QueryDefs collections, you can do so by using the name of the object, as shown in the following example. The name of the member of the collection is always enclosed in parentheses.

```
container.collection(name)
```

Suppose, for example, that you want to display the creation date of the Employees table in the current database. First, you refer to that table by using the phrase shown in the following line of code. Remember that you must enclose the name of the table, Employees, in quotation marks because it is a user given name.

```
Currentdb.TableDefs("employees")
```

You can also put this phrase into a command as shown in the following example. When you press Enter at the end of the command, Access displays the value of the DateCreated property of the Employees table on the next line of the Debug window.

```
? Currentdb.TableDefs("employees").DateCreated
11/11/96 10:26:58 AM
```

✔ **By index.** Access 97 assigns every object in a collection an *index number,* with 0 (that is, the number *zero*) being the index number of the first object. Note that the index number is enclosed in parentheses but not in quotation marks because it is a numeric value and not a user-given name. The phrase shown in the following example refers to the table in the current database, which has an assigned index number of 1.

```
Currentdb.TableDefs(1)
```

The following command displays the creation date of the table in the current database that Access 97 assigned index number 1.

```
? Currentdb.TableDefs(1).DateCreated
```

Collections in Access are *zero-based* — that is, the first item in the collection receives the index number zero, not the number one. The number of the last item in a collection is always one less than the total number of items in the collection. If, for example, the `Count` property of the `TableDefs` collection returns 15, the index numbers of the `TableDefs` range from 0 to 14. In Access 97 programming, you frequently refer to the last item in a collection by using the expression `Count -1`. As you see this expression throughout this book, the expression should remind you that collection index numbers are zero-based.

The name style of reference is useful if you know the name of a specific table with which you want to work. The index style of reference is useful if you're not sure about the names of the tables in a database. In such a case, you can still check out the properties of the tables by referring to their index numbers.

Interestingly, you can use the `Name` property to return the name of a table if you refer to the table by index number.

```
? Currentdb.TableDefs(1).Name
Employees
```

The index numbers that Access 97 assigns to objects aren't permanent assignments but *dynamic,* which means that as soon as you delete or add an object to a collection, the program reassigns the index numbers accordingly. So never write a program that relies on the index number of an object as a means of identification because that number may change. Always use the name of the object instead.

Another useful property of `TableDefs` objects is the `RecordCount` property. This property returns the number of records in each table. The following example causes Access 97 to display the number of records (5) in the Employees table:

```
? Currentdb.TableDefs("employees").RecordCount
5
```

Collections within objects

In the preceding section, I discuss how to refer to individual objects contained within a collection — for example, tables within the `TableDefs` collection. Individual objects such as tables, however, may themselves contain other objects — or even entire collections. Every Access user knows, for example, that tables contain one or more fields.

In terms of the Access object model, this characteristic means that any object in the `TableDefs` collection that contains fields also contains a `Fields` collection. The `Fields` collection consists of all the fields defined in a given table. You may recall from the discussion earlier in this chapter about properties and methods that every collection supports the `Count` property. You could, therefore, string together a series of objects and collections to determine values, such as the number of fields in the Employees table, as shown in the following example:

```
? Currentdb.TableDefs("employees").Fields.Count
6
```

What are the names of the six fields in the Employees table? You can obtain that information by selecting elements of the `Fields` collection for that table. The first field in a table would be `Fields(0)` — that nasty zero-based mentality again. The `Name` property returns the name of the field. If you put these elements together with the `TableDefs` object, you can find out the name of the field by using the following command:

```
? Currentdb.TableDefs("employees").Fields(0).Name
EmployeeID
```

Nesting object references

In some ways, programmers are a bit like detectives. In order to get the answer you seek you need to start with one clue which you then use to find the next clue. By putting all of the pieces together you arrive at the answer to the puzzle. In computer programming, *nesting* refers to a process by which you use one result or value to fill in a value used as part of another expression.

To see what's meant by nesting and why nesting is useful, imagine that your task is to display the name of the *last* field in the Employees table. Displaying the name of the *first* field is easy, because that's always item zero in the collection. But how do you know the index number of the last field?

You can get the name of the last field in the collection by breaking the problem down into two steps. Step 1 uses a statement like the following one to determine the total number of fields in the table.

```
? Currentdb.TableDefs("employees").Fields.Count '#1
```

You can add plain-English comments or notes to a command by inserting an apostrophe at the end of the actual command, and then adding your notes after the apostrophe. Access stops reading the command when it encounters the apostrophe. This technique is used in the following to label the command as step #1.

After you know the total number of fields, you can use that value in step 2 to figure out the index number of the last field in the collection. For example, if the preceding statement prints the number 6, the index number of the last field in the collection is 5 (because the first element in an object collection is 0, not 1). The following example uses the number obtained in step 1 to get the name of the last field in the collection.

```
? Currentdb.TableDefs("employees").Fields(5).Name '#2
```

The two-step approach has a significant weakness though: It requires that a human read the result of step 1 and then insert the appropriate value into the command used in step 2. A better approach is to combine the commands used in step 1 and step 2 into a single command in which the entire object phrase from step 1 becomes part of a larger command. In the following example you can see that the object name used in step 1 is inserted where the index number of the field appeared in step 2. Note that Count–1 is used because collection index numbers begin with zero, not 1. The result is the name WorkPhone which is the name of the last field in the Employees table. The result is thus obtained with one, not two, commands.

If you're entering very long commands such as the one that follows, you can break up the entry into more than one line by using the *line continuation character* (a space followed by an underscore) at the end of each line that you want to continue. The following example uses this technique to break the command into two lines. Remember that you must enter a space *and* an underscore to create such a line continuation.

```
? Currentdb.TableDefs("employees").Fields( _
Currentdb.TableDefs("employees").Fields.Count-1).Name
WorkPhone
```

This technique of placing a command inside another command is called *nesting*. When Access encounters a command that contains one or more nested commands it first calculates the values of the nested items and uses those values to figure out the value of the entire command. In this example, Access first calculates the number of fields in the table, and then uses that value to calculate the index number of the last field whose name becomes the result of the command. A command with nested commands is a sort of mini-program in which a number of separate calculations are written as a single command.

The primary value of nesting is that it allows you to write more generalized commands. A generalized command is one that is not limited to a specific object but can be applied to any object of the same type. In this example the Employees table was used. However, the statement would work exactly the same way for any table in any Access database. As an illustration, the following command is identical to the preceding example, except that this command replaces the name of the table ("employees") with index number 0. The result is that the command displays the name of the last field in the first table in the current database.

```
? Currentdb.TableDefs(0).Fields( _
Currentdb.TableDefs(0).Fields.Count-1).Name
CategoryName
```

Properties that return codes

Some object properties, such as Name or DateCreated, return information in the form of text or dates that you can immediately understand as you see them. Many properties, however, return numeric codes that correspond to various settings or attributes.

The following command, for example, returns the Type property of the first field in the Employees table:

```
? Currentdb.TableDefs("employees").Fields(0).Type
 4
```

The property returns the value 4. The 4 is not the actual field type — for example, Text or Yes/No — but a numeric code that stands for the field type. What type of field does 4 stand for? You can find the answer in the Access 97 VBA Help files. To access Help for the Type property, for example, perform the following steps:

1. **Double-click** Type **in the Debug window.**

   This action highlights the word.

2. **Press F1.**

   Access automatically performs a search of the help files for a topic that matches the highlighted word or phrase. This technique works in both the Debug window and in any code module window in Access.

   The Help screen explains how the coding system for field types operates in Access 97. Access 97 recognizes 20 field types. The Help screen, however, does not show the number codes for the field types. Instead, the screen lists a series of names, such as dbBigInt or dbBinary, next to the field types.

The names represent a built-in set of special names (called *constants*) that Access 97 recognizes as numeric values. The program uses these names because names are easier to remember than numbers.

Access 97 has some new features that make finding the names of special items such as constants even easier than looking in Help. Check Chapter 2 for a discussion of these new features.

When you finish looking at the Help screen, you need to return to Access 97 to continue working. Remember that in Windows, the Help screen displays are not part of the application (such as Access 97) but a separate program running in its own application window. One fast way to get back to the previous application window is the Alt+Tab shortcut key.

3. Press Alt+Tab.

Now you are back in Access where you can continue exploring the Access 97 object model.

Recall from the Type Property Help screen shown in Figure 1-5 that the Type property uses names such as dbText. What happens if you use this name in a command without any reference to the Type property? Enter the following and see what happens.

```
? dbText
 10
```

Access 97 returns the number 10, which is the value assigned to the constant dbText. Any field type property, therefore, that returns a value of 10 is a Text type field. It turns out that dbText is simply a term used in Access 97 to represent the number 10. The idea is that it is easier to remember the name dbText than it is to remember that the code number for text is 10. The use of names to represent numbers is a standard part of all forms of Visual Basic, including VBA in Access, Word, Excel, and PowerPoint.

But what about a field that returns a Type value of 4? Unfortunately, the information in the Access 97 Help screen doesn't answer this question, because the screen lists only the constants' names, not their actual numeric values. The only way that you can find the answer to this question is to print out the values of each constant to find out their numeric equivalents as done in the previous command. After you perform this task you end up with the information summarized in Table 1-1, which lists both the constant name and the numeric code value for each of the possible values the Type property returns. You can see, for example, that 4 indicates a *Long* (integer) type field.

Table 1-1	Field Type Values	
Type	*Constant*	*Value*
Boolean	dbBoolean	1
Byte	dbByte	2
Integer	dbInteger	3
Long	dbLong	4
Currency	dbCurrency	5
Single	dbSingle	6
Double	dbDouble	7
Date/Time	dbDate	8
Binary	dbBinary	9
Text	dbText	10
Long Binary (OLE Object)	dbLongBinary	11
Memo	dbMemo	12
GUID	dbGUID	15
VarBinary	dbVarBinary	17
Char	dbChar	18
Numeric	dbNumeric	19
Decimal	dbDecimal	20
Float	dbFloat	21
Time	dbTime	22
Time Stamp	dbTimeStamp	23

The OBJECTS.MDB file contains a simple VBA program that prints to the Debug window the information shown in Table 1-1. To run this program, type **ListTypeConstants** and then press Enter. You can then copy and paste the text into a word-processing document if you want a printed copy of the information.

Using the information in Table 1-1 you can determine the field type for the second field in the Employees table. You don't need to enter the entire command if you simply edit the last entry you made. Change `Fields(0)` to `Fields(1)`, as in the following example, and then press Enter.

```
? Currentdb.TableDefs("employees").Fields(1).Type
10
```

This time, Access returns `10`, indicating that the second field in the table —
`Fields(1)` — is a *Text* type field.

Properties that return numeric codes can prove rather inconvenient to work
with because you have no obvious, simple way to figure out the meaning of
the numeric code. Unfortunately, even with the use of the Access 97 Help
screen, you couldn't determine the meaning of the numbers that the `Type`
property returned without looking at the data in Table 1-1. In Chapter 4, you
discover how to use VBA to solve this problem.

Setting Properties

In previous sections of this chapter, all the operations I describe concerning
Access 97 objects, methods, and properties, display information about the
objects. Object commands, however, aren't limited to displaying information. You can also use such commands to actually change the value of
various properties of the objects in the database. The following command,
for example, displays the name of the first table in the current database:

```
? Currentdb.TableDefs(0).Name
Categories
```

You can set the value of a property by issuing a command that uses the form
shown in the following example. In this form, the name of the object property entered is set equal to the new value for that object. Notice that you
don't use the ? to set a property.

```
object.property = newvalue
```

The following example changes the `Name` property of the first table in the
current database from its current name (Categories) to *Table 1*. The command is the VBA equivalent of using the Edit➪Rename command to change
the name of a table. Figure 1-4 shows how the database window looks before
you change the name of the table.

You may or may not be able to see that database window in the background
as shown in Figure 1-4. The Debug window can be moved and sized just like
any other window. Feel free to drag or resize the window as needed.

Type the following command in the Debug window and press Enter to
execute the command:

```
Currentdb.TableDefs(0).Name = "Table 1"
```

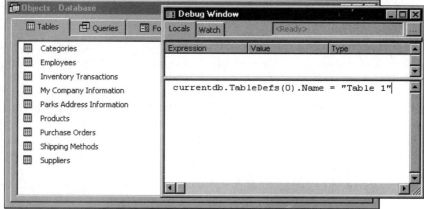

Figure 1-4:
The original
names of
the tables
before
renaming
the
Categories
table.

If the previous command worked, the names of the tables in the database window should have changed. But if you look at the database window (you may have to move the Debug window a bit to see it) you will see that it hasn't changed because Access 97 doesn't automatically update the database window to show new or altered objects.

To make Access 97 update the list of tables, you must switch to another tab — for example, the *Queries* tab — and then switch back. You can do so by pressing the following series of shortcut keys:

1. **Press Ctrl+F6.**

   The database window is now the active window.

2. **Press Ctrl+Tab to switch to the Queries tab.**

3. **Press Ctrl+Shift+Tab to switch back to the Tables tab.**

   Switching back to the Tables tab updates the list of table names to reflect any changes that may have been made by any VBA programs or commands.

4. **Press Ctrl+G to return to the Debug window.**

After Access 97 updates the list of tables, the renamed table, *Table 1,* appears at the bottom of the list, as shown in Figure 1-5.

An important point to keep in mind is that if you change such properties as the name of a table, the change affects the index numbering of the objects within the TableDefs collection. Before you renamed this table, it was the first table in the collection — that is, index value 0. But is the renamed table

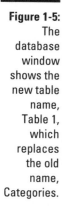

Figure 1-5:
The
database
window
shows the
new table
name,
Table 1,
which
replaces
the old
name,
Categories.

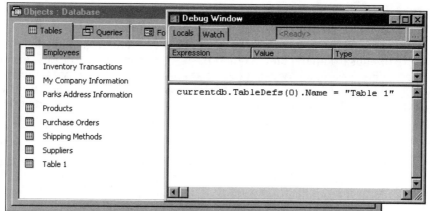

still the first in the collection? The following command checks to see what table is currently the first table in the collection:

```
? Currentdb.TableDefs(0).Name
Employees
```

The result shows that after you change the name of the Categories table, its position within the TableDefs collection changes, too. Now the Employees table is the first table in the collection.

You can reverse the process by renaming Table 1 back to its original name Categories, as in the following command:

```
Currentdb.TableDefs("Table 1").Name = "Categories"
```

Now check to see which table is the first table in the collection. The following example shows the command you use and the answer that returns:

```
? Currentdb.TableDefs(0).Name
Categories
```

The index order of the objects once again automatically adjusts to a change you make to the properties of one of the objects in the collection. The Categories table is now back at the top of the TableDefs collection.

Changes you make to collections, as shown in these examples, don't automatically appear in the database window. You need to click the Queries tab and then the Tables tab to force Access 97 to update the list of tables.

The DoCmd Object

Almost all the operations you can perform in Access 97 manually — by using menus, toolbars, and dialog boxes — you can also carry out through using VBA. You do so by using the `DoCmd` object. The `DoCmd` object provides VBA with command equivalents for all the actions that you can perform by using Access 97 macros. Your VBA programs, therefore, can include operations that range from maximizing windows to importing and exporting tables to and from other file formats.

Each type of macro action is a *method* of the `DoCmd` object. The Access 97 macro command `Maximize`, for example, maximizes the windows inside the Access 97 application window. The VBA equivalent of the `Maximize` macro action appears in the following example, where `Maximize` is a method of the `DoCmd` object. You can enter directly into the Debug window the equivalent of macro actions by using the `DoCmd` object and its methods. In the Debug window, you simply enter the following command:

```
DoCmd.Maximize
```

Access 97 responds to the command in the same way whether you manually maximize the window (with a mouse click or menu selection) or use a macro to perform the maximizing action. You can return the window to its normal size by using `DoCmd` to execute the `Restore` method. To restore the window to its previous size, type the object and a dot connector, as shown in the following example:

```
DoCmd.
```

Notice that as soon as you type the object and the dot connector, Access 97 provides a drop-down list of the methods this object supports.

In this case, because the object is `DoCmd`, the list of methods corresponds to all the macro actions that Access 97 macros support. Complete the command by either selecting `Restore` from this list or by typing the method in manually. (Remember to always press Enter at the end of the line to execute a command.) The completed command appears as follows:

```
DoCmd.Restore
```

The window returns to its normal size.

You can perform other types of operations by using the `DoCmd` object directly from the Debug window. You can, for example, open a table window by using the `OpenTable` method with `DoCmd`. Enter the following command in the Debug window. After you type `OpenTable`, press the space bar and then wait for a moment.

`DoCmd.OpenTable`

Access 97 automatically displays a box showing you the required and op-tional arguments that apply to the method you select, as shown in Figure 1-6. The purpose of this display is to guide you through the process of entering any *arguments* — required or optional — that apply to the selected method. (An argument is an item of information that determines how a given method is carried out.) The `OpenTable` method, for example, requires that you specify the name of the table you want to open. The name of the table is an argument of the `OpenTable` method.

Figure 1-6:
Access 97
automatically
displays the
syntax for
the method
you enter.

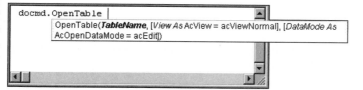

Access 97 (as well as other Microsoft Office 97 programs) uses a set of conventions in displaying the syntax of a method.

Like spoken and written languages, computer languages have a set of grammatical rules that apply to the way statements (sentences) should be written. Computer language *syntax* refers to the rules that tell you the proper way to write and punctuate programming statements.

- ✔ The names of the arguments appear in *italics*. In Figure 1-6, for example, the box that appears lists three arguments for the `OpenTable` method: `TableName`, `View`, and `DataMode`.

- ✔ Brackets ([ ]) enclose any optional arguments. Arguments not enclosed in brackets are required arguments for the method.

- ✔ Many of the arguments that Access 97 VBA methods use require numeric codes as arguments. To simplify the entry of the these codes, Access 97 supports the use of *constants*.

  A *constant* is a special name that represents a value that's always the same no matter where you use that value in Access 97. If you choose to open a table, for example, you can open the table in a normal window, in Design mode, or in Print Preview mode. The `OpenTable` method supports an argument called `View` that enables you to specify to Access 97 exactly how to open the table. Table 1-2 lists both the numeric codes and the Access constant names that you can use for this argument. Because the constant names indicate their meaning, these names are easier to understand and remember than are numeric codes.

Table 1-2	View Arguments for the OpenTable Method	
View Type	*Numeric Code*	*Constant Name*
Normal	0	`acViewNormal`
Design	1	`acViewDesign`
Print Preview	2	`acViewPreview`

> ✔ The syntax display shows the constant name of the default value for any arguments that require a numeric code. In Figure 1-8, for example, the syntax box shows *View As* `AcView=acViewNormal`. `AcView` is the name of the family of constants that you can use for this argument; `=acView Normal` indicates the default value for this argument. If you choose to omit the optional argument, the method uses the default value.

You can now continue to fill in the name of the table as the first argument in the command you are entering, as follows:

```
"employees",
```

After you type the comma after `"employees"` in this example, Access 97 automatically moves the highlight (bold type) in the syntax box to the next argument, `View`, and displays a list of the relevant constant names, as shown in Figure 1-7.

Figure 1-7:
Access 97
automatically
lists
constants
for the
current
argument.

Complete the entry by using the lists of constants that Access 97 provides, as described in the following steps:

1. To select the Normal view, double click `acViewNormal` **in the constant list.**

Access inserts the selected name into your command and removes the list from the screen.

2. **To add the next argument, type another comma.**

   Access 97 responds by displaying a new list of constants (acAdd, acEdit, and acReadOnly) that are appropriate for the current argument, the *DataMode* argument.

3. **Double click** acReadOnly **in this second list of constants and press Enter.**

   acReadOnly ensures that in this case the data can be read but not changed. acEdit allows editing and acAdd allows only new records to be entered (the equivalent of the Data Entry mode).

The Debug window always appears on top of any other windows open within Access 97, so the Debug window often covers portions of other windows, such as those containing tables, queries, or forms. You may need to move or close the Debug window to view the Employees table window. You can reopen the Debug window at any time by pressing Ctrl+G. The Debug window is unusual in that any commands entered or data displayed in the window are not erased when you close it. Access 97 maintains the information in the window so that the next time you open it you see all of your previous entries just as you left them.

You can open the Employees table by using the DoCmd object, exactly as if you manually open the table from the database window. Figure 1-8 shows the table window opened by the DoCmd method. Of course, you can't tell by looking at the window which method was used. This demonstrates that the DoCmd object is the functional equivalent of the Access menus. Notice that, because you selected acReadOnly as the DataMode argument, you can't edit the table.

Figure 1-8:
Open the
Employees
table by
using the
DoCmd
object.

Employee ID	First Name	Last Name	Title	Extension	Work Phone
1	Nancy	Davolio	President		(212) 555-9857
2	Andrew	Fuller	Treasurer		(212) 555-9482
3	Janet	Leverling	Executive Secre		(212) 555-3412
4	Margaret	Peacock	Accounting Mar		(212) 555-8122
5	Steven	Buchanan	Vice President		(212) 555-1189
(AutoNumber)					

employees : Table

Record: |◄| |◄| 1 |►| |►|| |►*| of 5

You can also close the window by using the DoCmd object. If necessary, switch back to the Debug window (by pressing Ctrl+G). This time, use the Close method to close the window by entering the command shown in the following example. Access 97 presents you with syntax help for this method if you pause momentarily as you enter each argument.

```
DoCmd.Close acTable,"employees"
```

Requesting syntax help

By default, Access 97 automatically displays lists of properties, methods, and syntax information as you enter a command into the Debug window (or any module window). After you type in the period following an object name such as DoCmd, for example, Access 97 displays a list of properties and methods associated with that object.

As you manually edit a command, however, you may want Access 97 to redisplay a list of the syntax information at a point where the program doesn't do so automatically. Table 1-3 lists the menu commands and short-cuts that you can use to display the language aids available in Access 97.

Table 1-3	Commands that Display VBA Lists and Syntax	
Information	*Menu Command*	*Shortcut Key*
Properties and Methods	Edit⇨List Properties/Methods	Ctrl+J
Constants	Edit⇨List Constants	Ctrl+Shift+J
Argument Syntax	Edit⇨Quick Info	Ctrl+I

If you want to stop Access 97 from automatically displaying the lists and syntax information, you can do so by changing the options that Access 97 uses for VBA modules. To do so, follow these steps:

1. **Choose Tools⇨Options from the menu bar to open the Options dialog box.**

2. **Click the Module table of the dialog box.**

3. **Remove the check mark from the Auto List Members check box to turn off the methods and properties lists.**

4. **Remove the check mark from the Auto Quick Info check box to turn off the syntax information display.**

5. **Click OK to close the dialog box and save the new options.**

Keep in mind that even after you turn off the automatic displays of the lists and syntax information, you can still view these displays by using the menu commands or shortcut keys listed in Table 1-3.

Using objects as arguments

If you're working with the DoCmd object, many of its methods, such as OpenTable or Close, require additional items of information, such as the name and the type of the object you want to use. You need to type this information in a list following the method's name. In computer languages, any items listed after a command or method are *arguments*. In the following command, *"employees"* is the argument for the OpenTable method.

```
DoCmd.OpenTable "employees"
```

In the preceding example, I entered the argument for the method *literally,* that is, I specified the exact name of the table I want to open as a name enclosed in quotation marks. You're not limited, however, to using just *literals* for arguments. One alternative is to use an object reference as an argument. Suppose, for example, that you want to open the first query in the QueryDefs collection of the current database. You can do so, even though you don't know the actual name of that query, by using an object reference to return the name.

The object name in the following example returns the name of the first query (index number zero) in the current database:

```
Currentdb.QueryDefs(0).Name
```

You can insert this object reference as the argument for the OpenQuery method of the DoCmd object. The following command opens the query window.

```
DoCmd.OpenQuery Currentdb.QueryDefs(0).Name
```

You can use a similar command to close the query window. Switch back to the Debug window. Instead of writing a new command, simply edit the previous command by changing the method from OpenQuery to Close and adding the object type argument, acQuery, as shown in the following example:

```
DoCmd.Close acQuery, Currentdb.QueryDefs(0).Name
```

Named arguments

The examples in the preceding sections show the use of methods that require the use of one or more arguments, such as those associated with the DoCmd object. Traditionally, you enter arguments as a list of items separated by commas, as shown in the following example. The ... at the end of the list indicates that you can add any number of arguments to the list.

```
object.method argument1,argument2,argument3...
```

This approach has several drawbacks:

  ✔ The meaning of the arguments is unclear because there is nothing in
    the commands that indicates or labels the purpose of each argument.

✔ The order of the arguments determines their meaning. The two OpenQuery commands that follow, for example, contain the same information. One of the commands, however, cannot work, because its arguments, although valid, appear in the wrong order. (Which one is incorrect? The first command. The query name must always be the first argument following the OpenQuery method.)

```
DoCmd.OpenQuery acViewDesign, "Parks By Region
DoCmd.OpenQuery "Parks By Region", acViewDesign
```

Starting with Excel version 5.0, Microsoft began a process by which new versions of VBA in other programs, such as Access 7.0 (Access 95) and Access 8.0 (Access 97), can support the use of *named* arguments. A *named argument* is one that begins with an *identifier*. Named argument identifiers always end with :=, which you then follow by the actual argument, as shown in the following example:

```
object.method name1:= argument1, name2:= argument2
```

Named arguments solve both of the problems that characterize traditional argument lists, as described in the following paragraphs:

✔ Each argument has a label that indicates its purpose and meaning in the command.

✔ Because each argument has a label, you can enter arguments in any order. You no longer need to enter the arguments in a specific sequence, which is especially useful if you want to skip over optional arguments.

The following command uses a named argument to specify the name of the query you want to open:

```
DoCmd.OpenQuery QueryName:= "Parks By Region"
```

In response to this command, a window opens that displays the data set defined by the `Parks By Region` query. You can close windows by using the `Close` method of the `DoCmd` object. The following command takes advantage of the fact that you can enter named arguments in any order. Normally, the object-type argument precedes the object name. By using named arguments, however, you can instead begin with the object name — which may seem more natural, because the `OpenQuery` method, used in the previous command to open the window, starts with the named argument. The named arguments give the two statements a similar construction and avoid the awkward fact that Access doesn't place the named argument first in the `Close` method.

```
DoCmd.Close ObjectName:= "Parks By Region", _
ObjectType:= acQuery
```

If you want to open the query in Design mode, you can do so by using either of the following commands, because the order of the named arguments is not significant. Notice that the use of the constant `acViewDesign` selects the Design mode display of the specified query. Figure 1-9 shows the query opened in the design window.

```
DoCmd.OpenQuery View:= acViewDesign, _
QueryName:= "Parks By Region"
```

```
DoCmd.OpenQuery QueryName:= "Parks By Region" _
, View:= acViewDesign
```

Figure 1-9:
A query
open in the
Design
mode.

Close the query window this time by using a command with named arguments, as follows:

```
DoCmd.Close acQuery, "Parks By Region"
```

The RunCommand method

The `RunCommand` method provides Access VBA with a means of executing the equivalent of the 336 commands that you can issue by using the various menus and toolbars supplied with Access 97. The `RunCommand` method is associated with the `DoCmd` object.

The `RunCommand` method and its corresponding constants replace the `DoMenuItem` method that previous versions of Access used. (Access 97 still recognizes the `DoMenuItem` method, however, to ensure compatibility with previous versions of Access.)

The following command, for example, performs the operation that occurs after you choose the menu command Window➪Cascade (arranging all open windows in cascade style):

```
DoCmd.RunCommand acCmdWindowCascade
```

Keep in mind that the RunCommand method executes commands from the Access 97 menu structure. Some of the method's operations, therefore, open dialog boxes that you must then manually manipulate. The following statement is the equivalent of the menu command Tools➪Options. After you execute the command, the Options dialog box opens.

```
DoCmd.RunCommand acCmdOptions
```

After the dialog box opens, you must manually close the dialog box.

You can find a full list of all the constants that the RunCommand method uses in the *Run Command Constants* table located in the OBJECTS.MDB database in which you find the examples for this chapter.

Chapter 2
Your First Program

● ●

In This Chapter

▶ What's a program?

▶ Displaying a message

▶ Getting user input

▶ Enumerating collections

▶ Evaluating If conditions

● ●

*C*hapter 1 illustrates how Visual Basic for Applications (VBA) can interact with a program such as Access, which consists of so many elements. From VBA's point of view, everything that makes up Access — the menus, tables, queries, fields, and so on — are all *objects,* each of which has a unique name. You can use special *properties* and *methods,* which you apply to specific objects, to manipulate these objects. As a result, you can write out a single VBA command that counts the number of fields in a table, for example, or opens a query window without the use of Access menus, toolbars, or shortcut keys. In this chapter, you move beyond one-line commands and begin writing some simple but useful VBA programs.

> *Database Folder: Access Prog Dummies \ Chapter 2*
> *Database File: BASIC.MDB*
> *Module: Basic*

If you don't feel like typing in all of the code shown in this chapter don't worry. You can avoid all of the typing by loading copies of the examples stored on the CD-ROM. To use these examples, perform the following steps:

1. **Open the database file BASIC.MDB.**

2. **Click the Modules tab.**

   You see a module named *Basic.*

3. **Click the Design button to open this module.**

   This module contains all 24 examples discussed in this chapter. The names in the module match the names of the examples in this chapter.

4. **To run an example, scroll down until you position the cursor in any part of the code that you want to execute.**

5. **Press the F5 key.**

   Access runs the code.

What's a Program?

Writing a computer *program* is merely a matter of writing a list of instructions. After you complete the list, you run the program by telling Access to start *executing* the list you created. Executing instructions refers to a process in which Access reads the instructions and then attempts to carry out the task described by the instruction.

Because all programs consist of *text,* writing programs is actually just another form of word processing. Access provides *module windows* which are specifically designed to facilitate the entry of programming text.

Module windows in Access provide a number of special features, such as Auto Property/Method Lists, which expedite writing programs the way that auto spell-checker feature in Word 97 facilitates writing standard English text. You may have encountered the Auto Property/Method Lists feature in Chapter 1 when you entered commands into the Debug window. Each time you began to enter a property or method for an object such as DoCmd, Access would display information about the syntax and constants in order to help you write a valid command.

If you're new to programming, take a look at the following list, which describes a few key terms that you often use in programming:

- **Code.** In programming, you call the instruction text that you enter in a module *code.* The name *code* reflects the fact that the programmer designs the syntax of the instructions so that the computer, not a person, understands the instructions. So that Access can carry out your instructions correctly, you must learn to express your ideas within the limits of the VBA language.

- **Statement.** A *statement* is one complete line of code that completes a single instruction. Statements are also known as *commands.* The term *command,* however, is considered a bit obsolete in languages such as VBA that encompass sophisticated programming concepts such as objects, properties, and methods.

- **Structure.** A *structure* is a set of statements that work together to perform a single action. `Sub` and `End Sub`, for example, are separate statements that work together to define the start and the end of a VBA procedure.

- **Procedure.** A *procedure* is a set of statements that form the smallest unit of code that VBA can execute. In VBA, the smallest possible procedure must contain three statements. Each procedure must have a unique name within the database. Names don't have to be fancy. They can be as simple as a single letter such as Q. In general, try to give your programs names that suggest what they do or what their purpose is, for example, `FindCustomerAddress` or `CalcSalesTax`.

- **Run.** If you *run* a procedure, Access reads the first statement in the procedure and carries out the operation specified by that statement. Access then reads the next statement in the procedure, if any, and performs the specified action. This process continues until Access reaches the last statement in the procedure. Procedures automatically terminate if Access cannot perform their instructions.

- **Error.** An *error* occurs if Access cannot perform the operation that a given statement describes. Access displays a message box that indicates the reason why the program can't carry out the instruction.

- **Debugging.** *Debugging* is the process of eliminating errors from your program. Access provides special tools to help you analyze why it can't carry out your instructions. (Debugging is described in more detail in Chapter CD2 on this book's CD.)

In Access, you enter and store VBA instructions in *modules*. The first step in writing a VBA program is to open a *module window*. To open a module window, follow these steps:

1. **If you have not already done so, open the BASIC.MDB file supplied on the CD.**

2. **When the database window is displayed, click the Modules tab.**

3. **Click the New button to open this module.**

After the module window opens, you see the following two lines of text already entered in the module:

```
Option Compare Database
Option Explicit
```

At this point, the meaning of the preceding text is obscure, rather technical, and not very significant for what you're about to explore in this chapter. If you're like most people, however, you hate to let anything go by without explanation as you're picking up something new, so here's a brief comment on both items:

✔ **Option Compare Database.** This statement ensures that any comparisons that the program performs in this module use the same set of comparison rules that Access uses in its database operations. Essentially, Compare Database means that sorting is not sensitive to the case of the characters. Table 2-1 shows that, if this command is missing, Access views the upper- and lowercase versions of the same word — for example, *Zebra* and *zebra* — as different terms. If Database comparison is active, Access treats the two versions of the word as logically equivalent.

Note that the examples used in Table 2-1 are enclosed in quotations. VBA requires text items to be marked with quotations so that they can be distinguished from other parts of the VBA language.

Table 2-1	How Option Compare Affects Access	
Option Compare	*Example*	*True or False*
None	"ZEBRA" = "zebra"	False
Database	"ZEBRA" = "zebra"	True

✔ **Option Explicit.** The purpose of this statement is to act as a kind of *spell checker* for programmers. In addition to all the object, property, and method names provided by Access, VBA enables programmers to create user-defined object names. The most common source of errors in programs turns out to be misspellings of user-defined names. To avoid such errors, the Explicit option requires that you register each user-defined object name using the Dim statement so that Access can automatically flag any unregistered names as errors. Although the Explicit option adds a few more steps to writing programs, this option can help programmers solve a lot of problems that spelling errors cause.

Defining Procedures

After you open a module window (as described in the preceding section), you're ready to take the next step in writing a program — defining a *procedure*. A procedure is a single list of VBA instructions. Although a module can contain one or more procedures, a procedure is the smallest unit of programming instruction that Access can execute.

Each procedure has a distinct starting and ending point. If you want to execute VBA commands, you do so by specifying a procedure name. Access then begins executing instructions, starting with the first instruction in the specified procedure, and then continues until the program reaches the end of the procedure.

VBA uses the following three types of procedures:

- ✔ **Sub.** Sub stands for *subroutine*. Subroutines enable you to break up a large program or task into a series of smaller segments. You execute a Sub procedure by entering the name of the procedure in the Debug window, or by entering the name within another procedure.

- ✔ **Function.** Function procedures return a value in the same way that built-in functions do (spreadsheet programs such as the functions built into Excel). You execute functions by including the function name within an expression that's part of a VBA command.

- ✔ **Class.** Class procedures are used to create custom-defined objects that have their own properties and methods. If you worked with Access before, you probably created forms and reports. When you add your own VBA procedures to objects like forms and reports, as you do in this book, you are creating Class modules.

If all these definitions seem obscure, don't be alarmed. Everything becomes clearer with time and a little experience.

In Chapter 1, you enter individual commands. To begin getting some experience with actual programming, start with a Sub type procedure.

You create a new procedure by typing **Sub** or **Function**, followed by the name of the procedure, in any part of the module. Here, I name the procedure Sub Basic1. Keep in mind that all the procedures in a database (regardless of the module) must have unique names:

To create a new Sub procedure, follow these steps:

1. **Type** Sub Basic1 **on the first available blank line.**

2. **Press Enter.**

   Access reacts to your entry by creating a new procedure. The program creates the procedure by adding two statements to the module, as shown in the following example:

   - The Sub statement does two things: First, the statement marks the starting location of the procedure, and second, this statement registers the name (for example, Basic1) as a procedure.

   - The End Sub statement marks the end of the procedure. After Access encounters the End Sub statement, the program stops executing instructions and ends the procedure.

In addition Access adds ( ) following the name of the procedure. The ( ) are a standard part of every procedure name. What you see in the following example is what should also appear on-screen:

```
Sub Basic1()

End Sub
```

Notice that you entered a blank line between the Sub and End Sub statements. The blank line indicates that you enter the instructions that make up the procedure there, between Sub and End Sub.

If you look carefully at the text in the Module window, you notice that some of the text, such as the words Sub and End Sub appear in blue. Others, such as Basic1, appear as black text. The folks at Microsoft designed Access to alter the color of the text in the module to help identify the meaning of the text. VBA keywords such as Sub and End Sub, for example, appear in blue, and identifiers such as Basic1 appear as black text. You can customize the color scheme for VBA code by using the Code Colors settings on the Module tab of the Tools⇨Options dialog box.

Displaying a Message

One of the most versatile statements in VBA is the MsgBox (or *message box*) statement. The statement displays a simple dialog box in the center of the screen. You can control the appearance of the message box by using any of the following three arguments. The arguments shown in brackets ([]) are optional.

- ✔ Prompt determines the text that appears within the message box.

- ✔ [Buttons] determines the number and type of button that appears. If you omit this argument, an OK button appears in the box.

- ✔ [Title] determines the text of the title bar at the top of the message window. If you omit this argument, the title bar contains the name of the current application — for example, Microsoft Access.

In the Basic1 procedure, insert the following MsgBox statement. This statement displays the text Hello in a message box. Notice that, in the following example, I indent the statement one tab inward from the Sub and End Sub statements. Indenting has no meaning to VBA or Access. Indenting does, however, make your programs easier for people (including you) to read.

```
Sub Basic1()
    MsgBox "Hello"
End Sub
```

You now have a simple but complete procedure. You can have Access execute the code in either of the following two ways:

- ✔ If your cursor is positioned anywhere within the procedure in the module window you can run the program by choosing Run⇨Go/Continue from the menu bar or by pressing F5.

- ✔ In the Debug window, type the name of the Sub procedure — for example, **Basic1** — and press Enter. (You can display the Debug window at any time by pressing Ctrl+G.)

As Access runs the procedure, a message box appears, as shown in Figure 2-1. This message box displays the text Hello that you specified in the MsgBox statement.

Figure 2-1:
The MsgBox statement displays a simple message box.

The window that the MsgBox statement displays is the type of window that doesn't enable you to select anything outside that window while it's open. To continue, you must select one of the buttons in the box or press Alt+F4. Access calls this type of window a *modal* window. In fact, you can define any dialog box as being a modal window because you must complete your dialog with the window before the program allows you to continue.

Access provides a number of *built-in functions*. These functions are actually procedures built directly into the Access program. You can use functions in Access tables, queries, forms, and reports, as well as in VBA to perform calculations, obtain information, or manipulate information. Most Access users are familiar with the Date function. This function returns the current date as maintained by the computer. The following procedure displays the current date, as shown in Figure 2-2:

```
Sub Basic2()
   MsgBox Date
End Sub
```

Figure 2-2:
The current
date
appears in
a message
box.

Almost all functions in Access require parentheses — () — following the function name. Exceptions are the Date (today's date) and Now (today's time and date) functions. If you enter **Date()** anywhere in Access, Access automatically removes the ().

Another source of information in any Access database is the information that various object properties return. Chapter 1 notes that you can obtain the name of the open database by using the Name property of the CurrentDB object. The following code example displays the full path name of the current database, as shown in Figure 2-3:

```
Sub Basic3()
    MsgBox CurrentDb.Name
End Sub
```

Figure 2-3:
The full
path name
of the
current
database
appears.

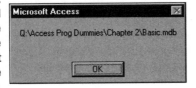

So far, the items appearing in the message box are all the results of simple arguments. You're not limited, however, to simple items. The following example uses the Pmt() function to calculate the monthly payment of a $10,000 loan for 36 months at 8.5 percent interest. The result appears in Figure 2-4.

In using functions such as Pmt() that use interest rates, remember that people usually express interest rates as APRs (annual percentage rates) but usually calculate payments on a monthly basis. Remember to divide the APR by 12 to get the correct monthly interest rate.

```
Sub Basic4()
    MsgBox Pmt(0.085 / 12, 36, -10000)
End Sub
```

In Access (and in Excel, too) functions that make calculations about loans, such as Pmt (monthly payment), Ppmt (the principal portion of a monthly payment), and IPmt (the interest portion of a monthly payment), express the amount of the loan as a negative number. These functions view the amount as the initial cash flow from the lender's point of view. (The *initial cash flow* in a loan is one in which the lender gives up a lump sum to the borrower and then, in return, receives a series of positive cash flows, usually in the form of monthly payments.) If you're more familiar with the Pmt function in products such as Lotus 1-2-3 or even Microsoft Works (which express the loan amount as a positive number), the Access approach may seem odd.

Figure 2-4:
The message box returns the result of a calculation.

Using the Format function

In the previous example, the data obtained by the Pmt( ) function was displayed as 315.675374235574. While this number may be accurate it may be a bit awkward to display to a user as the monthly payment amount. In a spreadsheet program such as Excel, you control the appearance of numbers like 315.675374235574 by using the Format Number command to apply a formatting style to the raw data.

In VBA, the Format ( ) function provides methods for controlling the appearance of the values calculated during a procedure. Format plays roughly the same role in VBA that Format Number does in Excel.

- ✔ Value. This is the text, number, or date value to format.

- ✔ Format. This is the name of a standard format — for example, Currency, Standard, Percent, or a custom-designed format template, such as 0.000%.

The following example uses the Format() function to convert the raw output of the Pmt() function to a currency style value, as shown in Figure 2-5. Notice that I insert the entire Pmt() function as the value argument for the Format() function. As described in Chapter 1, this technique is called *nesting*. In this case, the Pmt() function nests inside the Format() function, which in turn forms the argument for the MsgBox statement.

```
Sub Basic5()
        MsgBox Format(Pmt(0.085 / 12, 36, _
        -10000), "currency")
End Sub
```

Figure 2-5:
The
Format()
function
controls the
appearance
of the
number.

You can also apply the Format () function to dates as well as numbers. The following example uses the Long Date format to display the current system date — for example *Sunday, November 24, 1996* — in the message box:

```
Sub Basic6()
    MsgBox Format(Date, "Long Date")
End Sub
```

String expressions

So far in this chapter, the information appearing in the message box is the result of a single item, such as a function or an object property. You can improve the informational value of the message box display if you add a label or text explaining the meaning of the number or date that appears in the box.

You add a label or text to the message box by creating a *string expression*. You create string expressions by chaining together literal text, numbers, dates, functions, and/or calculations to form a single output. Suppose, for example, that you want to display a message box that reads Today is Sunday, November 24, 1996 (where 11/24/96 is today's date).

Text strings consist of two parts, as shown in the following example. The first part is a *text literal.* A *literal* is a value that looks the same in the code as it does after you run the program. Quotation marks always enclose text literals. The second part of the string involves the functions that generate the desired date.

```
"Today is "
Format(Date, "Long Date")
```

Remember that if you want to have a space between items when they are combined you have to add a space inside the quotation marks. For example, if you type **"Today is"** (without the extra space at the end) you might get something like Today isJuly 4, 1996 on the screen.

You can connect two or more different data items by using the & operator (also called the *concatenation operator*). Procedure Basic7 uses the & operator to combine text and date information into a single output, as shown in Figure 2-6.

The word *concatenation* comes from the Latin word *concate,* which means to forge into a chain. When you use a concatenation operator you are chaining together two or more items into a single block of text. The result of concatenation is always text.

The following example demonstrates how this text string appears in the Basic7 procedure:

```
Sub Basic7()
    MsgBox "Today is " & Format(Date, "Long Date")
End Sub
```

Figure 2-6:
The message box displays the result of the string expression.

You can apply the same technique to combinations of text and numbers. `Basic8` (the procedure shown below) combines text with the `Pmt()` calculation to produce the message box shown in Figure 2-7. Notice in the following example that `Basic8` uses the & twice. The second & inserts a period at the end of the expression to make the output a grammatically correct sentence.

```
Sub Basic8()
    MsgBox "The Monthly Payment is " _
    & Format(Pmt(0.085 / 12, 36, -10000), "currency") _
    & "."
End Sub
```

Figure 2-7:
Punctuation is added to the end of the message using the & operator.

Multiple-line text expressions

Sometimes, the information you want to appear in the message box may look better as several lines of text rather than as a single, long line of text stretching across the box. If you are typing text in a word processor, you start a new line by pressing Enter. But how do you insert a new line into a string expression?

The answer comes in the form of the `Chr()` function. Keyboards communicate with the computer through numeric codes. This procedure is true not only for the visible characters (A, z, 1, 2, $, and so on), but also for the invisible characters that you produce by pressing keys such as Enter or Esc. The letter *A,* for example, is equivalent to a numeric code of 65. The `Chr()` function enables you to specify a character by its code number. If, for example, you enter the following command in the Debug window, the result is the letter `A`:

```
? Chr(65)
```

The best-known coding system for the standard U.S. keyboard is the *American Standard Code for Information Interchange (ASCII)*. ASCII, which was the standard for teletype machines, contains 128 characters. Most PCs are and have long been capable of supporting more than 128 characters. The *American National Standards Institute (ANSI)* code, for example, expands the coding system to 256 characters. Many Windows fonts support the full 256-character ANSI code set.

You can create a multiple-line display in a message box by taking advantage of the character codes for the invisible characters, specifically the code produced by the Enter key, *13*. You can use Chr(13) to insert a new line into a string expression. Basic9 (the procedure shown below) employs this technique in the following example to create the multiple-line display shown in Figure 2-8:

```
Sub Basic9()
    MsgBox "Date: " & Date & _
    Chr(13) & "Time: " & Time
End Sub
```

Figure 2-8:
The Chr() function enables you to create a multiple-line string expression.

Basic10 shows how you can combine the concept of a string expression with the Access object model to create an expression that provides specific information about a database object — here, a table. The expression inserts the name of a table with the Name property and then uses the Fields.Count property to return the number of fields in that table, as shown in the following example:

```
Sub Basic10()
    MsgBox "The " & CurrentDb.TableDefs(0).Name _
    & " table contains " & _
    CurrentDb.TableDefs(0).Fields.Count _
    & " fields."
End Sub
```

What's interesting about Basic10 (the previous example) is the way that you can alter the object model reference to yield information about a different object. What do you need to change to create a procedure that displays the name and field count for the second table in the current database? The answer is only two characters — change the 0s to 1s, as in the following example, and you get the result shown in Figure 2-9:

```
Sub Basic11()
    MsgBox "The " & CurrentDb.TableDefs(1).Name _
    & " table contains " & _
    CurrentDb.TableDefs(1).Fields.Count _
    & " fields."
End Sub
```

Figure 2-9:
The message box displays information about table definition number 1.

The Employees table contains 6 fields.

Getting User Input

All the examples discussed so far in this chapter deal with displaying information that you define as you create the code for the procedure. Examples Basic10 and Basic11 use specific index numbers, for example 0 or 1, to refer to the table object used in the procedure. This means that each time you want to display information about a different table in the collection, you must either edit an existing procedure or create a new one that points at a different table in the collection. Typing the specific number or name of an object is called *hardwiring* your code. Hardwired code works, but only for the exact object you had in mind when you wrote the code.

A more productive approach is to find a way to create a procedure that you can use to display information about any table without having to rewrite the procedure each time. The idea is to leave a blank in the code where the index number of the table goes. Then, each time you run the procedure, you are asked to enter the index number of the table you want to use.

In contrast to the hardwired approach, this technique results in a generalized procedure that you can use to retrieve information about any table without having to rewrite your code each time.

To create this type of code, add the following two elements to your procedures:

- ✔ **Input.** You need a way to pause the execution of your code, enabling the user to enter a value, such as the index number of the table, into the procedure.

- ✔ **Temporary Storage.** You need a way to temporarily save the user's input so that it can then be inserted into other statements or expressions within the procedure that depend on the user's input. If the user enters **2** (for the third table in the collection) you must insert that value into the expression `CurrentDB.TableDefs(???)` where I have typed `(???)`.

Both of these needs involve the use of *variables*. A variable is an object that provides a place where you can temporarily store values. Temporary in this case means the time it takes to execute the program. Unlike complex objects such as tables or queries, a variable has only one property, that is, its value. You create variables using the `Dim` statement. The following example defines a variable called `TableNumber`:

```
Dim TableNumber
```

Dim is short for dimension. The name has very little to do with its function as shown here. `Dim` was originally used in BASIC to set the number of elements in a subscripted array such as x(1), x(2), x(3), and so on. In VBA, Dim is used to define variable names, and it still retains its old usage for arrays.

The concept of a variable is one of the harder ones to grasp mainly because you can never see a variable the way you can see a table or a form. To better understand variables, try to think of a variable as a storage box inside the memory of the computer. The `Dim` statement places a label on that box — for example, `TableNumber`. After you create this box, you can place text, numbers, or dates into the box. Later, you can retrieve the information from the box and use the same information in another statement.

Variables have roughly the same function as the Windows clipboard, which allows you to copy data from one location and then paste it into other locations. The main difference is that while Windows only has one clipboard (you can only copy and paste one item at a time), VBA allows you to have as many variables as your computer's memory can hold. In order to distinguish one memory box from another you must give each box (variable) a unique name.

VBA gives you wide latitude in creating variable names. The only limitations are that names must begin with an alphabetical character; can't be longer than 255 characters; and can't contain a period, a space, or the symbols *$*, *%*, *&*, or *!*. Variables aren't case-sensitive.

The goal in this example is to enable the user to input a value and then insert that value into a MsgBox statement, such as the one in examples Basic10 and Basic11. The simplest way to get user input is by using the Input statement. The simplest form of this statement uses InputBox to assign whatever the user entered to a variable name, as shown in the following example:

```
VariableName = InputBox(prompt)
```

Basic12 shows how you would use InputBox in a program. First, the Dim statement is used to create the variable *DateOfBirth*. This means that you have created a box in memory, labeled *DateOfBirth,* into which you can place some text, a date, or a number. InputBox is then used to insert whatever the user entered into the *DateOfBirth* box. Then, the MsgBox statement extracts the value stored in *DateOfBirth* and uses that value to calculate the age of the person whose date of birth was entered using the DateDiff function.

The DateDiff() function calculates the difference in time between two dates. The first argument in the function is a text code (yyyy = year, q = quarter, m = month, y = day of year, d = day, w = weekday, ww = week, h = hour, n = minute, s = second) that sets the unit of time calculated. In Basic12 the code "yyyy", as displayed in the following example, expresses the date difference in years:

```
Sub Basic12()
    Dim DateOfBirth
    DateOfBirth = InputBox("Enter your date of birth")
    MsgBox "You are " & DateDiff("yyyy", DateOfBirth, _
    Date)& " years old."
End Sub
```

After the Basic12 procedure runs, it displays a message box that pauses the execution of the procedure (see Figure 2-10). This pause enables the user to enter an appropriate value in the box — for example, **9/13/51**.

After the user makes this entry, a second message box appears, as shown in Figure 2-11. This time, the message box shows the person's age based on the entry made in the previous message box.

The key to how Basic12 works is the use of the variable *DateOfBirth*. Think of the variable as a kind of storagebox. InputBox deposits information into the storagebox. The MsgBox statement then looks in the storagebox to see what the user left and uses that date to perform the DateDiff() calculation.

Figure 2-10:
The
InputBox
enables the
user to
enter a
value that
other
statements
in the
program
can use.

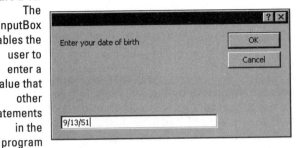

Figure 2-11:
The user's
input
determines
the content
of the
message
box.

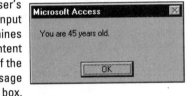

What happens to the storagebox after the procedure ends? Access destroys it. The next time the procedure is run, Access creates a new storagebox for DateOfBirth when it executes the Dim statement again. It may seem wasteful to destroy the storageboxes each time. However, destroying them (the variables) at the end of each procedure prevents data from one run affecting the next run of the same procedure. Each time the procedure is run, it starts with a clean slate.

To summarize, Basic12 illustrates the three steps involved in writing an interactive procedure:

✔ Create a variable for each item of data the user needs to enter.

✔ Use InputBox to fill the variables with the user's input.

✔ Use the data stored in the variables to produce new information and display that information within a message box.

Interacting with Database Objects

The procedure Basic12 illustrated the basic approach to interactive programming. Interactive programming creates procedure that require the user to make an entry. More importantly, the entry they make actually determines the result of the procedure.

Of course, the simple message displayed by Basic12 doesn't accomplish much. The next task is to apply the interactive programming to the database objects found in Access. The structure of Basic13 is identical to the structure of Basic12 in that it contains the three basic steps of interactive programming: Create variables, fill with user input, and obtain and display the specified data.

Figure 2-12 shows the dialog boxes that generate this procedure. The input box asks the user to enter the index number of the table that the user wants analyzed. Access stores the value the user enters in the variable *TableName*. The program then inserts the variable into the object expression where the index number normally appears. Thus, whatever number the user enters determines which table Access summarizes. You now have a single procedure that you can use to find the field count of any table in the open database, as shown in the following example:

```
Sub Basic13()
    Dim TableName As Integer
    TableName = InputBox("Enter the table index number")
    MsgBox "The " & CurrentDb.TableDefs(TableName).Name _
    & " table contains " & _
    CurrentDb.TableDefs(TableName).Fields.Count _
    & " fields."
End Sub
```

Figure 2-12:
User input
determines
which
TableDef
object
Access
analyzes.

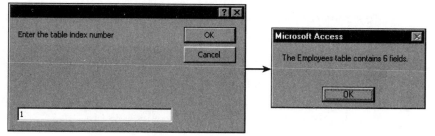

One technical change appears in `Basic13` that did not appear in `Basic12`. The difference occurs in the `Dim` statement. In `Basic12` the variable was not assigned a specific data type (text, number, date, and so on). If you mention no specific data type, VBA creates a generic type of variable called a *variant*. Variants can store text, numbers, or dates. You don't need to decide in advance which type of variable to use.

On the other hand, as the programmer, you know in advance that the entry made by the user is going to be the index of an object in a collection. Access requires that the index number be an integer-type (a whole number). Adding the `As Integer` keywords to the `Dim` statement, as shown in the following example, ensures that Access converts any user input into a whole number value which will be compatible with the rest of the statements in the procedure:

```
Dim DateOfBirth              'Basic12
Dim TableName As Integer     'Basic13
```

One problem with `Basic13` is that the user doesn't know the maximum index number for the current database. In Chapter 1, I explain how entering an index number that exceeds the actual number of tables (minus one) causes an error. The object reference shown in the following example returns the maximum index value possible for tables in the current database:

```
CurrentDb.TableDefs.Count - 1
```

You can alert the user to the range of valid entries by inserting that object reference into the `InputBox` prompt to form a phrase such as `Enter a number from 0 to 17` in the box, as shown in the following example:

```
TableName = InputBox("Enter a number from 0 to " & _
CurrentDb.TableDefs.Count - 1)
```

`Basic14`, as shown in the following example, displays a message that alerts the user to the range of valid index numbers for the current database.

```
Sub Basic14()
   Dim TableName As Integer
   TableName = InputBox("Enter a number from 0 to " & _
   CurrentDb.TableDefs.Count - 1)
   MsgBox "The " & CurrentDb.TableDefs(TableName).Name _
   & " table contains " & _
   CurrentDb.TableDefs(TableName).Fields.Count _
   & " fields."
End Sub
```

One problem with Basic14 is that for most users the index numbers of the tables aren't very meaningful. It would be more user-friendly if the user could enter the name of the table instead of its index number.

Basic15 enables the user to enter the name of the table for which the program can count fields. Notice that, in the following example, the Dim statement you use to define the variable drops the As Integer keywords. This change enables the variable to store text data, such as the name of a table.

```
Sub Basic15()
    Dim TableName
    TableName = InputBox("Enter the table name" & _
    CurrentDb.TableDefs.Count - 1)
    MsgBox "The " & CurrentDb.TableDefs(TableName).Name _
    & " table contains " & _
    CurrentDb.TableDefs(TableName).Fields.Count _
    & " fields."
End Sub
```

One interesting point about Basic15 is that the user still has the option to enter either an index number or a name to specify a table despite what the prompt in the input box says. As long as the variable TableName contains either a valid index number or name, the procedure will be able to run without error.

Procedures Basic13, Basic14 and Basic15 illustrate how user input can be used to select an object from a collection, such as a table, by using the input as either the object's index value or the object's name.

Enumerating Collections

In all the procedures you've worked with in this chapter, you've dealt with one member of a collection at a time. You selected that member either by using its index number within the collection or by referring to the name of the object — for example, the name of a table. But what about the collections themselves? How would you deal with all of the members of a collection?

The process of dealing with all of the members of a collection is called *enumerating* the collection. Enumerating is a programming technique that deals with all the members of a collection, starting with the first member (index number 0) and continuing through to the last member.

VBA provides a structure that's specifically designed to help you enumerate all the members of a collection. The For Each and Next statements create a structure that repeats one or more operations for each element in a collection.

```
For Each object In collection
...
Next
```

The procedure shown in the following example, ENumCollection1, illustrates how you can use a For Each structure to perform the same action once for every member of a collection. As an example, suppose the collection is the set of tables contained in the TableDefs collection. You can use this structure to display the name of every table that is a member of the collection.

To make this work, you use the Dim statement to create a variable that the For Each statement uses as a temporary container for each member of the collection. Remember that to assign an object such as a table, query, field, form, or report to a variable you must specify the object type in the Dim statement (for example, TableDef or QueryDef). Because ENumCollection1 processes table definitions, the variable *T* is defined as a TableDef type variable.

```
Sub ENumCollection1()
    Dim T As TableDef
    For Each T In CurrentDb.TableDefs
      MsgBox T.Name
    Next
End Sub
```

The selection of *T* as the name for the object variable has no special significance. The variable could be anything — for example, *TName*, *TableName* or *NameOfTable*. I use *T* here because it is the simplest possible name (a single character) and the simplicity makes the code a bit easier to understand. On the other hand, a longer, more descriptive name might be easier to understand when you haven't looked at the code in a long time. If a procedure is using only a single variable of a given type, my own preference is to use simple names like *T* for TableDef, *R* for a Recordset, and *Q* for a QueryDef. Professional programmers often add prefixes to their variable names that identify their meaning such as tbl for a Table, rs for a Recordset and qry for a QueryDef. For example, tblCompany would refer to a TableDef, rsCompany would refer to a Recordset, and so on. These prefixes are useful when your code contains several different variables of the same type.

After this procedure runs, the result is a series of message boxes. Each message box displays the name of one of the members of the collection. You need to click the OK button 18 times (once for each mesage box that is displayed) to work your way through the entire collection.

In `ENumCollection1`, the keywords `TableDef` and `TableDefs` both appear. Is this a mistake? What's the difference? If you have a collection of objects such as tables, the name that ends with s refers to the entire collection. The name without the s refers to a single member of the collection. `TableDefs` refers to the entire collection of tables. `TableDef` refers to a single table within the collection.

Building a text string

Although `ENumCollection1` does succeed in displaying the name of each table in the database, the procedure does so in a rather inconvenient way. Clicking through a long series of boxes, each of which carries only a single item of information about the collection, can quickly become annoying. Creating a single box that lists all the tables in the database is a much better idea.

You can accomplish this by using the same techniques (the & operator and variables) that have earlier been introduced in this chapter. The difference is that you will put them together in a slightly different way.

The trick involves using a variable to store not just one name, but all of the table names. If all of the names are stored in one variable, you can display all of the names in one message box at the end instead of a series of message boxes with one name in each.

Because this technique is a bit unintuitive, it may be useful to play around with some variables in the Debug window before you try to use this technique in a procedure. Perform the following steps:

1. **Activate the Debug window by pressing Ctrl+G.**

2. **Move the cursor to the first blank line at the bottom of the Debug window.**

3. **Create a variable by entering** `people = "John"`.

   Remember to press Enter after each entry.

4. **Enter** `? people` **to display the value of the variable.**

   Access displays `John` on-screen. This response confirms that the variable `people` contains the name `John`. What happens if you assigned a different name to the same variable?

5. **Type** `people = "Mary"`.

6. **Type** `? people`.

   Not surprisingly, Access replaces the old contents of the variable (`John`) with the newly assigned value, `Mary`. Each time you assign a new value to a variable, Access erases the old value. But suppose that you actually want to *add* a value to an existing variable *without* erasing the old value. How? The solution appears following Step 8. Enter the commands in Steps 7 and 8 and see what happens.

7. **Type** `people = people & "John"`.

8. **Type** `? people`.

The screen displays `MaryJohn`. Access added `John` to `Mary` instead of replacing one with the other. The statement `people = people & "John"` means that `people` can contain whatever is currently stored in `people` — plus the characters `John`. Because the variable name `people` appears on both the left and the right side of the `=`, Access adds the new text to the existing text.

Of course the variable's result would look more like a list if each name appeared on a separate line. Remember, to create multiple-lined text displays, insert `Chr(13)` into the text whenever you want to start a new line. Try Steps 9 and 10.

9. **Type** `people = people & Chr(13)& "Sue"`.

10. **Type** `? people`.

The display shows that the new name, `Sue`, appears on a line separate from the previous text, as in the following example:

```
MaryJohn
Sue
```

With this technique in hand, you can return to the problem of listing the table names. (Press Ctrl+F4 to close the Debug window.)

`ENumCollection2` applies this technique to the `TableDefs` collection. You use a variable called *TableList* to accumulate a list of the table names that the `TableDefs` collection contains. Keep in mind that nothing appears on-screen until all the names are stuffed into the `TableList` variable. Notice the use of `Chr(13)` in the following example to add a new line after each name. The result is shown in Figure 2-13, where the message box contains a full list of the tables contained in the current database.

```
Sub ENumCollection2()
    Dim T As TableDef, TableList
    For Each T In CurrentDb.TableDefs
        TableList = TableList & T.Name & Chr(13)
    Next
    MsgBox TableList
End Sub
```

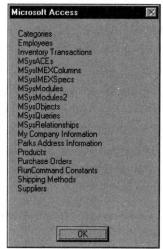

Figure 2-13:
The
message
box shows
a list of all
the tables in
the current
database,
each on
its own
separate
line.

You can expand the amount of information gathered about the members of the collection to include the number of fields as well as the table names. In the following example, ENumCollection3 adds T.Fields.Count to the text stored for each table to produce a list of tables with the number of fields in each one, as shown in Figure 2-14.

```
Sub ENumCollection3()
    Dim T As TableDef, TableList
    For Each T In CurrentDb.TableDefs
        TableList = TableList & T.Name _
        & " - " & T.Fields.Count & Chr(13)
    Next
    MsgBox TableList
End Sub
```

You can use the same logic to show a variety of information. In the following example, ENumCollection4 replaces the Fields.Count property with the RecordCount property to list the number of records in each table.

```
Sub ENumCollection4()
    Dim T As TableDef, TableList
    For Each T In CurrentDb.TableDefs
        TableList = TableList & T.Name _
        & " - " & T.RecordCount & Chr(13)
    Next
    MsgBox TableList
End Sub
```

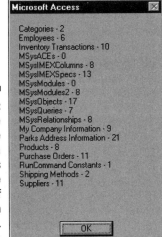

Figure 2-14:
The
procedure
produces a
list of tables
and the
number of
fields in
each table.

You can also apply the concept of nesting — that is, of putting one programming structure inside another — to For Each loops. Tables and fields, for example, represent nested collections. This means that inside the TableDefs collection are individual tables, each of which contains a collection of fields.

ENumCollection5 uses two For Each structures, one nested inside the other, to process all the fields in all the tables, as shown in Figure 2-15.

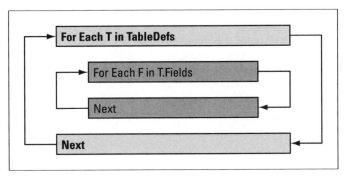

Figure 2-15:
The Fields
collection
nests
inside the
TableDefs
collection.

Specifically, ENumCollection5 generates one message box for each table in the current database. Included in each message, however, is a complete list of all the fields in that table.

Notice that the program contains two statements that affect the content of the *TableInfo* variable, as shown in Figure 2-16.

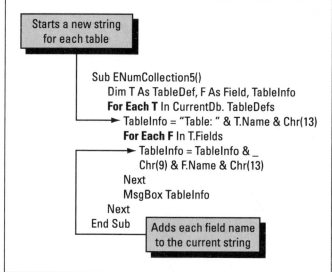

Figure 2-16:
Statements
that control
the
contents
of the
TableInfo
variable.

✔ Access executes the first statement each time you select a new
TableDef. This statement erases the previous contents of the variable,
if any, and inserts the name of the current table in the collection.

✔ The second statement that deals with *TableInfo* uses the string-
building technique to combine the names of all the fields in the current
table into a single variable.

The result of the procedure is a series of message boxes, similar to the one
shown in Figure 2-17, which lists all the fields in each table.

Figure 2-17:
The
message
box for
each table
summarizes
the fields in
that table.

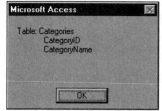

Evaluating If Conditions

Chapter 1 notes that, among the tables in the TableDefs collection of any
database, one set of eight tables normally doesn't appear in the database
window. These tables are special *system* tables that Access uses. After you

enumerate the `TableDefs` collection, however, the database window includes these tables. Suppose, however, that you could limit the tables that Access selects during a procedure to only those tables that do appear in the database window — that is, the *user-defined tables* only. Such a limitation may prove useful.

Access maintains a set of tables called *system tables.* Access uses these tables internally to keep track of the user-defined objects (tables, queries, forms, reports, and modules). These tables are not meant to be altered by the user since incorrect changes can corrupt data. For this reason the tables are hidden from the user. However, when you enumerate the `TableDefs` collection they are included. In most cases you want to avoid using the system tables in your programs.

The first step in creating a procedure that can select only user-defined tables is to figure out how you can logically differentiate between user tables and system tables. Access provides a table property called `Attributes`. The purpose of the `Attributes` property is to identify the special characteristics of database objects such as tables and fields. In the following example, `ENumCollection6` lists the `Attributes` value for all the tables in the current table, as shown in Figure 2-18.

```
Sub ENumCollection6()
    Dim T As TableDef, TableInfo
    For Each T In CurrentDb.TableDefs
        TableInfo = TableInfo & T.Name & " = " _
        & T.Attributes & Chr(13)
    Next
    MsgBox TableInfo
End Sub
```

If you look at the list of attributes shown in Figure 2-18, you may notice a pattern. All the user-defined tables — that is, those tables having names that appear in the database window list of tables — have an attribute of 0. This means that if you limit the tables included in the list to only those with an `Attributes` value of 0, you get a list of only the user-defined tables.

The solution to this and a whole range of similar problems is to use an `If ... Then ... End If` structure. In this type of structure, you follow the `If` statement with a *logical expression.* A logical expression is one that is either true or false, as shown in Figure 2-19. If the expression evaluates as true, Access executes any statements that follow the `If` statement. On the other hand, if the expression evaluates as false, the procedure skips all the statements following the `If` statement and resumes with the first statement following the `End If` statement. By using `If ... Then ... End If` therefore, you can create a procedure that skips certain statements under specific circumstances.

Figure 2-18:
The
Attributes
property
value for
each table
appears
in the
message
box.

Figure 2-19:
Using the If
statement
enables you
to execute
statements
selectively
based on
the truth or
falsity of an
expression.

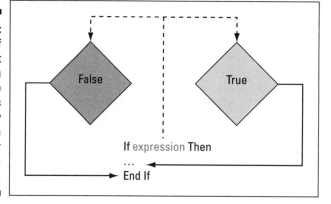

In this case, the task is to include information about a table only if the Attributes property is zero. This idea is expressed in VBA code as shown in the following example of code. The If statement is true if the current table definition is a user-defined table and false in all other cases.

```
If T.Attributes = 0 Then
```

The procedure *ENumCollection7* shows how an If … Then … End If can be applied to the current problem. The If structure is placed inside a For Each structure. As each member of the TableDefs collection is processed, the Attributes property of the TableDef is tested by the If statement. When the value of the Attributes property is zero, the name and record count of the table are added to the *TableList* variable. Conversely, when the value is not zero, the procedure skips the statement that adds information to *TableList*. See Figure 2-20.

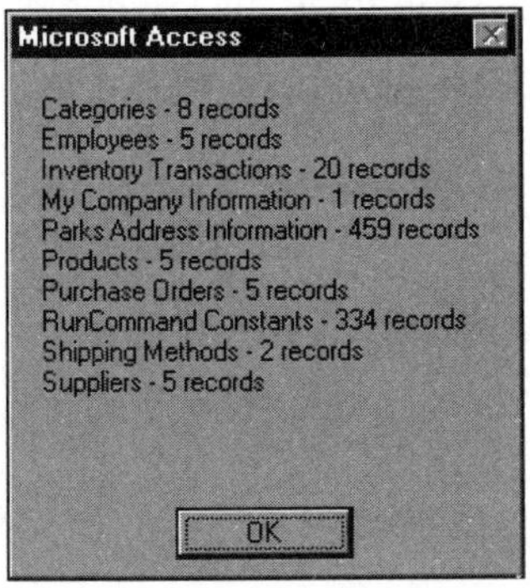

Figure 2-20:
The table
information
now
includes
only the
user-
defined
tables in
the current
database.

Microsoft Access

Categories - 8 records
Employees - 5 records
Inventory Transactions - 20 records
My Company Information - 1 records
Parks Address Information - 459 records
Products - 5 records
Purchase Orders - 5 records
RunCommand Constants - 334 records
Shipping Methods - 2 records
Suppliers - 5 records

OK

```
Sub ENumCollection7()
    Dim T As TableDef, TableList
    For Each T In CurrentDb.TableDefs
        If T.Attributes = 0 Then
            TableList = TableList & T.Name _
            & " - " & T.RecordCount & " records" _
            & Chr(13)
        End If
    Next
    MsgBox TableList
End Sub
```

Using DoCmd in a Procedure

In Chapter 1, I describe how the DoCmd object enables you to execute Access macro actions and menu commands. In Chapter 1 you entered the VBA code equivalents of these actions directly into the Debug window. You can also use these same commands within a procedure in which you want to execute a macro command or a menu operation.

Suppose, for example, that you want to open a table (such as the Employees table) and sort that table according to its LastName field. You can accomplish this task by using the VBA equivalents of the macro and menu operations you would use if you were performing the task manually.

The following example uses three DoCmd object methods to open and sort the table. First, the example uses OpenTable to open a window containing the contents of the specified table. Then the example uses GoToControl to select the sort field. In an open table or query window, this command moves the cursor to a specific field column. In this case, the cursor moves to the LastName field. The RunCommand method of the third example executes the equivalent of the Records⇨Sort⇨Sort Ascending menu command by using the constant `acCmdSortAscending` as its argument. The display that results is shown in Figure 2-21.

```
Sub DoCmd1()
    DoCmd.OpenTable "Employees"
    DoCmd.GoToControl "LastName"
    DoCmd.RunCommand acCmdSortAscending
End Sub
```

Editing macro actions in VBA code is usually quite simple. To change the sort order of the records from LastName to Title, for example, all you need to do is edit the name of the field that you use as an argument for the `GoToControl` method, as shown in the following example:

```
Sub DoCmd2()
    DoCmd.OpenTable "Employees"
    DoCmd.GoToControl "Title"
    DoCmd.RunCommand acCmdSortAscending
End Sub
```

You can easily use VBA code to express such operations as applying a filter to a table. In the following example, `DoCmd3` shows the use of the `ApplyFilter` method to select only those records from the Parks Address Information table that have a `State` value of `PA`.

```
Sub DoCmd3()
    DoCmd.OpenTable "Parks Address Information"
    DoCmd.ApplyFilter WhereCondition:="State = 'PA'"
End Sub
```

If you want to insert a text literal as part of a text item, you can use apostrophes (`' '`) around the text literal, as is the case in `DoCmd3`, where you use the expression `"State = 'PA'"` to filter records.

Figure 2-21:
Access 97
sorts the
table by the
LastName
field.

	Employee ID	FirstName	LastName	Title	Extension	Work Phone
▶	5	Steven	Buchanan	Vice President		(212) 555-1189
	1	Nancy	Davolio	President		(212) 555-9857
	2	Andrew	Fuller	Treasurer		(212) 555-9482
	3	Janet	Leverling	Executive Secre		(212) 555-3412
	4	Margaret	Peacock	Accounting Mar		(212) 555-8122
*	(AutoNumber)					

⊞ Employees : Table

Record: ◄◄ ◄ 1 ► ►► ►* of 5

Chapter 3
The SQL Story

In This Chapter

▶ Using SQL to retrieve sets of records

▶ Using SQL keywords

▶ Sorting records with ORDER BY

▶ Selecting records with WHERE

▶ Adding calculated columns

▶ Creating queries with parameters

*O*ne of the most powerful tools available in database management software is *SQL (Structured Query Language)*, typically pronounced *sequel* — you know, like a newer (usually worse) version of a movie. This chapter explains what SQL is, why it's important in Access 97, and how you can use SQL to manipulate the data stored in Access tables.

> **Database Folder: Chapter 3**
> **Database File: SQL.MDB**
> **Module: Object Example**

Before you begin, do the following:

1. Open the database for Chapter 3, SQL.MDB.

2. Click on the Queries tab.

This tab lists 52 queries that correspond to those named in this chapter.

3. Open the specified query form in the design mode.

This, of course, is optional. You can choose to enter the commands as they appear in the book, if you'd rather.

While running the previously entered queries saves time, some people feel that actually doing the typing helps them to understand what they are entering.

Why SQL?

SQL? Isn't this a book about Access 97 programming? Why am I introducing another language in Chapter 3?

It turns out that you can't do much Access programming without encountering SQL. SQL was originally designed back in the neolithic age of computers to help average human beings access data stored on their mainframe computers. The goal was to allow people to request sets of data by writing sentences like "select these fields from that table."

While it may be possible to write Access programs and not directly use SQL, you will find that the most efficient way to write Access programs is to combine the objects discussed in Chapters 1 and 2 with SQL operations explained in this chapter.

Using the SQL View

Unlike most desktop applications (such as Word or Excel), Access is actually a collection of several different applications bundled together in a single user interface. Table 3-1 lists the six basic parts of the Access interface that correspond to the six tabs in the database window (Tables, Queries, Forms, Reports, Macros, and Modules).

What's interesting about this list is that only three of the six components (Forms, Reports, and Macros) are designed specifically for Access and only Access. The other three (Tables, Queries, and Modules) are components that Access uses and can also function outside of Access as part of other applications. For example, the tables used in Access conform to the Microsoft DAO (Data Access Objects) model. This means that in addition to accessing the tables stored in an MDB (Microsoft DataBase) file through Access, you can use those same tables with other applications, such as Excel, or from programs written in Visual Basic or Visual C++.

Table 3-1   Component Parts of the Access System

Access Name	Other Name	Acronym	Function
Tables	Data Access Objects	DAO	Defines the structures in which data is entered and stored.
Queries	Structured Query Language	SQL	Provides a standard method for retrieving sets of data.
Forms	Access Form Objects	none	Provides screen windows in which data can be viewed and edited.

Access Name	Other Name	Acronym	Function
Reports	Access Report Objects	none	Provides paginated output forms for printing sets of data.
Macros	Access Macros	none	Provides a macro language to customize Access Forms and Reports.
Modules	Visual Basic for Applications	VBA	Provides a standard programming language that can be used to manipulate all of the elements in Access and the Microsoft Office suite.

The subject of this chapter is SQL — a component behind the Access Query feature (as listed in Table 3-1). Access uses SQL in a variety of ways to select sets of data based on logical criteria. The data sets can then be displayed in forms, printed on reports, or used to calculate summary information.

FAQs about SQL

Before you dig into the details of SQL, it may be useful to clarify a few points about the Access/SQL personality split.

Where did SQL come from?

SQL is not new. The language was developed over a decade ago to make it simpler for users to retrieve information from mainframe databases. At that time, users needed to learn a different set of commands for retrieving data from each database they wanted to access.

The goal of SQL is to provide a single set of commands that you can use to retrieve data from any database. As a result, SQL eliminates the need to learn a variety of database commands or languages and allows a user or programmer to apply his knowledge of SQL to a wide array of data resources. For example, Microsoft sells two different database products: Access and SQL Server. However, because both products support SQL, each of the products can process the same commands.

What is a query language?

Table 3-1 lists two types of languages in Access: SQL and VBA (Visual Basic for Applications). SQL is called a query language because its set of commands is limited to entering, updating, and retrieving sets of data — or *querying*. While this is an important function, languages such as VBA provide the user with a broad set of functions. These functions can control all aspects of an application, including the user interface, data security, and printed reports.

If SQL is so important, why don't I see it when I use Access?

While SQL is not a difficult language to learn, it's still a computer language. Languages, no matter how simple, require the user to write out a structured command that includes specific terms placed in the correct order, and with the correct punctuation. To make Access data easy to retrieve, Access hides SQL behind its query grid interface.

As an example, look at Figure 3-1 which shows the Access query grid. The grid contains a visual representation of a query that will retrieve four fields (*Customer ID, Part No, Quantity,* and *Unit Price*) from the Orders table.

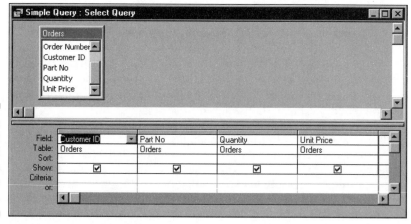

Figure 3-1:
A typical query laid out in the Access query grid.

Query: Simple Query

However, behind every Access query grid is an equivalent SQL command, also called a *statement*. You can change the display of the query window to reveal the SQL statement that corresponds to the query you've designed.

Do this by selecting SQL View, using the View icon on the Design toolbar (shown in Figure 3-2), or by using the View⇨SQL View command.

Figure 3-2:
The SQL
View
command
as found on
the Design
toolbar.

When you select either of these commands, the contents of the query window change to reveal the SQL statement (see Figure 3-3) that is equivalent to the query you created in the design grid.

While the query grid may be a useful and easy way to specify the data you want to retrieve, it's actually the text of the SQL statement that Access processes.

Figure 3-3:
The query
window
shows the
text of
the SQL
statement.

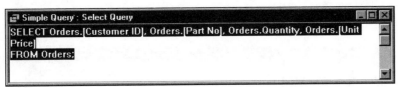

Why would I need to use SQL instead of the query grid?

You may find that in some cases it's easier to create or modify a query by editing the SQL statement instead of manipulating the objects in the query grid. In addition, you may find that you can integrate sets of data in forms, reports, and within VBA code by writing the SQL statements. Throughout this book, SQL statements are used to execute a range of data-related operations.

Defining a Data Set with SQL

The key concept behind SQL is the concept of a *data set*. A data set is a set of rows and fields. In Access data sets are displayed in Datasheets. The SQL statement is a definition of the type and amount of data that should be included in a data set. When a SQL statement becomes processed, the result is a set of rows and columns that matches the details specified in the SQL statement.

The simplest possible SQL statement consists of two parts:

- ✔ SELECT. The section begins with the keyword SELECT followed by a list of fields that you want to include in the data set. Commas separate the names in a field list. If you want to include all the fields in a table, you can type an asterisk (*) instead of a field list.

- ✔ FROM. This portion begins with the keyword FROM. It specifies the table or tables from which the fields are to be drawn.

The following SQL statement shows how to generate a data set that consists of the names and cities for all the records in the Customers table. The results of this statement appear in Figure 3-4.

```
SELECT name,city
FROM customers;
```

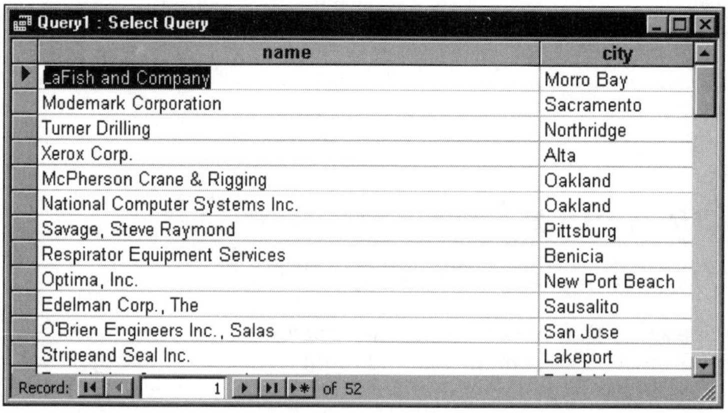

Figure 3-4:
The data set resulting from a simple SQL statement.

name	city
LaFish and Company	Morro Bay
Modemark Corporation	Sacramento
Turner Drilling	Northridge
Xerox Corp.	Alta
McPherson Crane & Rigging	Oakland
National Computer Systems Inc.	Oakland
Savage, Steve Raymond	Pittsburg
Respirator Equipment Services	Benicia
Optima, Inc.	New Port Beach
Edelman Corp., The	Sausalito
O'Brien Engineers Inc., Salas	San Jose
Stripeand Seal Inc.	Lakeport

Query1 : Select Query

Record: 1 of 52

Query: SQL Example 01

You should make note of a few points about the way you write a SQL statement.

✔ SQL statements processed in Access always end with a semicolon (;).

  The semicolon is characteristic only of SQL in Access. Other forms of SQL — such as Transact SQL, supported by Microsoft SQL Server — do not use the semicolon at the end of the SQL statement.

✔ SQL is not case-sensitive. You can write a SQL statement in any combination of upper- or lowercase characters.

✔ While it's true that SQL statements are not case-sensitive, it's a widely followed convention that SQL keywords are written in uppercase, and field and table names are written in lowercase. Another traditional element is that the SELECT and FROM keywords are typed on separate lines. The following example shows the traditional style of writing SQL statements.

```
SELECT name, city
FROM customers;
```

✔ You can write SQL statements on one or more lines within the query window. As shown in the following code, you have the option to combine the SELECT and FROM keywords on a single line. Or you can go the other direction and add more lines to spread out the statement onto three, four, or more lines. SQL also ignores additional white space such as tabs or extra blank spaces. This allows you the freedom to arrange the elements in a SQL statement in any way you like, without affecting the meaning of the statement. The second example below places the keywords on lines by themselves. The semicolon also is placed on a separate line. This style clearly differentiates the keywords (which are always the same) from the table-specific names (which will vary).

```
SELECT name, city FROM customers;
SELECT
    name, city
FROM
    customers
;
```

🖊 If you want to include all the fields from a table within a SQL data set, you can avoid typing in all the names by typing an asterisk (*) in place of the field list.

```
SELECT *
FROM customers;
```

> **Query: SQL Example 02**

Using the WHERE keyword

The simplest SQL statements require only the SELECT and FROM keywords. However, this type of query will always include all the records in the specified table. In order to select records based on logical criteria, you need to add the WHERE keyword followed by a *logical expression*. A logical expression is one that compares two or more values and yields either a True or False value. For example, state = "CA" can either be True or False depending upon the actual value of the state field.

The following SQL statement returns the name and city fields from the Customers table when the value for the state field is TX. The WHERE keyword, plus the logical expression (for example, WHERE state = "TX"), is often called a *WHERE clause*. You can see the data set resulting from the query in Figure 3-5.

```
SELECT name, city
FROM customers
WHERE state = "TX";
```

Figure 3-5:
Customer
records
selected by
a WHERE
clause.

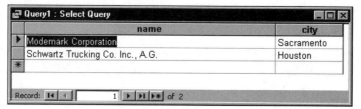

🖊 Access SQL, like most forms of SQL, allows the use of single-quotation marks (' ') or apostrophes to enclose text items, as shown in the following example. The characters that are used to enclose literal text items are called *delimiters*.

```
SELECT name, city
FROM customers
WHERE state = 'TX';
```

> *Query: SQL Example 03*

Using expressions with SELECT

In addition to lists of fields, the SELECT keyword can operate with any valid Access *expression*. Expressions can include arithmetic operations and built-in functions, as well as string operations. For example, the following statement retrieves data stored in the city, state, and zip fields. The result is a record set that contains separate columns, as shown in previous examples.

```
SELECT city, state, zip
FROM customers;
```

On the other hand, you often see this information expressed as a single item in which city, state, and zip, are combined with punctuation to form a single phrase. The technical term for combining two strings is *concatenate*. The following statement uses the & (concatenation) operator to combine the contents of the fields with text literals (the items enclosed in quotation marks). This combination creates a data set consisting of a single column based on the concatenation expression, as shown in Figure 3-6.

```
SELECT city & ", " & state & " " & zip
FROM customers;
```

> *Query: SQL Example 04*

Figure 3-6:
The data set contains the single-column result of an expression.

Expr1000
Morro Bay, WA 70461495
Sacramento, TX 95240
Northridge, CA 94612
Alta, CA 92311
Oakland, CA 95061
Oakland, CA 95454
Pittsburg, CA 95352
Benicia, CA 95616
New Port Beach, CA 6002
Sausalito, CA 94903

Setting column names

As you may have noticed when Access processes a SQL statement, it uses the field names as the column headings in the resulting data set. If you use an expression to generate a column, as is the case in Figure 3-6, Access generates a generic name, `Expr1000`, as the column heading.

SQL allows you to specify a different name for a column by using the `AS` keyword with either a field name or an expression. The following example uses the `AS` keyword to assign `Customer Name` to the `name` field and `Location` to the expression `city & ", " & state & " " & zip` as shown in Figure 3-7.

```
SELECT name AS [Customer Name],
city & ", " & state & " " & zip AS Location
FROM customers;
```

Customer Name	Location
LaFish and Company	Morro Bay, WA 70461495
Modemark Corporation	Sacramento, TX 95240
Turner Drilling	Northridge, CA 94612
Xerox Corp.	Alta, CA 92311
McPherson Crane & Rigging	Oakland, CA 95061
National Computer Systems Inc.	Oakland, CA 95454
Savage, Steve Raymond	Pittsburg, CA 95352
Respirator Equipment Services	Benicia, CA 95616
Optima, Inc.	New Port Beach, CA 6002
Edelman Corp., The	Sausalito, CA 94903

SQL Example 05 : Select Query

Record: 1 of 52

Figure 3-7:
Column names defined using the AS keyword.

Note that you can use the `AS` keyword to assign a multiword name to a column as long as brackets enclose the name, for example, `[Customer Name]`. Keep in mind that the case of the characters used with the `AS` keyword affect the names appearing as column headings.

Query: SQL Example 05

Sorting records

You can control the order of the records returned in the data set by using the `ORDER BY` keyword to specify which field, fields, or expression to use to determine the order of the records. The following example uses the `ORDER BY` keyword to sort the records in the resulting data set alphabetically by city. You can see the sorted data set in Figure 3-8.

```
SELECT name, street, city
FROM customers
ORDER BY city;
```

name	street	city
Xerox Corp.	1000 Broadway #612	Alta
Kirtley Overhead Doors	PO Box 1348	Alviso
Dressel Enterprises	1410 Cedar St.	Anderson
Sierra Research, Inc.	385 Higuera St.	Bakersfield
Sequoia Construction Specialties	2840 Howe Rd. #C	Barstow
Respirator Equipment Services	2325 E. 30th St.	Benicia
Steel Mill Supply Co. Inc.	4121 Dale Rd.	Benicia
Langworthy Construction Co.	35 Nagog Park	Canonsburg
Curtis & Tompkins LTD	PO Box 1710	Central Point
Circuit Breaker Sales Inc.	PO Box 2327	Chico
Hofmann Construction Co. Inc.	32 Henry St.	Chico

Figure 3-8:
The
ORDER BY
keyword
used to sort
data by city.

Query: SQL Example 06

When a SQL statement contains both a WHERE and an ORDER BY keyword, the WHERE clause must precede the ORDER BY keyword. The following example limits the records to state = "CA" while sorting the records by city.

```
SELECT name, street, city
FROM customers
WHERE state = "CA"
ORDER BY city;
```

Query: SQL Example 07

By default, the ORDER BY keyword assumes an ascending (low to high) order. You can specify a descending (high to low) order by adding DESC to the statement following the sort fields. The following example sorts the records in descending order by zip.

```
SELECT name, city, zip
FROM customer
WHERE state = "CA"
ORDER BY zip DESC;
```

Query: SQL Example 08

Sorting on multiple keys

In some cases, you may need to sort records by several key fields in order to arrange the records in the desired sequence. U.S. addresses offer a common example of this kind of sorting because locations in the United States are sorted first by state, and then within state by city.

In a SQL ORDER BY clause, multiple sort keys are listed in the order of their priority. In the following example, records are sorted first by state, and then within state by city when you use the phrase ORDER BY state, city, as shown in Figure 3-9. Keep in mind that the order of the field names is important. The phrase ORDER BY city, state would produce a record-set sorted first by city and then by state.

```
SELECT name, city, state
FROM customer
ORDER BY state, city;
```

Figure 3-9: Locations sorted by state and then by city.

name	city	state
ADE Construction & Development	Vacaville	CA
Smith & Gysbers	Visalia	CA
Parallax Marketing Research	Walnut Creek	CA
Nemat Management and Product	Wheeling	CA
Curtis & Tompkins LTD	Central Point	CO
Pan-Marine Constructors Inc.	Fairfield	IL
Union Flights Inc.	Stockton	OK
Hofmann Construction Co. Inc.	Chico	OR
Schwartz Trucking Co. Inc., A.G.	Houston	TX
Modemark Corporation	Sacramento	TX
LaFish and Company	Morro Bay	WA

SQL Example 09 : Select Query

Record: 1 of 52

Query: SQL Example 09

Dealing with null values

A special type of criterion concerns whether a field contains data or is blank. In SQL, blank fields are called *null values,* or simply *nulls.* SQL supports special keywords for dealing with nulls.

✔ IS NULL. Use this phrase to select records that have blank values in a specific field.

✔ IS NOT NULL. Use this phrase to select records that have an entry other than a blank value in a specific field.

Nulls occur in text, memo, and date fields. In a number or currency field, a blank entry is treated as a value of zero. In Yes/No fields, a blank is always a No (false) value.

The following statement selects records with a blank value in the contact field.

```
SELECT name, contact
FROM customers
WHERE contact IS NULL;
```

Query: SQL Example 10

Conversely, you can exclude records based on a blank value in a specific field. The following example inverts the logic of the previous statement by adding NOT to the IS NULL phrase. The result is that records with an entry other than a blank are included in the resulting data set.

```
SELECT name, contact
FROM customers
WHERE contact IS NOT NULL;
```

Query: SQL Example 11

Blanks and null

In most cases, a blank entry requires no special treatment or interpretation. For example, say you encounter a blank field for a zip code or a social security number. If you live in the United States you can assume the field is blank because you were missing the necessary information for the field when you entered the data — a safe assumption because every U.S. location has a zip code, and U.S. most citizens (over the age of 2) have social security numbers.

On the other hand, some blanks in some fields may suggest other meanings. In the previous example, the contact field in some records is blank. The blank could mean missing data — you didn't know the name of the contact for that company at the time you entered the data. However, it may also mean that no contact exists for this company. In this case, the blank doesn't mean *unknown at the time of entry* but *not applicable to this company.* In some cases, the difference between unknown and not applicable may be significant. Access and Access SQL support the ability to distinguish between two types of blank fields: (1) a *null* value that means unknown at the time of entry, and (2) a *zero-length string* that means the value is known and its value is blank (not applicable) for that record.

Enter a zero-length string by typing `""`, in a field — a pair of double-quotation marks with no space between them. Follow that by a press of the Enter key.

Keep in mind that when you enter a zero-length string in a field, the `""` appear only for a moment while you make the entry. As soon as you move to another field, the `""` disappear and the cell appears blank. You have no way to determine visually whether or not a field contains a null or a zero-length string. However, SQL statements can distinguish between the two types of entries.

By default, Access *does not permit* you to enter zero-length strings into database fields. If you want to allow zero-length strings, you must alter the property sheet of the field.

1. **Open the table in the Design mode.**

2. **Select the field where you want to enter the zero-length strings.**

3. **On the General tab of the field properties sheets (in the lower-half of the screen), you see the Allow Zero-Length property; change this from No to Yes.**

4. **Save the changes to the table's design.**

   You can now enter zero-length strings.

Zero-length strings can cause problems when you import tables stored in certain non-Access files. In some cases, the programs that originally created the data will designate empty fields as `""`. Access treats these values as zero-length fields. If the table into which you are importing does not permit zero-length strings, you may get an error message during the import process telling you that Access does not allow zero-length strings. If you encounter this type of error while importing, change the structure of the table you're importing into to allow zero-length strings. You can then reimport the data without error.

An example of a table that contains both nulls and zero-length strings is the Customers 1 table in the SQL.MBD database on this book's CD. The following SQL statement performs a query that selects records based on the contact field. In this case, it includes records that don't have a null value. Because the Customers 1 table includes records that have zero-length strings in the `contact` field, some of the records selected by the query have blanks in the `contact` column, as shown in Figure 3-10.

Figure 3-10:
Query
excludes
null values
but
includes
zero-length
strings.

name	contact
Modemark Corporation	Eric Simons
Turner Drilling	Gary Christofferson
Xerox Corp.	
McPherson Crane & Rigging	
Optima, Inc.	Leslie Schoon
Edelman Corp., The	
O'Brien Engineers Inc., Salas	Gina Mullin
Pan-Marine Constructors Inc.	Doug Krause
Steel Mill Supply Co. Inc.	
Circuit Breaker Sales Inc.	John McCarthy
Town & Country Fencing	Jim Pillsbury

Nulls 01 : Select Query

Record: 1 of 31

```
SELECT name, contact
FROM [customers 1]
WHERE contact IS NOT NULL;
```

Query: Nulls 01

Another way to produce a similar result is to select records that have a zero-length string in the `contact` field. The following SQL statement uses " " to specify a match for a zero-length string rather than a null value.

```
SELECT name, contact
FROM [customers 1]
WHERE contact <> "";
```

Query: Nulls 02

If you want to retrieve only those records that have a visible entry — that is, exclude both nulls and zero-length strings — use a compound criterion with the WHERE keyword, as shown in the following example:

```
SELECT name, contact
FROM [customers 1]
WHERE contact <> ""
AND contact IS NOT NULL;
```

Query: Nulls 03

SQL Comparison Operators

SQL statements support the use of the common logical operators (for example, =, <>, >, <, <= and >=). In addition, SQL supports three special operators that simplify the syntax required to perform selections based on multiple possible matches.

- ✔ LIKE. Use this operator to select records based on a pattern match rather than an exact match.
- ✔ IN. Use this operator to match one item from a list of items.
- ✔ BETWEEN … AND. Use this operator to select records based on an inclusive range of values.

The LIKE operator

The LIKE operator provides a number of simple ways to match text items based on patterns rather than exact matches. The LIKE operator permits the use of *wildcard* logic in expressions. Wildcards are symbols that define patterns used to select fields containing text that matches the pattern. If you have used file-specification wildcards in DOS, for example, *dir *.doc,* you find that the LIKE operator functions similarly.

The pattern can contain any sequence of characters, plus the wildcards *, ?, and #. The * lets you match any group of characters. The ? matches any one character, and # matches any one digit. For example, suppose you want to select all the items in the Parts table that contain *sparc* as part of their description. (*Sparc* is the brand name of computer workstations from Sun Microsystems.) The following example uses the expression description LIKE "sparc*" to select any record that begins with those characters, regardless of what other characters, if any, are in the description field. You can see the resulting data set in Figure 3-11.

```
SELECT [part no], description
FROM parts
WHERE description LIKE "sparc*";
```

| Query: Like 01 |

If you place the * at the beginning of the pattern, it signifies a match for the characters at the end of a field. The following statement matches any part of the description that ends with the word *monitor*. Figure 3-12 shows the result.

Figure 3-11:
Using LIKE
with a
wildcard to
select
records
with
specific
characters.

part no	description
ACC:S20FX1-151-32-P95	Sparc20, 150Mhz, 32MB, 17" Color, 2.1GB Disk
ACC:S20S-151-32-P97	Sparc 20,150Mhz,32MB,2.1GB Disk,CDROM 2 Plus
ACC:S5F24-110-32-P95	Sparc5, 110Mhz, 32MB, 17" Color, 2.1GB Disk
ACC:S5S-110-32-P98	Sparc5, 110Mhz, 32MB, 2x2.1GB, 2plus CDROM
ACC:SF2411095	Sparc5 110MHZ 32MB 17" Monitor

Record: 1 of 5

```
SELECT [part no], description
FROM parts
WHERE description LIKE "*monitor";
```

Figure 3-12:
LIKE used
to select by
the text at
the end of
a field.

part no	description
ACC:SF2411095	Sparc5 110MHZ 32MB 17" Monitor

ON THE CD

Query: Like 02

An * before and after a group of characters causes a *substring search*. A substring search is one that locates the character at any position within the field. The following statement locates any item with a description that contains the characters *cdrom* in any part of the field, as shown in Figure 3-13.

```
SELECT [part no], description
FROM parts
WHERE description LIKE "*cdrom*";
```

Figure 3-13:
LIKE used
to select
the text in
any part of
a field.

part no	description
ACC:A11-UBA1-9S-	Sun Ultra 1,167MHZ, 64MB, 2.1GB Disk,
ACC:S20S-151-32-	Sparc 20,150Mhz,32MB,2.1GB Disk, CDROM 2
ACC:S5S-110-32-P98	Sparc5, 110Mhz, 32MB, 2x2.1GB, 2plus
ACC:X560A	Internal CDROM Drive
ACC:X578	2Plus Internal CDROM Drive
ACC:X6153A	Sun CD 4 Internal CDROM Drive
MOT:17314	VANGUARD CDROM MOTOROLA;

Query: Like 03

You can also use pattern matching with date fields. The following example selects records for a specific month, for example, March 1996, by using the * as a wildcard for the day portion of a m/d/yy format date.

```
SELECT [Order Number], [Order date]
FROM orders
WHERE [Order Date] LIKE "3/*/96";
```

Query: Like 04

Another useful form of pattern matching is the use of ranges within a pattern. You can specify a range by enclosing the characters in [ ]. For example [a-g] would match characters *a* through *g* for any one position in a pattern. The following statement uses this range to match a range of characters for the first character in the city field. The query selects records with city names such as Alta, Alviso, Anderson, Bakersfield, Barstow, Benicia, Canonsburg, Central Point, Chico, Chula Vista, Cotati, Danville, Delray Beach, Denver, Eureka, Fairfield, and Gilroy.

```
SELECT name, city
FROM customers
WHERE city LIKE "[a-g]*";
```

Query: Like 05

You can specify a specific set of characters by entering a list in the [ ]. The next example uses a list of characters, [a,m,w], to select cities that begin with either *a, m,* or *w.* When the query is processed, the records selected include the cities Alta, Alviso, Anderson, Martinez, Morro Bay, Mt. Aukum, Walnut Creek, and Wheeling.

```
SELECT name, city
FROM customers
WHERE city LIKE "[a,m,w]*";
```

Query: Like 06

You can also use ranges with date values. The following query is designed to select records with order dates in the first quarter of 1996. This is not accomplished directly because the date format does not directly specify quarter. However, you can pick out first-quarter dates by selecting for a range of months, 1-3, in the month portion of the m/d/yy format.

```
SELECT [Order Number], [Order date]
FROM orders
WHERE [Order Date] LIKE "[1-3]/*/96";
```

Query: Like 07

The IN operator

Use the IN operator to determine whether or not an item is in a list of
values. The following statement compares the contents of the city field to
the contents of a list of items, for example, "Bakersfield","Benicia",
"Cotati". The resulting data set will contain only records whose cities
match one of the items in the list.

```
SELECT name, city, state
FROM customers
WHERE city IN("Bakersfield","Benicia","Cotati");
```

Query: IN 01

The BETWEEN ... AND operator

The BETWEEN ... AND operator is useful when you want to specify a range of
values as a criterion for selecting records for a data set. The following
statement selects records by the Unit Price field. Records are included if
the Unit Price is between 100 and 500. Note that a between range includes
the values (for example, 100 and 500) that sets the scope of the range.

```
SELECT [Part No], [Unit Price]
FROM orders
WHERE [Unit Price] BETWEEN 100 AND 500;
```

Query: BETWEEN 01

You can also use the BETWEEN ... AND operator to select a range of dates as
shown in the following code where the Order Date field is used to select
records from 3/1/96 to 3/15/96.

```
SELECT [Part No], [Unit Price]
FROM orders
WHERE [Order Date] BETWEEN #3/1/96# AND #3/15/96#;
```

Query: BETWEEN 02

Distinct values

Normally, a query returns all the records and fields that fit the specifications that you enter in the SQL statement. Often this means that the same value appears in more than one record.

In some cases you want to limit the items returned to a list of *distinct* values so that the data set includes only one occurrence of each unique value. For example, suppose you want to get a list of the cities from which your customer base is derived. The following statement lists the names of the cities.

```
SELECT city
FROM customers;
```

However, this list may contain duplicates because several customers may reside in the same city. Adding the DISTINCT keyword eliminates the duplicates from the data set.

```
SELECT DISTINCT city
FROM customers;
```

Query: Distinct 01

If one or more records have a blank (null) value, the blank will be included at the top of the data set. In most cases you'll want to eliminate the blank from the list by adding a WHERE clause as shown next.

```
SELECT DISTINCT city
FROM customers
WHERE city IS NOT NULL;
```

Query: Distinct 02

The DISTINCT keyword can also function with a list of fields. The statement produces a data set that contains a list of the unique combinations of city and state. When you run this query, you now get two records for Chico, one for California and one for Oregon: Chico CA, Chico OR.

```
SELECT DISTINCT city, state
FROM customers;
```

Query: Distinct 03

An added benefit of using the DISTINCT keyword is that the items are automatically sorted in ascending order. This occurs because Access must sort the items in order to eliminate the duplicate items from the listing. Thus, all DISTINCT data sets are also sorted data sets.

Calculated Columns

SQL allows you to generate columns in a data set by using expressions to define the contents of the column. In Access, SQL expressions can include any operator or function that Access supports. You can use these functions to manipulate text, dates, or make special match calculations such as the Pmt() function that calculates loan payments.

Access SQL supports built-in Access functions such as Month(), Left(), Pmt(), and so on. Standard SQL (for example, SQL supported by Microsoft SQL Server) has very limited sets of functions.

You can find a typical example using the Orders table, which contains fields for Quantity and Unit Price but not a field for the total for the order. This probably is a good strategy for minimizing the size of that table. Because you can easily calculate the total by multiplying the quantity times the price, you don't need to explicitly store the total.

The following SQL statement generates a new column named *Total* (by means of the AS keyword) that performs the calculation for each record in the data set, as you can see in Figure 3-14.

```
SELECT Quantity, [Unit Price],
Quantity*[Unit Price] AS Total
FROM orders;
```

Figure 3-14:
An
expression
generates a
calculated
column.

Quantity	Unit Price	Total
2	$1,917.00	3834
8	$537.00	4296
1	$2,097.00	2097
1	$1,079.40	1079.4
1	$153.00	153
1	$34.00	34
1	$597.00	597
2	$1,400.00	2800
2	$241.00	482
4	$244.00	976

| **Query: Calc 01** |

In addition to basic arithmetic, calculated columns are often handy for manipulating date information. For example, suppose you want to display a column with the month and year rather than the full date of each order. The following example uses the built-in functions Year and Month to manipulate the Order Date field to display a month designation (in the form *m/yyyy*) in the data set as shown in Figure 3-15.

```
SELECT Month([Order Date]) & "/" &
Year([Order Date]) AS Period
FROM orders
ORDER BY [Order Date];
```

Figure 3-15:
The date
function
manipulates
date
information.

Order Number	Period
2952	1/1996
5921	1/1996
3455	1/1996
2952	1/1996
2952	1/1996
3883	1/1996
3616	1/1996
5921	1/1996
5921	1/1996

Query: Calc 02

In looking at the data set represented in Figure 3-14, you may wonder why the Unit Price column is formatted as currency while the Total column is displayed without currency formatting. Unit Price appears as currency because the data was entered into a field defined as a currency type field in the table design. On the other hand, `Total`, which is a calculated field, is automatically treated as a number with no special formatting.

In most cases you needn't be concerned about the difference in formatting because a form or a report often displays the result of the query. In such cases, you have the opportunity to select the formatting style for the calculated field from the property sheet of the control used to display the field. On the other hand, to simply print the results of the query without having to build a form or a report, apply a format to the calculation using the `Format` function described next.

```
Format (value, format-spec)
```

- `value` is the field or calculation that supplies the value to be formatted
- `format-spec` is the name of a predefined format, for example, `currency`, or a format string, for example, `####,####.00`.

The following example applies the currency format to the calculated column Total. You can see the resulting data in Figure 3-16.

```
SELECT Quantity, [Unit Price],
Format(Quantity*[Unit Price],"currency") AS Total
FROM orders;
```

| Query: Calc 03 |

One oddity that occurs when you use Format in a query is that the formatted numbers are left-aligned, not right-aligned in the column. This is because the Format function always returns a text value. Since Access automatically left-aligns text columns, the formatted numbers end up left-aligned.

Figure 3-16:
The format
function
applies
formatting
to a
calculated
column.

Quantity	Unit Price	Total
2	$1,917.00	$3,834.00
8	$537.00	$4,296.00
1	$2,097.00	$2,097.00
1	$1,079.40	$1,079.40
1	$153.00	$153.00
1	$34.00	$34.00
1	$597.00	$597.00
2	$1,400.00	$2,800.00
2	$241.00	$482.00
4	$244.00	$976.00

You should avoid using Format in a query that you will use later as the record source for a form or a report. Use Format only when you want to output the results of the query directly without using a form or report.

You can also use Format to manipulate dates. You can also produce the data set pictured in Figure 3-15 by using the following example.

```
SELECT [Order Number],
Format([Order date],"m/yyyy") AS Period
FROM orders
ORDER BY [Order Date];
```

| Query: Calc 04 |

SQL Aggregate Functions

In SQL, the term *aggregate* refers to all data included in the resulting record data set generated by a query. The SQL aggregate functions listed in Table 3-2 summarize values in a data set.

Table 3-2	SQL Aggregate Functions
Function Name	*Operation*
Avg()	Arithmetic average of the values
Count()	Number of records
First()	Value of the first record in the set
Last()	Value of the last record in the set
Min()	Smallest value in the set
Max()	Largest value in the set
Sum()	Total of all records
STDev()	Standard deviation (nonbiased)
StDevP()	Standard deviation (biased)
Var()	Variance (nonbiased)
VarP()	Variance deviation (biased)

You can use aggregate functions in two ways:

- ✔ Summarize All. This type of query returns a single row of information. Each column displays a summary value used on all of the records that qualify for the data set by meeting the criteria established by the WHERE clause. If you don't use a WHERE clause, the entire table is summarized.
- ✔ Summarize By Group. This type of query returns one row of summary values for each unique member of a group. For example, you may want to calculate the totals for each customer. You can accomplish this by using the GROUP BY keyword with aggregate functions.

Summarizing all records

The simplest type of aggregate query is one that summarizes all the records in a table. The following statement summarizes the Quantity field. The result is a data set with a single column and row with the value 6632.

```
SELECT Sum(quantity) AS Total
FROM Orders;
```

Query: Agg 01

You can also summarize the result of a calculation with the aggregate functions. For example, in the Orders table you need to multiply *Quantity* by *Unit Price* to calculate the total for each order. The following statement summarizes the totals for each record and produces a single row containing the total for all orders — 5151133.6882.

```
SELECT Sum(quantity*[Unit Price]) AS Total
FROM Orders;
```

Query: Agg 02

You can use the WHERE clause to limit the records included in the aggregate. The following example totals only those records with an *Order Date* in September, 1996.

```
SELECT Sum(quantity*[Unit Price]) AS Total
FROM Orders
WHERE [Order Date] LIKE "9/*/96";
```

Query: Agg 03

The Min() and Max() functions locate the smallest and largest values in field. When used with date fields, they locate the earliest and latest dates entered into a field. The following statement produces two dates, 1/2/96 and 12/31/96, representing the range of dates found in the table.

```
SELECT Min([Order Date]), Max([Order Date])
FROM Orders;
```

Query: Agg 08

Summarizing by group

You can generate a data set that summarizes information by group by adding a GROUP BY keyword to the query statement. The following example generates a total for each part included in the Orders table as shown in Figure 3-17.

```
SELECT [Part No], Sum(quantity*[Unit Price]) AS Total
FROM Orders
GROUP BY [Part No];
```

Query: Agg 04

When you construct a group aggregate query you need to keep in mind that if a field name (which is not part of an aggregate function) appears in the SELECT portion of the statement, that field name *must* also be included in the GROUP BY list.

You can also use the aggregate functions to determine the order of the records. The following statement produces the same set of data shown in Figure 3-17 but orders the records so that the parts are ranked according to which have the largest volume of sales.

Part No	Total
ACC:A11-UBA1-9S-064CB	10381
ACC:A14-UCB2-1E-256DB	33831.65
ACC:NS-91-01009	1584.04
ACC:NZ-11102415	313
ACC:S20FX1-151-32-P95	24783.3
ACC:S20S-151-32-P97	11721.65
ACC:S5F24-110-32-P95	28458.25
ACC:S5S-110-32-P98	6026.65
ACC:SF2411095	5691.65
ACC:SOL-MEDIA	0

Figure 3-17: Summary values produced by group.

```
SELECT [Part No], Sum(quantity*[Unit Price]) AS Total
FROM Orders
GROUP BY [Part No]
ORDER BY Sum(quantity*[Unit Price]) DESC;
```

Query: Agg 05

Adding a WHERE clause restricts the summary to specific sets of records. The following example limits the summary to the month of September, 1996.

```
SELECT [Part No], Sum(quantity*[Unit Price]) AS Total
FROM Orders
WHERE [Order date] LIKE "9/*/96"
GROUP BY [Part No]
ORDER BY Sum(quantity*[Unit Price]) DESC;
```

Query: Agg 06

It's often useful to perform more than one summary calculation on the same record set. For example, you may want to calculate the total dollar amount of sales for each part, and also count the number of sales for that part. The following statement adds a second aggregate function, Count(), to the query in order to produce the data shown in Figure 3-18. Note that when you count records, the field specified is not important because Count() is merely counting the number of records in each grouping. You can simply use * as the field name to simplify the query.

Figure 3-18: Multiple summary calculations performed on a data set.

Part No	Total	Sales
CIS:4500-M	23400	1
CIS:NP-4T	17940	1
CIS:2503	11017.5	2
CNSC:Install/Config	9850	2
Install	9738.8	47
CIS:NP-1F-D-MM	9550	2
CIS:NP-2E	7800	1
CIS:SF25C-10.2.5	7020	1
SL5	6672.96	8
CIS:SF-G45C-10.3.2	6630	1
CIS:1004	6500	1
CIS:SF1004C4-10.3.3	6500	1
CIS:WS-X5213	6496.75	1

```
SELECT [Part No], Sum(quantity*[Unit Price]) AS Total,
        Count(*) AS Sales
FROM Orders
WHERE [Order date] LIKE "9/*/96"
GROUP BY [Part No]
ORDER BY Sum(quantity*[Unit Price]) DESC;
```

Query: Agg 07

Subqueries

In all the query examples in this chapter that use WHERE clauses to select records, the criterion used is a known value. The following statement (used to generate the data set shown in Figure 3-5) specifies a specific, literal value, for example, TX, to which the state field will be compared.

```
SELECT name, city
FROM customers
WHERE state = "TX";
```

But suppose you don't know in advance the exact item you want to use as a criterion. For example, suppose you have a customer whose contact name is Gina Mullin, and you want to know if you have any other customers in the same town as Gina. The query statement to use would look like the following one. The problem is you don't know the name of the city you want to match; all you know is the name of the contact — Gina Mullin.

```
SELECT name
FROM customers
WHERE city = ????;
```

One way to solve the problem is to use a separate query to find the name of
the city based on the contact name. The following statement returns the
name of the city. Once you have that, you can complete the previous statement and get the data you desire.

```
SELECT city
FROM customers
WHERE contact = "Gina Mullin";
```

SQL offers a shortcut. Instead of performing two separate queries, you can
insert the preceding query in place of the *????* in the previous query
statement. When you combine the two, you get a statement that looks like
the following one in which the criterion used in the first WHERE clause is a
complete SQL statement. When you enclose a SQL statement inside another
statement, it's called a *subquery*. When the statement is processed, the
subquery first returns its data — here, the name of the city — which in turn
is used as the primary query to select the list of companies, shown in
Figure 3-19.

```
SELECT name
FROM customers
WHERE city = (SELECT city
FROM customers
WHERE contact = "Gina Mullin");
```

Figure 3-19:
A data set
generated
by a query
that
contains a
subquery.

name	city
O'Brien Engineers Inc.	San Jose
Brune, Charlie and Reisender	San Jose
California, State of Dept. of Water & Air Inc.	San Jose

Query: Sub 01

Because a subquery is a complete SQL statement that can be evaluated
independently of the primary query, the subquery doesn't have to refer to
the same table as the primary query. Suppose you want to retrieve information from the Orders table for the company for which Gina Mullin is the

contact. The following statement is incomplete because the Orders table doesn't contain the contact name. Instead, you classify orders by Customer ID.

```
SELECT [Part No], Quantity*[Unit Price] AS Total
FROM orders
WHERE [Customer ID]= ????
```

You can solve the problem by using a subquery to search the Customers table for the ID of the record in which Gina Mullin is the contact. The result is a query like the following one in which the subquery extracts data from the Customers table while the primary query selects data from the Orders table.

```
SELECT [Part No], Quantity*[Unit Price] AS Total
FROM orders
WHERE [Customer ID]=(SELECT id
FROM customers
WHERE contact = "Gina Mullin");
```

Query: Sub 02

You can use subqueries as part of summary queries. The following statement uses the same subquery to locate the ID number of a company by matching the name of a contact (Gina Mullin). The primary query in this case summarizes the orders for this customer by Part No.

```
SELECT [Part No], Sum(Quantity*[Unit Price]) AS Total
FROM orders
WHERE [Customer ID]=(SELECT id
FROM customers
WHERE contact = "Gina Mullin")
GROUP BY [Part No];
```

Query: Sub 03

Using IN with subqueries

The previous examples of subqueries use subqueries that return a single row of information. SQL allows the use of subqueries that return multiple rows of data by using the subquery to generate a list of values for the IN operator (discussed in the section "SQL Comparison Operators," earlier in this chapter).

For example, suppose you want to calculate the total volume of sales outside the state of California. One solution is to use a subquery to generate a list of customer ID numbers that can select records in the Orders table for summing. The following statement produces the required list of ID numbers.

```
SELECT id
FROM customers
WHERE state<>"CA"
```

Because the subquery will return more than one row, the subquery is inserted in an `IN` operator in place of a static list of items. When executed, this query returns the total of all orders outside California, 243090.5.

```
SELECT Sum(Quantity*[Unit Price])AS TotalNonCal
FROM Orders
WHERE [Customer ID] IN (SELECT id
FROM customers
WHERE state<>"CA");
```

Using Parameters in Queries

In the SQL query statements discussed so far, the values used as criteria have been entered as part of the SQL statement in the form of text, date, or numeric literals. The following statement is typical of this approach. It selects records that match the text literal, `CA`.

```
SELECT name, city, contact
FROM customers
WHERE state = "CA";
```

Parameters allow you to create a query where you do not directly enter the criteria into the SQL statement, but can enter the criteria in a dialog box prior to the execution of the statement. In the following statement, the literal criterion for the `state`, for example, *CA,* was replaced with a place-holder that consists of a ? enclosed in [ ].

```
SELECT name, city, contact
FROM customers
WHERE state = [?];
```

When Access executes this query, it finds that there is no field in the Customers table named `?`. This causes Access to assume that `[?]` is a placeholder for a parameter. Access then displays a dialog box, shown in Figure 3-20, that allows you to type in a value.

Figure 3-20:
Access
displays a
box for
entering the
value of a
parameter.

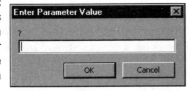

Query: Param 01

The value you enter passes through to the query where it's used to replace the placeholder identifier, for example, [?], with an actual value. For example, if you typed **co** into the dialog box shown in Figure 3-20, the query returns the data set shown in Figure 3-21.

Figure 3-21:
The data
set returned
when the
user enters
co as the
query
parameter.

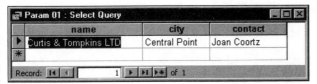

Each time you execute the query, you are asked to enter the parameter. The resulting data set will vary depending upon what value you enter each time. Parameters are significant because they provide a way to create a single query statement that you can use with a number of different criteria.

You should keep in mind the following points when dealing with SQL parameter queries:

✔ The name of the parameter placeholder appears in the dialog box as the prompt text. In order to aid users in filling in parameters, you can add placeholder names that read like sentences or questions. The following example uses Please enter the 2 letter state code: as the name of the parameter identifier. When you execute this statement, the dialog box, Figure 3-22, displays a prompt that actually explains what data the user should enter.

```
SELECT name, city, contract
FROM customers
WHERE state = [Please enter the 2 letter state code:]
```

Query: Param 02

✔ If you want to provide the user the option of selecting all the records rather than entering a specific criterion, you can modify the query to use a LIKE operator instead of an = operator as shown in the following example below. If the user does not want to select for a particular state, then she can type *. Becaue the * is a wildcard recognized by the LIKE operator, the statement will retrieve all the states if * is entered as the parameter.

```
SELECT name, city, contact
FROM customers
WHERE state
LIKE [Enter the 2 letter state code or * for all:];
```

Query: Param 03

Figure 3-22:
You can phrase parameter names to appear as useful prompts in input boxes.

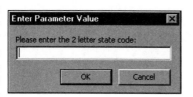

✔ You can enter as many placeholders as you desire in a statement. The following example uses a parameter for Start Date: and one for [End Date:]. When the query executes, Access displays a separate dialog box for each parameter. This example requires a dialog box for Start Date: and one for End Date:. The boxes appear in the order in which the placeholders are encountered in the SQL statement. Because Start Date: is the first placeholder, its dialog box is the first displayed.

```
SELECT [Order Number], [Order Date]
FROM orders
WHERE [Order Date] Between [Start Date:]
AND [End Date:];
```

Query: Param 04

✔ You *cannot* use parameters to insert field names into the SQL statement. The following statement seems to allow a parameter to determine the name of the second field in the SELECT list. However, if you enter a field name, for example, Street, Access does not insert the Street field name in the statement. Rather, the text "Street" is entered, resulting in a column that lists the word Street on each row.

```
SELECT name, [?], contact
FROM customers;
```

✔ Spelling mistakes are often interpreted as parameters. For example, suppose you enter contract instead of contact as a field name. Access reacts to the misspelling by assuming that contract is a parameter and displaying a dialog box asking you to type in the value for that parameter. The problem goes away when you correctly enter the field name.

In the previous examples, simply adding placeholders to the query established parameters. Access tries to automatically resolve problems in SQL statements by treating any identifier that cannot be matched with a field or column, as a parameter. This is a handy feature in Access but it's not a standard SQL feature. Other programs that also process SQL statements, such as Microsoft SQL Server, cannot resolve this type of statement.

The standard SQL approach to using parameters is to add a *parameters* section to the SQL statement. The parameters section begins with the PARAMETERS keyword followed by a list of one or more parameter identifiers. Each identifier must be assigned a specific data *type* such as text, DateTime, integer, or double.

The following statement follows the standard SQL format for a parameter query by adding a parameters section that defines the parameter Please enter the 2 letter state code: as a text parameter. Note that the name of the parameter must be identical each time it's used in the statement. In this example, the parameter name includes a punctuation character, a colon. The words must include that character each time the parameter is referenced, or else Access treats the two as different parameters.

```
PARAMETERS [Please enter the 2 letter state code:] text;
SELECT name, city, contact
FROM customers
WHERE state = [Please enter the 2 letter state code:];
```

Query: Param 05

If you want to use multiple parameters in a statement, each parameter must be listed following the PARAMETERS keyword in the parameters section of the statement. The following example allows for entry of two parameters, Start Date and End Date, each of which is defined as DateTime type values.

```
PARAMETERS [Start Date:] DateTime, [End date:] DateTime;
SELECT [Order Number], [Order Date]
FROM orders
WHERE [Order Date] Between [Start Date:]
AND [End Date:];
```

> **Query: Param 06**

The order in which the parameters are listed in the parameters section determines the order of the dialog boxes displayed for the parameters. However, you may insert the parameter names into the SELECT section of the statement in any order.

Domain Aggregate Functions

All the examples presented so far in this chapter have shown the use of SQL within Access query forms. However, Access allows SQL statements to be used in a variety of ways within forms, reports, and VBA modules. One of the simplest and most powerful ways to integrate SQL data retrieval operations in forms, reports, macros, or modules, is through the use of *domain aggregate functions*.

Domain aggregate functions are a special form of SQL statement that is embedded within the standard Access function format. Domain aggregate functions allow you to execute a SQL summary query. The function performs a SQL operation on the specified table and returns the summary value as the value of the function. Table 3-3 lists the domain aggregate functions available in Access.

Table 3-3	**Domain Aggregate Functions**
Function Name	*Operation*
DAvg()	Arithmetic average of the values
DCount()	Number of records
DFirst()	Value of the first record in the set

Function Name	Operation
DLast( )	Value of the last record in the set
DMin( )	Smallest value in the set
DMax( )	Largest value in the set
DSum( )	Total of all records
DSTDev( )	Standard deviation (nonbiased)
DStDevP( )	Standard deviation (biased)
DVar( )	Variance (nonbiased)
DVarP( )	Variance deviation (biased)

All of the domain aggregate functions share the same structure and syntax.

```
DFunction(expression, domain criteria)
```

The argument actually corresponds to the elements in a SQL query. The first argument corresponds to the field name or expression that follows the SELECT keyword. The second argument is called the *domain* in the name of the table from which the records will be retrieved, which corresponds to the FROM keyword. The last argument, which is optional, corresponds to the expression used with the WHERE clause to select records to be included in the summary.

```
DFunction (SELECT..., FROM... WHERE...)
```

If you understand SQL you can translate a SQL statement as it might appear in a query form, and write it as a domain function. For example, take a SQL statement used earlier in this chapter to show the use of an aggregate function. The query calculates the sum of the Quantity field in the Orders table.

```
SELECT Sum(quantity)
FROM Orders;
```

    Query: Agg 01

Instead of using a query form to execute the calculation, you can enter the equivalent domain aggregate function, DSum( ), in any part of Access (Form, Report, Macro, or Module) that allows Access functions.

If you remove all the standard SQL keywords and syntax, what you have left are the *expression* and *domain* arguments for the DSum( ) function.

The function would be written like this:

```
DSum("quantity" ,"orders")
```

Note that each of the arguments is entered as a *text literal* — that is, they are enclosed in quotation marks.

You can use the DSum() function in almost any part of Access where calculations can be performed. In this case you can use the Debug window to execute the statements just as I explain in Chapter 1.

Access displays the number 6632 in the Debug window, which represents that sum of the Quantity field in the Orders table. You may recall that this is exactly the number that was returned by the SQL statement discussed earlier in this chapter under SQL aggregate functions.

You can summarize calculated columns with the domain aggregate functions. The SQL statement shown next sums the quantity times unit price value for each record in orders.

```
SELECT Sum(quantity*[Unit Price])
FROM Orders;
```

Query: Agg 02

Enter the equivalent *domain aggregate* function (shown next) in the Debug window.

```
? DSum("quantity*[unit price]","orders")
```

The function returns the value 5151133.6882, which is identical to the result achieved with the SQL statement used earlier in this chapter.

If you want to apply a domain aggregate function to a specific set of records, you can add the optional third argument, which is equivalent to the expressions used with the SQL WHERE keyword. Eliminating the SQL keywords from the following statement shows the items that should be used as the arguments for the DSum() function.

```
SELECT Sum(quantity*[Unit Price])
FROM Orders
WHERE [Order Date] LIKE "9/*/96";
```

Enter the following in the Debug window:

```
? DSum("quantity*[unit price]", "orders", "[Order Date]
          LIKE '9/*/96'")
```

Because the WHERE argument, [Order Date] LIKE "9/*/96", contains double-quotation marks, you need to change them to apostrophes so that you can enclose the entire phrase in double-quotation marks. This allows you to insert a text literal, for example, '9/*/96', inside a larger text item.

This function returns the value 224182.54, which is the total sales volume for September, 1996.

If you are using the Dcount() function, you can simply type * for the first argument because the field name in a count operation is not significant. The statement returns the number of records, 217, that have order dates in September, 1996.

```
? DCount("*", "orders", "[Order Date] LIKE '9/*/96'")
```

> **Module: Domain Examples:**
> **Sub: DomainSamples**

Working with Automatically Generated SQL Statements

When you're working in a Query form, you have the option to view the query as a layout grid or as SQL text. In many cases it's faster and simpler to use the layout grid with its drag-and-drop interface than it is to write out complicated queries directly.

Conversely, there are times when it's easier to edit the SQL text in order to make changes than it is to update the items in the grid. You can view and edit all the columns and criteria expressions in a single window.

When you create a query with drag-and-drop and then switch to the SQL view, you may find that the statement is written in a slightly different style than if you had manually typed the query.

The following statement shows how you might enter a query that lists the order number, part number, and total for all of the records from September, 1996 sorted by order number.

```
SELECT [Order Number],[Part No],
[quantity]*[unit price] AS Total
FROM Orders
WHERE [Order Date] LIKE "9/*/96"))
ORDER BY [Order Number];
```

Creating a similar query with the drag-and-drop interface and then switching to the SQL view would reveal a statement that looks like this:

```
SELECT Orders.[Order Number], Orders.[Part No],
        [quantity]*[unit price] AS Total
FROM Orders
WHERE (((Orders.[Order Date]) Like "9/*/96"))
ORDER BY Orders.[Order Number];
```

In general, Access tends to create a more verbose SQL statement than is absolutely necessary. The additional items, while not required, provide a safety factor to ensure that when you switch between the grid and SQL text views, all changes are correctly accounted for in the query. When you type in the text of a SQL statement directly, you want to type the minimum number of characters needed to get the job done. When Access generates the statement based on your grid layout, you'll notice a few small items that aren't required in all cases.

- ✔ Access automatically attaches the table name to the field names as a prefix joined to the field name by a period. This is the standard SQL syntax for referring to a field in a specific table. Note that the use of the table name as a prefix is optional as long as the field reference is unambiguous. An *ambiguous* field reference occurs when a SQL statement includes several tables containing fields with the same name. In order to avoid this possibility, Access automatically adds the table prefix to each field that you drag and drop onto the grid.

```
Orders.[Order Number]
```

- ✔ Access does not automatically add prefixes to field names entered into expressions such as [quantity]*[unit price]. If Access finds that one or more of these names is ambiguous, an error occurs when you execute the statement. In calculated fields, you are responsible for adding table prefixes when needed.

- ✔ Access tends to add unneeded parentheses around the statements in the WHERE clause. Regardless of the type of expressions used, Access encloses the entire WHERE clause expression in a set of parentheses. The extra parentheses do no harm. Access adds them to ensure that the SQL statement you created with drag-and-drop correctly evaluates the expressions in the WHERE clause.

Part II
Educating Access

The 5th Wave   By Rich Tennant

"I'LL BE WITH YOU AS SOON AS I EXECUTE A FEW MORE COMMANDS."

In this part . . .

Access 97 is used by most Access users as a finished application. Only a small percentage of those users (unfortunately for my book sales) ever get around to taking advantage of the programming language built into Access. That is a shame for two reasons. First, I've always wanted a convertible. Second, Access programming enables you to take the plain old vanilla Access program that comes out of the box (off the CD actually) and educate that program about how you and your colleagues actually work.

The chapters in Part II explore how you can use Access 97 programming to educate Access so that it can respond more intelligently to your requests for information, reports, or calculations.

Chapter 4

Making Smart Forms

*F*orms are the basic structure by which users interact with database information. You can use Access VBA to go beyond simple data-entry forms and create *smart forms* that can carry out many of the required tasks automatically.

> **Database Folder: Chapter 4**
> **Database File: SMTFRM.MDB**

If you want to use the examples on the CD, open the database for Chapter 4, SMTFRM.MDB. Then, click the Forms tab to see the list of forms that I use in this chapter. The On the CD icons indicate which form goes with which example.

Smart Calculations

Among the most useful features of Access forms is a form's ability to perform calculations automatically for each record you display. You typically accomplish this by creating a *calculated field*. A calculated field is an unbound control that contains an expression as its `Control Source` property. On an Access form, a control is a text box, list box, label or button.

An *unbound control* is a control on a form that's not linked directly to a field in the underlying table or query. The value of the control isn't directly related to the data in any table. A *bound control* is one that's directly linked to a field in the underlying table. The contents of the field and table to which it's bound determine the contents of a bound control.

Figure 4-1, for example, shows a format that displays information from the Parts table. The table contains the following three fields that concern the pricing of parts:

- ✔ List Price. This field contains the suggested retail price of the part that the manufacturer supplies.

- ✔ Discount. This field contains the dealer discount that the manufacturer offers. The discount can be expressed as a percentage or as a decimal value depending on how the users choose to enter it into the field.

- ✔ Cost. The manufacturer doesn't supply the Cost, as he does the values for the ListPrice and Discount fields. Instead, you calculate Cost by applying the Discount percentage against the ListPrice.

Figure 4-1 shows the property sheet for the Cost control. The Control Source property contains the expression =[ListPrice]*(1 [Discount]), which automatically calculates the cost each time a new record appears in the form.

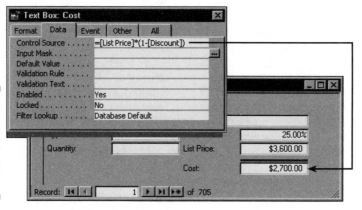

Figure 4-1:
Calculated
controls
display their
results on
forms.

> **Form: Calc 01**

A simple way to calculate the discounted price of an item is to multiply the item by 1 minus the discount percentage. In this case, the number 1 is the equivalent of 100 percent. Multiplying by 1 – 30 percent, for example, is the same as multiplying by 70 percent, which calculates the final cost of the item.

This approach, however, has one drawback. The value for the cost that appears on the form isn't actually a part of the table. The expression that the unbound control uses does display the calculated value for Cost on-screen but doesn't actually store that calculated value in the table, as shown in Figure 4-2. This figure demonstrates that the Cost field in the Parts table doesn't display any calculated costs.

Calculated controls do not fill fields with data ⌐

Part No	Description	Type	Discount	Cost	List Price ▲
ACC:5FX111046	SUN SPARC 110 T	Server Part	25.00%		$3,600.00
ACC:A11-UBA1-9S-064	Sun Ultra 1,167MH	Router	33.00%		$10,381.00
ACC:A14-UCB2-1E-25E	Sun Ultra 2, 2x200l	Router	33.00%		$33,831.65
ACC:FIR-1GW-ALA	Server Part	Server Part	33.00%		$5,120.00
ACC:NS-91-01009	Netscape Commeri	Server	33.00%		$796.00
ACC:NZ-11102415	NZ-11102415 Maint	Server	33.00%		$313.00
ACC:S20FX1-151-32-PS	Sparc20, 150Mhz,	Server Part	28.00%		$12,391.65
ACC:S20S-151-32-P97	Sparc 20,150Mhz,3	Router	28.00%		$11,721.65
ACC:S5F24-110-32-P9S	Sparc5, 110Mhz, 3	Router	33.00%		$5,691.65
ACC:S5S-110-32-P98	Sparc5, 110Mhz, 3	Server Part	28.00%		$6,026.65
ACC:SF2411095	Sparc5 110MHZ 32	Router	33.00%		$5,691.65 ▼

Parts : Table — Record: 1 of 705

Figure 4-2: Calculated controls don't store their results in the table's Cost field.

Table: Parts

Why is this a problem? In theory you have no absolute necessity to store a value such as the Cost, which you can always instruct Access to calculate from other stored values (for example, List Price and Discount). In practice, however, you may find that storing the value in the Cost field is useful, because, that way, the value is immediately available if you use the table in other forms, reports, queries, and so on. Calculating a value only when you need it (the cost, for example) is usually feasible, but you can save a lot of time and effort if you just store the value in the table at the time you enter the original data.

TIP

If you plan to export or link data from an Access 97 table for use with some other application (for example, Word to create form letters), your best bet is usually to store these calculated values in the tables; making calculations in word-processing programs is *much* more cumbersome than doing so in Access 97.

Storing Calculated Values

How can you get Access to actually write the result of the calculation into the field instead of just showing it on the form? The answer lies in *event procedures*. An event procedure is an Access VBA procedure that automatically executes every time a specific *event* takes place.

Whenever the user interacts with Access — that is, by pressing a key, clicking the mouse, or performing a combination of the two — he triggers one or more events. The two most important events for most of the tasks you perform on Access 97 forms are as follows:

- OnCurrent. This event takes place just before a new record appears on a form. Each time you click the navigation buttons to move to the next or previous record, for example, the OnCurrent event takes place.

- AfterUpdate. The AfterUpdate event takes place after you enter and save new information. Two types of AfterUpdate events actually take place on a form. Each control generates an AfterUpdate event after you enter a new or modified item of information. If, for example, you enter a new value into the Discount control and then move to another control on the form, the Discount control triggers an AfterUpdate event.

  In addition to the AfterUpdate event for each control, Access registers an AfterUpdate event for each record. This event occurs before you move to a new record after making any changes to one or more of the controls on the current record.

What good are these events anyway? The purpose of an event is to provide an opportunity for you to instruct Access 97 to perform some action automatically every time the user interacts with the form in a specific way. You implement this automatic action by linking the execution of a VBA procedure with the occurrence of a specific event.

To return to the example of the Cost calculation, what events require the recalculation of the Cost? The events in the following list relate to Cost because they affect the values Access 97 uses to calculate the cost. If either of these changes takes place, you need to instruct Access to recalculate the cost value and then update the value stored in the field.

- The user changes the value in the *Discount* control (field).
- The user changes the value in the *List Price* control (field).

For the sake of simplicity you can assume that each of the fields involved is bound to a text box control that has the same name. In this case you can think of the terms *field* and *control* interchangeably.

Assuming that you have already opened the database for Chapter 4, follow these steps to edit the event procedure for the first event you want to control, that is, a change value in the Discount control:

Form: Calc 02

1. **Open the form you want to change.**

   In this example, open the form Calc 02 in the Design mode.

2. **Click the** Discount **control.**

3. **Display the property sheet (if not already open) by choosing View⇨Properties.**

4. **Click the Event tab.**

   The Event tab, as shown in Figure 4-3, lists all the events that can occur as a user interacts with the selected control. In this case, you're interested in the event that occurs after you make a change to the Discount control — that is, the AfterUpdate event.

5. **Click the After Update property box.**

6. **Click the drop-down list arrow to the right of this property box and select [Event Procedure] from the drop-down list.**

7. **Click the Build button (...), located to the right of the drop-down list.**

If you select the listing to create an Event Procedure as the value of an event property, Access 97 automatically opens a module window for the current form, and generates a new procedure within that module, as shown in Figure 4-4, when you click the Build button. If the property is blank, Access 97 allows you to choose to create an expression, a macro, or a procedure for the event property.

The module created for the form is a special module designed to hold Access VBA procedures that relate to this specific form. The program stores the code for these procedures along with the form. The module that Access 97 stores with the form isn't listed on the Modules tab of the database. You can access the module only through the form after you open the form in Design mode.

Control name   Event name   Event procedure

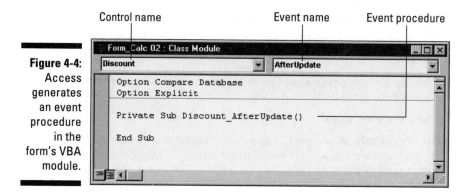

Figure 4-4:
Access
generates
an event
procedure
in the
form's VBA
module.

You need to understand the following three points about the automatically generated procedure shown in Figure 4-4:

- ✔ `Private`. The keyword `Private` means that only other procedures in the module can access this procedure — that is, the current form. The event procedures created for a form are meant only for that form and aren't recognized outside of that form. Access automatically defines all of the event procedures in a form module as Private.

- ✔ `Sub`. All event procedures are `Sub` type procedures.

- ✔ `Name`. The program automatically creates the name of the procedure by combining the name of the event with the name of the control — for example, `Discount_AfterUpdate`.

Notice the two drop-down list boxes at the top of the module window (refer to Figure 4-4). The list box on the left shows the name of the control, and the list box on the right shows the name of the event. You can use these drop-down lists to navigate around the module to view or create additional procedures without returning to the form window. Simply select the name of a control from the left box and the name of the event from the right box and Access displays the procedure for that control/event combination. If there isn't already a procedure for that control/event combination, Access 97 creates one.

After you create the procedure, you can add one or more VBA statements that you want to execute whenever the event occurs (here, updating the `Discount` control). In this case, you want to calculate the Cost and store that value in the `Cost` control. The statement I've inserted into the following procedure makes that calculation and places the results in the `Cost` field. The `Cost`, therefore, is a permanent part of the table — not just a value appearing on the form.

```
Private Sub Discount_AfterUpdate()
   [Cost] = [List Price] * (1 - [Discount])
End Sub
```

In addition to executing the calculation whenever the Discount changes, you also need to perform the same operation whenever you update the List Price control. You can generate an After Update procedure for the List Price control from within the module window by selecting the event and control names from the drop-down list boxes at the top of the window. To do so, follow these steps:

1. **Click the arrow of the left drop-down list box and select** List Price **from the list that appears.**

   Access automatically generates a new procedure, shown below, for the Before Update event of the List Price control. Before Update is the default event for a Text box type control.

   ```
   Private Sub List_Price_BeforeUpdate(Cancel As Integer)


   End Sub
   ```

   However, you want to work with the After Update event of the List Price control.

2. **Click the arrow of the right drop-down list box and select** AfterUpdate **from the list.**

What should you do about the List_Price_BeforeUpdate procedure? Nothing! Access changes the name of the procedure to match the event you select. Enter the same statement into the following procedure as you did in the Discount_AfterUpdate procedure.

```
Private Sub List_Price_AfterUpdate()
    [Cost] = [List Price] * (1 - [Discount])
End Sub
```

Access actually creates an empty List Price_BeforeUpdate procedure that remains part of the form module. Because the procedure is empty, however, it has no effect on how the form operates. If you're a compulsive sort, you may want to find these empty procedures and delete them. To remove a procedure, simply highlight the Sub through End Sub statements and press the Delete key.

You've now set up the form to automatically calculate the cost whenever you make any change to either the Discount or List Price controls. To see how this works, open the form and change the value of the Discount control — from 25 percent on the first record, for example, to 33 percent. Remember that, to activate the After Update event, you must save the new value. You can do so by tabbing to the next control. The result is that the form automatically calculates the new cost, as shown in Figure 4-5.

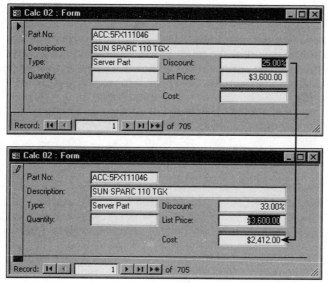

Figure 4-5:
Access
automatically
calculates
the cost
after you
save the
new
discount
rate.

Form: Calc 02

If you were to open the table window for the table (Parts) associated with the form, you'd see that the calculated cost actually appears in the Cost field of the table, shown in Figure 4-2.

Isolating Business Rules

In the example described in the preceding section, you created two event procedures that use the same basic calculation to determine the cost of an item based on its list price and manufacturer discount. The following example illustrates these two event procedures:

```
Private Sub Discount_AfterUpdate()
    [Cost] = [List Price] * (1 - [Discount])
End Sub

Private Sub List_Price_AfterUpdate()
    [Cost] = [List Price] * (1 - [Discount])
End Sub
```

In these procedures, the statement that actually calculates the cost plays the role of a *business rule*. A business rule is a calculation, procedure, or other action that a business defines as the standard of conduct for the organization. In this example, the business rule is a simple calculation that defines the meaning of *cost* by using an arithmetic formula. In other cases, the business rule may be a complex set of related calculations that determine credit limits for customers or estimated taxes.

Regardless of the complexity or simplicity of the rule, all business rules share something in common — you're supposed to apply them consistently. In the current example, several events require you to apply the *cost business rule*. The rule itself (the formula for cost), however, is always the same.

To ensure that you apply a business-rule calculation consistently, no matter how many different events trigger that rule, you want to isolate the business rule from the event procedures. The following example demonstrates a simple procedure called CalcDiscount that encapsulates the business rule you use to calculate the cost of an inventory item.

```
Sub CalcDiscount()
    [Cost] = [List Price] * (1 - [Discount])
End Sub
```

After you create the business-rule procedure, you can *call* that rule from any of the event procedures that require the calculation of the cost. The term *call* refers to a statement that you enter into one procedure that itself executes another procedure. The following example shows an event procedure that doesn't contain a specific business-rule calculation. Instead, this event procedure contains a Call statement that executes the procedure CalcDiscount.

```
Private Sub Discount_AfterUpdate()
    Call CalcDiscount
End Sub
```

You can call only Sub type procedures. Function and Property procedures execute by using different methods.

In VBA, the keyword Call is optional, and most programmers don't bother to use it. With or without Call, the procedure behaves in exactly the same way.

You can rewrite the code module of the form (Calc 02) so that each event procedure contains a call to the business rule procedure CalcDiscount, as shown in the following example:

```
Option Compare Database
Option Explicit
Sub CalcDiscount()
    [Cost] = [List Price] * (1 - [Discount])
End Sub
```

(continued)

(continued)

```
Private Sub Discount_AfterUpdate()
    CalcDiscount
End Sub

Private Sub List_Price_AfterUpdate()
    CalcDiscount
End Sub
```

Form: Calc 03

Why is it important to isolate the business rules portion of a procedure from the rest of the event procedures? There are three reasons for this:

- ✔ **Apply rules consistently.** Using a single business-rule procedure and then calling that procedure in each event that requires that rule en-sures that you're applying the same rule in all cases. If you attempt to write code for each event requiring the calculation, you run the risk of making mistakes or changes in one instance that aren't the same as another. This inconsistency may cause variations in results.

- ✔ **Make changes easily.** If you need to change the way a business rule carries out its calculation or analysis, you need only go to a single procedure to make the change.

- ✔ **Add new events.** If you isolate the business-rule from the event proce-dures, you can easily include another event in the set of event proce-dures that triggers the business-rule calculation.

Using On Current to update records

You may already have guessed that the example requires performing CalcDiscount on a third event. You may recall that, after you opened the form, you saw only blanks in all the Cost boxes in existing records. These boxes remain blank because Access triggers the After Update procedures for Discount and List Price only if you actually change the value in one of those controls. Recall, too, that Access didn't trigger the cost calculation shown in Figure 4-5 until after you entered a new discount rate.

Because the table contains more than 700 records, forcing the calculation of the cost by editing each of the Discount or List Price controls for each record would prove awfully cumbersome. An easier method is to take advantage of the On Current event. This event takes place every time a new record appears. Typically, you use this event to evaluate the current state of the records and perform any updates required before the record appears on-screen.

You could, for example, use the On Current event to check to see whether the Cost field is empty. If the field is empty, the event calls the CalcDiscount procedure to calculate the cost. The effect is that every displayed record appears with a calculated cost.

The On Current event is an event linked to the Form object. To create an OnCurrent procedure, follow these steps:

1. **Open the form in the Design mode.**

2. **Press Ctrl+R to select the Form object.**

3. **Display the property sheet, if not already open, by choosing View⇨Properties from the menu bar.**

4. **Click the Event tab of the property sheet.**

5. **Click the On Current property box.**

6. **Click the drop-down list's arrow and select [Event Procedure] from the list.**

7. **Click the Build button (...).**

In this example, the procedure you need to write must check the contents of the Cost control to see whether the control is empty — that is, whether the control contains a null value.

How do you check for nulls? The correct way to evaluate null values in Access is through the use of the IsNull() function. The *Form_Current* procedure in the following example uses the IsNull() function to determine whether to call the *CalcDiscount* procedure.

```
Private Sub Form_Current()
If IsNull([Cost]) Then
     CalcDiscount
   End If
End Sub
```

Form: Calc 04

More business rules

The business rule implemented in the CalcDiscount procedure is the simplest possible rule — that is, a simple arithmetic calculation that you can apply across the board to all the records in the table. In most cases, you can implement very simple business rules just as well by using expressions in unbound fields.

Other business rules are more complex, requiring additional types of programming logic that you can implement only by using event procedures that call business-rule procedures. Figure 4-6, for example, shows three new fields added to the parts inventory form: *Installation, 1 Year Maintain,* and *3 Year Maintain.* Although you can price these additional service items many different ways, many businesses establish rules or formulas for calculating the cost of these items if sold in conjunction with a specific piece of equipment.

As an example, suppose that the following business rules apply if you calculate the service-item prices for one type of products (for example, Internet routers):

✔ *Installation* equals 17.5 percent of margin — that is, *List Price – Cost.*

✔ One-year maintenance contract (*1 Year Maintain*) equals *Installation +* 38 percent of the *Installation.*

✔ Three-year maintenance contract (*3 Year Maintain*) equals *Installation +* 10 percent of the installation price each year.

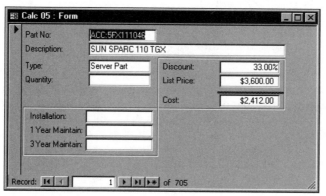

Figure 4-6:
Additional
business
calculations
now appear
on the
inventory
form.

You can express these rules in VBA code, as shown in the `CalcService` procedure in the following example:

```
Sub CalcService()
    If [Type] = "Router" Then
        [Installation] = 0.175 * ([List Price] - [Cost])
        [1 Year Maintain] = [Installation] * 1.38
        [3 Year Maintain] = [Installation] * 1.1 * 3
    End If
End Sub
```

After you add this business-rule procedure to the form's module, the next task is to call the procedure from the appropriate event procedures. You could execute a call for the CalcService procedure, for example, from the Form_Current procedure if the Installation control on the current form is null. The following example shows how different procedures can be called based on null values in specific controls (fields).

```
Private Sub Form_Current()
    If IsNull([Cost]) Or [Cost] = 0 Then
        CalcDiscount
    End If
    If IsNull([Installation]) Then
        CalcService
    End If
End Sub
```

Additionally, because the service calculations depend on the value of the Cost field, which in turn depends on Discount and List Price, any change you make to Cost requires that CalcService execute. To ensure the accuracy of the data, you need to find every place in the program that calls CalcDiscount and then add a call to CalcService, as shown in the following code sample. The program now calls two procedures each time a change is made to either the discount amount or the list price.

```
Private Sub Discount_AfterUpdate()
    CalcDiscount
    CalcService
End Sub
Private Sub List_Price_AfterUpdate()
    CalcDiscount
    CalcService
End Sub
```

You have, however, a simpler and more reliable way to ensure that any change in Cost ripples through to the service values: Insert a call for the CalcService procedure in the CalcDiscount procedure, as shown in the following example. Here, one business rule calls another business rule. This structure establishes a relationship between various business rules that interact with one or more common values.

```
Private Sub Discount_AfterUpdate()
    CalcDiscount
End Sub
Private Sub List_Price_AfterUpdate()
    CalcDiscount
```

(continued)

(continued)

```
End Sub
Sub CalcDiscount()
    [Cost] = [List Price] * (1 - [Discount])
    CalcService
End Sub
```

Figure 4-7 shows how effective these simple code examples can be in generating information based on the business rules embedded in the VBA module of a form. When the user displays the record shown in the figure, the procedures automatically evaluate the contents of the record and fill in the required installation and maintenance values.

> **Form: Calc 05**

Figure 4-7:
After you display a router record, Access 97 automatically calculates the values for service products.

```
Calc 05 : Form                                          _ □ ×

Part No:        ACC:A11-UBA1-9S-
Description:    Sun Ultra 1,167MHZ, 64MB, 2.1GB Disk, CDROM

Type:           Router          Discount:              25.00%
Quantity:                       List Price:         $10,381.00

                                Cost:                $7,785.75

Installation:        $454.17
1 Year Maintain:     $626.75
3 Year Maintain:   $1,498.76

Record: |◄| |◄|         2 |►| |►I| |►*| of 705
```

Using Select Case

In the preceding section, the business rule in the `CalcService` procedure accounts for a single product type — *router* — by using an `If` statement to determine the type of product appearing in the current record. The following statement tests the value of the `Type` control (field) to see if it contains *Router*.

```
If [Type] = "Router" Then
```

Suppose that additional business rules apply to different product types — for example, DSU, Server, and others. Table 4-1 shows a sample table of values that your program will use to calculate the cost of the service products for each type of product.

Table 4-1	Values for the Business Rules for Calculating Service Prices		
Type	_Installation_	_1 Year Maintain_	_3 Year Maintain_
Router	17.5%	38%	10%
DSU	15%	40%	25%
Server	22.5%	35%	20%
All Others	none	none	none

Just to show how with-it I really am, I have chosen as my example database a company that sells networking technology. Of course it really doesn't matter what type of products are used as examples — widgets are widgets. However, some of you won't rest unless they know what all these parts are. A _router_ is the device that make the Internet possible. Routers are intelligent devices that can determine the best path for sending data from a computer on one network to a computer on another network. A _DSU_ (digital service unit) is a device that connects network devices like bridges and routers to a digital quality transmission line. A _server_ is a computer that provides data to other computers on a network.

One way to accommodate a series of options — in this example, based on the type of product — is to use a Select Case...End Case structure. The diagram in Figure 4-8 shows how this structure works.

In the first statement in the structure the Select Case statement is assigned a value from a field, control, or an expression. The Select Case statement is followed by a series of one or more Case statements. Each Case statement is assigned one or more values that represent a possible match for the value assigned to the Select Case statement.

If Access finds that the value assigned to a Case statement matches the value that Access has assigned to the Select Case statement, then Access will execute any additional statements that are grouped under that Case.

You can also add an optional Case Else statement. If none of the specific cases turn out to be a match for the expression, Access 97 selects Case Else and executes the statements in that group.

The order in which you list the cases is significant. In a Select Case structure, VBA always selects the _first_ matching case if more than one of the cases can be true at the same time. The program ignores all other cases that follow the first match, even if they also match the expression.

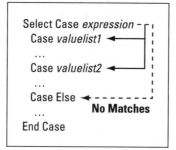

Figure 4-8: A Select Case structure evaluates any number of specific cases.

```
Select Case expression
    Case valuelist1
    ...
    Case valuelist2
    ...
    Case Else          No Matches
    ...
End Case
```

The following example is a revised version of the `CalcService` business-rule procedure. This example uses the values shown in Table 4-1 to calculate the service-product prices for specific product types. Notice that the `Case Else` inserts Null values into the fields of all products that aren't of the specified types — that is, router, DSN, or server.

```
Sub CalcService()
    Select Case [Type]
        Case "Router"
            [Installation]=0.175 * ([List Price] - [Cost])
            [1 Year Maintain]=[Installation] * 1.38
            [3 Year Maintain]=[Installation] * 1.1 * 3
        Case "DSU"
            [Installation]=0.15 * ([List Price] - [Cost])
            [1 Year Maintain]=[Installation] * 1.4
            [3 Year Maintain]=[Installation] * 1.25 * 3
        Case "Server"
            [Installation]=0.225 * ([List Price] - [Cost])
            [1 Year Maintain]=[Installation] * 1.35
            [3 Year Maintain]=[Installation] * 1.2 * 3
        Case Else
            [Installation]=Null
            [1 Year Maintain]=Null
            [3 Year Maintain]=Null
    End Select
End Sub
```

Form: Calc 06

The revised `CalcService` procedure now automatically fills in values for the additional product types as you enter the product types or as they appear on-screen, because the event procedures that monitor user interaction with the form call this procedure.

This is a good example of isolating business rules in procedures separate from the event procedures that may call them. Making changes to a single business-rule procedure causes those changes to automatically flow through to all the event procedures that call `CalcService`.

Using Local Variables

If you look at the code that the `Select Case` structure uses in the preceding section, you may notice that a great deal of the code is repetitious. You must repeat the basic formula for calculations, for example, in each example. If you look carefully at the code, you can see that each calculation is identical to the other, with the exception of the specific percentage you use. If you remove the percentages, however, and replace them with *????* as a placeholder, you get a general pattern for the calculations, as shown in the following example:

```
[Installation]= ???? * ([List Price] - [Cost])
[1 Year Maintain]=[Installation] * (1 + ???? )
[3 Year Maintain]=[Installation] * (1 + ???? ) * 3
```

You can greatly simplify the code required to perform the `CalcService` business-rule procedure by using local variables to insert the required percentages into the formulas instead of repeating the entire formula for each case. A local variable is a temporary object that you define within a procedure and then discard after the procedure finishes. You can assign variables a value throughout the procedure. You can then use the variable name to insert the value assigned to that variable into other statements.

The code fragment in the following example shows the basic way that you use local variables. First you use the `Dim` statement to define a local variable name. Then you assign to that variable name (`RateInstall`, in this example) a value — for example, **.175**. Then you insert the variable name into a calculation where the variable supplies its current value to the formula.

```
Dim RateInstall
RateInstall = .175
[Installation]= RateInstall * ([List Price] - [Cost])
```

The abbreviation *Dim* is short for *dimension*. The designers of BASIC originally used the `Dim` statement to create arrays of values. An *array* is a set of variables that share the same name but are differentiated by number — for example, *x(1)*, *x(2)*, *x(3)*, and so on. The *dimension* of an array is the total number of numbered elements in the array.

Using local variables, you can rewrite the code for the `CalcService` procedure as shown in the following example. In this example, you assign three
local variables (`RateInstall`, `Rate1Year`, and `Rate3Year`) different rates,
depending on the type of product in the `Select Case` structure. At the end
of the procedure, a single instance of the formulas used to calculate the
installation and maintenance prices can calculate those values using the
rates supplied by the local variables. Using this approach you don't have to
include a formula under each case.

Using local variables greatly reduces the amount and complexity of the
code. This example states the actual formulas only once in the procedure
instead of repeating the formulas after each `Case` statement. This method
improves the code by eliminating the possibility of anyone incorrectly or
inconsistently entering the formula in some of the cases. This method also
isolates the specific rates from the formula that uses the rates, which makes
changing the business rules easier and reduces the possibilities of introducing errors because of typing mistakes.

```
Sub CalcService()
    Dim RateInstall, Rate1Year, Rate3Year
    Select Case [Type]
        Case "Router"
            RateInstall = 0.175
            Rate1Year = 0.38
            Rate3Year = 0.1
        Case "DSU"
            RateInstall = 0.15
            Rate1Year = 0.4
            Rate3Year = 0.25
        Case "Server"
            RateInstall = 0.225
            Rate1Year = 0.35
            Rate3Year = 0.2
        Case Else
            RateInstall = Null
            Rate1Year = Null
            Rate3Year = Null
    End Select
    Installation]=RateInstall * ([List Price] - [Cost])
    [1 Year Maintain]=[Installation] * (1 + Rate1Year)
    [3 Year Maintain]=[Installation] * (1 + Rate3Year) * 3
End Sub
```

Form: Calc 07

Look at the two statements that follow. Suppose that your task is to change the rate the statement uses from 25 percent to 30 percent. You can see that editing the second statement is much simpler than changing the first statement. More significant, because the second statement doesn't actually contain the formula, you don't run the risk that you may accidentally delete some part of the formula while entering a new value.

```
[3 Year Maintain]=[Installation] * 1.25 * 3 'hard to edit
Rate3Year = 0.25 'easy to change
```

The revised `CalcService` procedure produces exactly the same results, but the code is much easier to read and maintain.

Using Lookup Tables with VBA

The two previous versions of the `CalcService` procedure were based upon the data listed in Table 4-1. That table appears in this book because it displays in a simple and straightforward manner the essential values that define the business rules that `CalcService` implements.

This is a clue! If that table works well in this book, perhaps an Access table may prove useful in the database as a source for the values you need to implement the business rule. At this point, Access 97 stores the specific values (the percentages the program uses to calculate the prices) in the actual VBA code of the `CalcService` procedure. Suppose that your company decides to change its servicing pricing values. Which course do you think is easier — to edit the VBA code module or to edit values in a table?

The obvious answer is that anyone familiar with Access can edit the table, but you can expect or trust only someone who understands programming to edit the VBA code. Putting the values in an Access 97 table enables anyone to change the percentages without needing to touch the procedure code at all.

But how can you accomplish this? One way is to take advantage of the Domain Aggregate functions I discuss in Chapter 3. These functions enable you to perform the equivalent of a full SQL query as part of some expression or formula. The Domain Aggregate functions make combining table-based operations, such as queries with VBA statements, simple.

Figure 4-9 shows the data from Table 4-1 entered into an Access table called Rates with fields called `ID`, `Type`, `Install`, `1 Year`, and `3 Year`.

ID	Type	Install	1 Year	3 Year
1	Router	17.50%	38.00%	10.00%
2	DSU	15.00%	40.00%	25.00%
3	Server	25.00%	35.00%	20.00%
(AutoNumber)				

Record: 1 of 3

You can use the DLookUp() function to extract specific values from the table. The following example, which you can enter into the Debug window, extracts the *Install* percentage for the router product type.

```
? DLookup("[Install]","Rates" ,"Type ='Router'")
 0.175
```

The arguments of the DLookUp() function correspond to the SELECT, FROM, and WHERE keywords in a SQL statement. The SQL statement in the following example is the equivalent of the DLookUp() function shown in the preceding example.

```
SELECT [Install]
FROM Rates
WHERE Type = 'Router'
```

If you use the DLookUp() function inside the CalcService procedure, the procedure looks a bit different from the version shown in the preceding example, because the WHERE clause expression isn't a literal entry — such as *router* — but instead is the text you stored in the Type field. The expressions in the following examples show how you can insert the value of the Type field into the DLookUp() function. The first example uses the apostrophe (') to insert the quotation inside the double quotation marks (" "). The second example uses the Chr() function to perform the same task. You can use either style. In this book, I use the apostrophe (') in most cases, because this character is the simplest to enter — although the apostrophe is sometimes hard to pick out if you're reading the text off the screen.

```
"Type = '" & [Type] & "'"
"Type = " & Chr(34) & [Type] & Chr(34)
```

Using the DLookUp() function to query the Rates table for the required values results in a CalcService procedure such as the one shown in the following example.

Notice that this example lists three values ("Router", "DSU", "Server") for the first Case statement. Items separated by commas are called a *list*. When you use a list with a Case statement the program selects the case if any one of the listed names matches the value of the Type field.

The DLookUp() function then queries the Rates table to acquire the appropriate percentages for the installation and maintenance calculations. The remainder of the procedure is unchanged from the previous example shown in the section titled "Using Local Variables."

```
Sub CalcService()
    Dim RateInstall, Rate1Year, Rate3Year
    Select Case [Type]
        Case "Router", "DSU", "Server"
            RateInstall = DLookup("Install", "rates", _
            "Type = '" & [Type] & "'")
            Rate1Year = DLookup("[1 Year]", "rates", _
            "Type = '" & [Type] & "'")
            Rate3Year = DLookup("[3 Year]", "rates", _
            "Type = '" & [Type] & "'")
        Case Else
            RateInstall = Null
            Rate1Year = Null
            Rate3Year = Null
    End Select
    [Installation]=RateInstall * ([List Price] - [Cost])
    [1 Year Maintain]=[Installation] * (1 + Rate1Year)
    [3 Year Maintain]=[Installation] * (1 + Rate3Year) * 3
End Sub
```

Form: Calc 08

Time-Stamping Entries

The use of a separate table to contain the rates that the business-rule procedure CalcService uses raises an important issue: Suppose that someone edits the Rates table and changes the installation percentage for routers from 17.5 percent to 20 percent. What effect does or should this change have on the inventory form?

The answer is that any change to the Rates table potentially invalidates some of or all the values stored in the Parts table. However, the program you originally created assumed that updates would only be triggered by users making changes to the data when it was displayed in a form. Now you have the possibility that updates may need to be triggered by events that take place outside the context of a form. How can you account for this type of event?

One answer is to *time-stamp* the records in both tables. If you time-stamp a record, you store the date and time that you make a change to that record. You can then compare the time-stamps of two records to determine whether one is out of sync with the other.

Because time-stamping involves two tables, Rates and Parts, you must add a field to each table in which you intend to store the time-stamp for each record. Table 4-2 lists the time-stamp fields you need to add to each table.

Table 4-2	Time-Stamp Fields
Table	*Time-Stamp Field*
Rates	EnteredOn
Parts	ServiceUpdate

How do you make sure that records receive a time-stamp showing a date each time you change those records? The only way to make sure that time-stamping occurs is to create a form that you can use for editing the Rates table and then use an event procedure to automatically enter the time stamp value whenever you make any changes to a record. Figure 4-10 shows the form I used for editing the percentages in the Rates table.

Figure 4-10:
A form you can use for editing the Rates table.

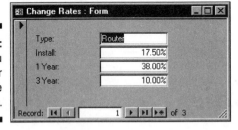

Form: Change Rates

To time-stamp each record, you must create an event procedure for the BeforeUpdate event of the Form object. This procedure, as shown in the following example, contains a single statement that inserts the current time and date into the EnteredOn field (by using the Now keyword).

```
Private Sub Form_BeforeUpdate(Cancel As Integer)
   [EnteredOn] = Now
End Sub
```

The reason I chose the `Before Update` event for the preceding example, instead of the `After Update` event, is subtle but important. First, review the timing of the two events, as described in the following paragraphs:

- ✔ `Form_BeforeUpdate` **event.** This event takes place after the user performs any action, such as moving to a new record or pressing Shift+Enter, that saves the data in the form to the underlying tables.

- ✔ `Form_AfterUpdate` **event.** This event takes place after the user saves the data in the form to the tables linked to the form.

What happens if the `Form_AfterUpdate` event executes the statement `[EnteredOn] = Now`? The `Form_AfterUpdate` takes place after you save the data. But here, as soon as you save the data, the statements in the `AfterUpdate` procedure change the record. The result is that a new value is inserted into the record just as it's supposed to have been saved. Ironically, this means that the record has changes that weren't saved.

This is a bit of a contradiction, because the `Form_AfterUpdate` event assumes that all the edits in the form are saved. Access 97 reacts to this situation by preventing you from moving to the next record — by *"freezing"* the current record. The reason for this freeze is that, each time Access 97 attempts to close out the record by saving any pending changes, the `Form_AfterUpdate` procedure edits the record, something it by definition should not be allowed to do because it negates its function of saving all of the changes to the record.

As a general rule, *never* put a statement into the `Form_AfterUpdate` event procedure that changes any of the controls on the form or any of the fields in the underlying table.

Using the `Form_BeforeUpdate` event works because the procedure inserts the time-stamp prior to saving the change to the record. The value that the procedure inserts is simply lumped together with any changes the user enters. Then Access saves the entire record with both the user-made and procedure-made changes.

You've now completed half the time-stamp solution for ensuring accurate updates. The second part is to change the `OnCurrent` event procedure of the inventory form to check the time-stamp field in the Parts table so that you can see whether you need to update the record.

The procedure shown in the following example adds an Else structure that contains another If. The If statement checks the time-stamp field, ServiceUpdated, to see whether it needs to adjust the values in the service price field to match any new rates in the Rates table. The procedure employs a Dlookup() function to extract the time-stamp from the Rates table to determine whether the record is out of sync. If the time-stamp field is a null, Access 97 automatically updates the record.

Notice in the example, too, the use of the variable WhereClause which inserts the WHERE clause expression into the Dlookup() function. Because the expression *"Type = '" & [Type] & "'"* is a bit awkward to read, using a variable makes the code easier to read.

```
Private Sub Form_Current()
    Dim WhereClause
    WhereClause = "Type = '" & [Type] & "'"
    If IsNull([Cost]) Or [Cost] = 0 Then
        CalcDiscount
    End If
    If IsNull([Installation]) Then
        CalcService
    Else
        If IsNull([ServiceUpdated]) Or _
        [ServiceUpdated] < _
        DLookup("[EnteredOn]", "Rates", WhereClause) Then
            CalcService
        End If
    End If
End Sub
```

The final modification is to make sure that the records in the Parts table receive a time-stamp as you update them. Typing **[ServiceUpdated] = Now** at the end of CalcService inserts the current date and time in the ServiceUpdated field which ensures the accurate time-stamping of the records.

```
Sub CalcService()
    Dim RateInstall, Rate1Year, Rate3Year
    Select Case [Type]
        Case "Router", "DSU", "Server"
            RateInstall = DLookup("Install", "rates", _
            "Type = '" & [Type] & "'")
            Rate1Year = DLookup("[1 Year]", "rates", _
            "Type = '" & [Type] & "'")
            Rate3Year = DLookup("[3 Year]", "rates", _
```

```
           "Type = '" & [Type] & "'")
      Case Else
          RateInstall = Null
          Rate1Year = Null
          Rate3Year = Null
    End Select
    [Installation] = RateInstall * ([List Price] - [Cost])
    [1 Year Maintain]=[Installation] * (1 + Rate1Year)
    [3 Year Maintain]=[Installation] * (1 + Rate3Year) * 3
    'TimeStamp records
    [ServiceUpdated] = Now
End Sub
```

| Form: Calc 09 |

Entering Percentages

Most of the examples shown so far in this chapter involve the use of percentages. Percentages pose an interesting problem in entering data. If asked to enter a percentage, you have two possible choices: Enter the percentage as a whole number (for example, **17.5**) or enter the percentage as a decimal number (**.175**).

Which way is the right way to go? The answer depends on the assumptions you make at the time you design the database. Making sure that the people using your database are going to recognize or remember how to enter percentages into your forms or tables, however, is often quite a bit more difficult than simply choosing how to enter the values.

In using event procedures, you can circumvent this problem by realizing that people may enter percentages in either form. The code fragment in the following example shows how to deal with an entry made into the Discount field. The If statement checks the value the user enters into the field. If that value is greater than 1, the program assumes that the user entered the percentage as a whole number. In that case, the program is designed to convert the entry to a decimal value and inserts the value back into the field. If the entry is less than 1, the program assumes that the entry is in decimal format and needs no adjustment.

```
If [Discount] > 1 Then
    [Discount] = [Discount] / 100
End If
```

The following example shows this technique in context as part of the AfterUpdate event procedure for the Discount control:

```
Private Sub Discount_AfterUpdate()
    If [Discount] > 1 Then
        [Discount] = [Discount] / 100
    End If
    CalcDiscount
End Sub
```

Form: Check Entry

Keep in mind that this technique isn't perfect. If, for example, someone enters a percentage less than 1 percent — such as .5 percent — the procedure doesn't convert .5 to .005 but leaves the value as .5, which is 50 percent.

Changing the Form's Appearance

In addition to performing calculations, you can use event procedures to alter the appearance of the form. In the inventory form discussed earlier in this chapter under "Isolating Business Rules," for example, no information appears in the Installation, 1 Year Maintain, and 3 Year Maintain fields for many of the items in the Parts table. On those records, the form displays empty text boxes.

Because these text boxes aren't meaningful for these records, the more sensible course is to make sure that those controls don't appear on records without data for those fields. You can hide a control by setting the control's Visible property to False. Conversely, you can make a hidden control visible again by setting the Visible property to True. The following example uses a Select Case structure to determine which set of controls is visible on the form, based on the value in the Type field.

Note that the name of the control that draws the box around the service controls is called Box15. The program includes this control as part of the group of controls that displays service information.

```
Private Sub Form_Current()
' existing code not shown
' hide unused controls
    Select Case [Type]
        Case "Router", "DSU", "Server"
            [Installation].Visible = True
            [1 Year Maintain].Visible = True
            [3 Year Maintain].Visible = True
            [Box15].Visible = True
```

```
        Case Else
            [Installation].Visible = False
            [1 Year Maintain].Visible = False
            [3 Year Maintain].Visible = False
            [Box15].Visible = False
    End Select
End Sub
```

Form Calc 10

If you have trouble remembering the exact names of the controls and fields in the form as you enter code, you can open the Expression Builder window by right-clicking the module window and choosing Build from the shortcut menu.

Figure 4-11 shows the effect of the new section added to the Form_Current procedure. The entire services section (four controls) remains hidden if the product type doesn't match one of the specified criteria. The display adjusts itself each time you move to a new record. When the type does match one of the specified types, the form returns to the full display as shown in Figure 4-7.

Figure 4-11:
The
OnCurrent
procedure
hides some
controls
based on
the type of
product
being
displayed.

Calc 10 : Form		
Part No:	ACC-FIR-1GW-ALA	
Description:	Server Part	
Type:	Server Part	Discount: 33.00%
Quantity:		List Price: $5,120.00
		Cost: $3,430.40

Record: 14 | 4 | 4 | ▶ | ▶I | ▶* | of 705

Using the Tag property

In the last example in the preceding section, your task was to change the value of a property — specifically, the Visible property for a group of controls. In that example, the only way to refer to the controls that you want to change is to specify by name each control belonging to the group.

Access controls have a special property called Tag that you can use to define a group of related controls. Tag is a special property, because Tag actually has no function at all. The purpose of Tag is to provide a means of defining a group of controls by giving all the controls the same value as in the Tag property. Figure 4-12 shows the Other tab of the Installation control's property sheet. The name *Service* appears in the Tag property. Table 4-3 lists the controls that form a group because their Tag properties all have the same value.

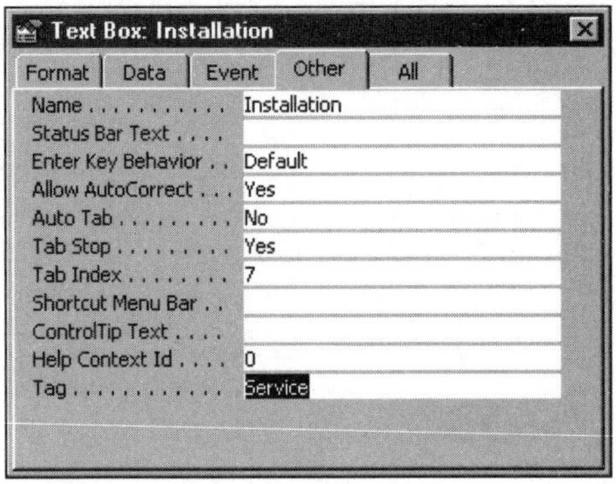

Figure 4-12:
You can use
the Tag
property to
define a
group of
controls.

Text Box: Installation

| Format | Data | Event | Other | All |

Name	Installation
Status Bar Text	
Enter Key Behavior . .	Default
Allow AutoCorrect . . .	Yes
Auto Tab	No
Tab Stop	Yes
Tab Index	7
Shortcut Menu Bar . .	
ControlTip Text	
Help Context Id	0
Tag	Service

Table 4-3	Settings for the Tag Property
Control	*Tag Property*
Installation	Service
1 Year Maintain	Service
3 Year Maintain	Service
Box15	Service

What's the point of tagging controls? Using Tag enables you to write procedures that operate on just the members of that particular group of controls. The Tag property allows you to arbitrarily form a group by giving each control the same value in its Tag property. The following example hides all the controls on a form that display a Tag property value of *Service*. Take special notice of the following points in this example:

✔ **The Me object.** The Me object refers to the currently active Form or Report object. You can use Me to refer to any property, method, or collection within the form. The Me object can also serve as a prefix to any control or field in the current form. The following statement refers to the Installation control on the current form:

```
Me![Installation].Visible = True
```

In most cases, you don't need to specify the Me object, because Access 97 assumes that any reference to a control or field in a form module refers to the Me object. The Me object is only available in a form or report module. Standard modules, that is, modules created from the Modules tab of the Database window cannot use the Me object.

✔ **The** For Each **Structure.** You use this structure to enumerate all the controls on the form. This structure enables you to inspect the Tag property for each control and pick out those that belong to the Service group.

```
Dim C As Control
   For Each C In Me.Controls
      If C.Tag = "Service" Then
         C.Visible = False
      End If
   Next
```

Utilizing For Each…Next, you can develop a procedure that shows or hides the controls based on the Type of part being displayed. The program fragment shown in the following uses For Each to enumerate all of the controls on a form. The program tests the Tag property of each control to determine which, if any, belong to the Service group.

```
Dim C As Control
   Select Case [Type]
      Case "Router", "DSU", "Server"
         For Each C In Me.Controls
            If C.Tag = "Service" Then
               C.Visible = True
            End If
         Next
      Case Else
         For Each C In Me.Controls
            If C.Tag = "Service" Then
               C.Visible = False
            End If
         Next
   End Select
```

Form: Calc 11

The primary advantage of using For Each to examine the Tag property of each control is that your code is no longer locked into a specific list of control names. You can easily include or exclude controls from the group simply by changing their Tag property instead of editing your code.

Dealing with controls as a group also eliminates errors that can arise if you fail to keep the hide and show control lists identical. In the previous example (`Calc 11`), the code required you to have two identical lists of controls entered under different `Case` statements. If the two lists were not identical, some controls would fail to hide or reappear when they were supposed to do so.

Passing parameters to a procedure

If you examine the statements included within the `Case` statements in the preceding section, you may notice that the code is almost identical in all the statements, with the exception that one case uses the `False` value and the other a `True` value. If you replace the True or False with a placeholder, *????,* you find that you have a block of code that you can use to either show or hide a group of similarly tagged controls.

```
Sub GroupShow()
    For Each C In Me.Controls
        If C.Tag = "Service" Then
            C.Visible = ????
        End If
    Next
End Sub
```

But how can you avoid fixing the function of the code by specifying either True or False? The answer is to create a procedure that places a variable in the location where the True or False should go. In the following example I insert the variable `Show` into the code in place of a specific True or False value.

```
Sub GroupShow()
    For Each C In Me.Controls
    Sub GroupShow()
        If C.Tag = "Service" Then
            C.Visible = Show
        End If
    Next
End Sub
```

If `Show` equals True, the `GroupShow` procedure shows the controls in the group. Conversely, if `Show` equals False, the procedure hides the controls. But how can you assign a value to a variable in a procedure called from another procedure? The rules that govern the scope of local variables prevents variables defined in one procedure from being available in any other procedure.

The solution lies in the capability of VBA to *pass* parameters between procedures. When you pass a value you send the a value defined in one procedure to another procedure that you are calling. A *parameter* is the value that the procedure passes to the procedure it is calling. You define parameters by placing a list of the parameters inside the ( ) that follows the procedure name in the Sub statement. The following example defines a parameter called Show that's required for the GroupShow procedure.

```
Sub GroupShow(Show)
    For Each C In Me.Controls
    Sub GroupShow()
        If C.Tag = "Service" Then
            C.Visible = Show
        End If
    Next
End Sub
```

If you want to execute the GroupShow procedure, you use a Call statement that specifies the name of the procedure to call and the value of the required parameter.

```
Call GroupShow True
```

Figure 4-13 shows what happens when you use a parameter in calling a procedure. In this case, the value that is passed to the GroupShow procedure is a True value. When the GroupShow procedure receives the value, the GroupShow procedure assigns the value to the variable name, Show, specified in the Sub statement. Within the GroupShow procedure, Show has the value of True.

You're limited to passing a single parameter. The following example requires two parameters: GroupName and Show. You can use the procedure to show or hide and group of controls that share the same Tag property.

```
Sub GroupShow(GroupName, Show)
    For Each C In Me.Controls
    Sub GroupShow()
        If C.Tag =GroupName Then
            C.Visible = Show
        End If
    Next
End Sub
```

Figure 4-13:
The
parameter's
value
passes
to the
procedure.

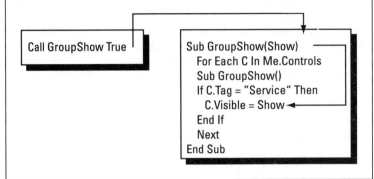

To execute the procedure, you enter the following statement in another procedure. Notice that you generally omit the optional keyword `Call`.

Be aware that the order of the parameters you write as a list must match the order of the variables in the `Sub` statement of the procedure you're calling. In this case, the group name comes first and the True/False value second.

```
GroupShow "Service", True
```

Access 97 also enables you to specify arguments for user-defined procedures as *named arguments*. (Named arguments are introduced in Chapter 1.) The names of the arguments are the names specified in the `Sub` statement of the procedure you're calling. The following statement shows the use of named arguments. If you use the named argument form, the order of the parameters isn't important.

```
GroupShow Show:= True, GroupName:= "Service"
```

The following block of code shows how you can call the same procedure, `GroupShow`, to show or hide a group of controls:

```
Private Sub Form_Current()
'other statements not shown
Select Case [Type]
    Case "Router", "DSU", "Server"
        GroupShow GroupName:="Service", Show:=True
    Case Else
        GroupShow GroupName:="Service", Show:=False
  End Select
End Sub


Sub GroupShow(GroupName, Show)
   Dim C As Control
```

```
     For Each C In Me
         If C.Tag = GroupName Then
             C.Visible = Show
         End If
     Next
 End Sub
```

Form: Calc 12

Working with color

Another way to enhance the appearance of your forms is to use color. You can add colors at design time to make the form more interesting to look at. You can also use procedures to alter the original color of the form, based on the actual data the form displays.

Suppose, for example, that you want to use color as a visual indicator of the level of manufacturer discount for each item. The idea is that, by changing the color of the controls based on the discount percentage, you can tell at a glance which products offer the best margins.

To work with colors, you need to use the following types of properties:

✔ ForeColor/BackColor **properties.** Each control that displays text (labels, text boxes, combo boxes and list boxes) has both a foreground color (ForeColor) and a background color (BackColor) property. You can set these properties in the control's property sheet at the time you design the form or later on by using a VBA procedure to change colors while the finished form is on-screen. The following statement, for example, sets the background color of the Part No control on the Calc 13 form to red:

```
 Forms![Calc 13]![Part No].BackColor = 255
```

You can test out various color combinations by opening a form — for example, Calc 13 — and using the Debug window (which you open by pressing Ctrl+G) to enter statements such as the preceding example. These kinds of statements temporarily change the color of the controls on the form. Using this procedure is faster than making changes while in Design mode and then displaying the form. You can try out the color combinations until you find one you like.

✔ **The** RGB()/QBColor() **functions.** Two functions help generate the colors in VBA: The RGB() — red-green-blue — function calculates the value of a color by using three values ranging from 0 to 255 for the primary colors red, green, and blue. The QBColor() — QuickBasic — function generates the 16 basic colors supported by all Windows devices.

Table 4-4 shows the 16 basic colors, the QBColor number code, the RGB combinations, and the decimal number that produces the color. The three statements that follow all produce the same result — they set the background color of the control to gray.

```
Forms![Calc 13]![Part No].BackColor = QBColor(8)
Forms![Calc 13]![Part No].BackColor = RGB(128,128,128)
Forms![Calc 13]![Part No].BackColor = 8421504
```

Table 4-4   The Values for Generating the Basic 16 Colors

QBColor #	Color	Decimal	RGB argument
0	Black	0	(0,0,0)
1	Blue	8388608	(0,0,128)
2	Green	32768	(0,128,0)
3	Cyan	8421376	(0,128,128)
4	Red	128	(128,0,0)
5	Magenta	8388736	(128,0,128)
6	Yellow	32896	(128,128,0)
7	White	12632256	(192,192,192)
8	Gray	8421504	(128,128,128)
9	Light Blue	16711680	(0,0,255)
10	Light Green	65280	(0,255,00)
11	Light Cyan	16776960	(0,255,255)
12	Light Red	255	(255,0,0)
13	Light Magenta	16711935	(255,0,255)
14	Light Yellow	65535	(255,255,0)
15	Bright White	16777215	(255,255,255)

The color system on a computer screen is an *additive system*. In an additive system, combining all the colors produces white. If you combine equal amounts of red, green, and blue at any level from 0 to 255 you produce a gray tone. If, for example, you combine 128, 128, and 128, you get a 50 percent gray tone.

Although the controls on a form combine to create a single collection, Controls, that collection can consist of a number of different kinds of controls. The TypeOf keyword provides a means by which you can distinguish the different types of controls. The following statement is true if the control named *Installation* is a text box but false if Installation is any other type of control — for example, a Label.

```
If TypeOf [Installation] Is TextBox Then
```

The AdjustColors procedure shown in the following example alters the colors of all the text boxes on the form, based on the value of the Discount field. The first section uses a Select Case structure to pick color combinations based on the Discount amount. The second part of the procedure uses a For Each loop structure to apply the color combination to the controls. The example uses the TypeOf…Is keywords to select only the text box controls for the color change. The text is also set to bold — by using the FontBold property — because white letters need to be bold to show up against a colored background.

```
Sub AdjustColors()
    Dim FG, BG, C As Control
    Select Case [Discount]
        Case 0 To 0.28
            BG = RGB(0, 255, 0) 'green
            FG = RGB(255, 255, 255) 'white
        Case 0.28 To 0.4
            BG = RGB(255, 0, 0) 'red
            FG = RGB(255, 255, 255) 'white
        Case Is > 0.4
            BG = RGB(0, 128, 128) 'cyan
            FG = RGB(255, 255, 255) 'white
    End Select
    For Each C In Me
        If TypeOf C Is TextBox Then
            With C
                .ForeColor = FG
                .BackColor = BG
                .FontBold = True
            End With
        End If
    Next
End Sub
```

This procedure needs to be called from two event procedures. The first is the Form_Current procedure. The Form_Current procedure ensures that each time a record appears on-screen, the color of the text boxes changes to fit the current discount amount.

```
Private Sub Form_Current()
' other statements not shown
    AdjustColors
End Sub
```

Because the Discount field controls AdjustColors, any changes to that field requires that the Discount_AfterUpdate call the AdjustColors procedure, as shown in the following procedure, to ensure that the colors are updated if the user should change the Discount value.

```
Private Sub Discount_AfterUpdate()
    CalcDiscount
    AdjustColors
End Sub
```

| Form: Calc 13 |

Using colors to indicate something about the information on-screen can prove very effective, because people react to colors much more strongly than they react to text. In addition, color offers a way to convey a message without adding something to the screen that takes up more room, such as a label or a text box.

About colors in VBA

Windows uses a color system that blends red, green, and blue pigments to create color combinations. Each color has 256 (0 to 255) different intensities, where zero represent none of that color and 255 represents full intensity. The color combinations fall in a range from 0 to 16,777,215, which is the total number of different possible combinations of three 256 colors. (The number 16,777,216 is 2 raised to the 24th power.) If you want to set each pixel on the screen to any one of the 16,777,216 possible colors, you need to reserve 24 bits (three bytes) of memory for each pixel. A 24-bit color system is one with sufficient video memory available to allocate 24 bits (three bytes) for each pixel. If you're using a resolution of 640 x 480, you need about 0.9 MB of memory to display 24-bit color. Systems that don't support the full 16,777,216 possible colors simply substitute the closest color available if someone uses an unsupported combination.

Chapter 5

Working with Lists

● ●

In This Chapter

▶ Eliminating unnecessary data entry

▶ Creating dynamically updating lists

▶ Creating special handling for new records

▶ Linking the values in several lists to each other

▶ Generating random selections of data

● ●

*O*ne of the biggest differences between databases designed by people who can write Access 97 on programs and those designed by people who cannot write Access 97 programs is the use of lists to eliminate direct data entry. In this chapter you discover a number of ways to make the forms you create easier for people to use and less prone to normal typographical errors.

Selection versus Entry

In any database system the most critical section of the application is *data acquisition* — or more simply, those segments in the program involving the input points for the data. PCs support any number of interesting ways to acquire data — from bar code readers to downloads from other computer databases — but data acquisition's bread and butter still remains the keyboard, the mouse, and a user's hands.

Any programmer's most important task is to use those tools available in Access 97 (including VBA programming) to create a user interface that maximizes the chances for data to be entered quickly and accurately. One of the best ways to do this is to try to eliminate *direct data entry* — typing information into text boxes — by selecting data from lists of various types. While there is no way to eliminate all text entry, you can greatly reduce the amount of typing (and subsequently the number of typing errors) by taking advantage of the rich set of tools available to the Access 97 programmer.

> *Database Folder: Chapter 5*
> *Database File: list.mdb*

To get ready to begin this chapter, open the database for Chapter 5, LIST.MDB. When you have opened the database, click on the Forms tab to display a list of the forms discussed in this chapter. In addition, you may find other objects such as queries, modules, or tables, that are relevant to understanding the example. I specify these objects, when relevant, next to the On the CD icon.

Self-Referencing Lists

The first rule for making better entry forms is to eliminate, wherever possible, the user having to enter information that he can simply select. As an example, look at the form shown in Figure 5-1. This form displays 11 text box controls that you use to display and enter data.

If you look carefully at the items included in the form you see in Figure 5-1, you'll notice that some of the items tend to repeat from record to record. For example, the city, state, and zip code information for a company may be the same in many respects as the city, state, and zip of a previously entered record.

Figure 5-1:
A standard
style form
that uses
text boxes
for all data
entry.

Entry Form 01 : Form			
Company:	20th Century Insurance		
Address:	6301 Owensmouth Ave., 5th Flr.		
City:	Woodland Hills	State: CA	Zip: 91367
Name1:	Jack Semler	Name2:	
Phone1:	8187043723	Phone2:	
Phone1_Ext:		Phone2_Ext:	

Record: 1 of 333

> *Form: Entry Form 01*

One way to simplify the entry of these items is to create a *self-referential* combo box control. The term self-referential refers to the fact that the data source for the combo list box is not a separate lookup table (a separate table that contains only city names) but the same table, for instance, *Businesses,* which is the record source for the form itself.

To illustrate, Figure 5-2 shows a form similar to the one in Figure 5-1. The only exception is that the control displaying the City field was changed from a text box to a combo box with a drop list. This drop list shows the names of all the cities previously entered into other records in the same table. If the city name to be entered next is already in this list, the user can pick it from the list rather than manually enter it.

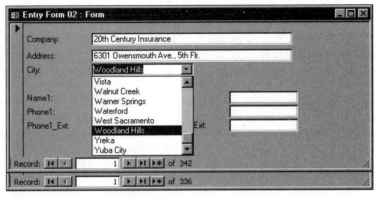

Figure 5-2:
A self-referential combo box used for selecting city names.

> **Form: Entry Form 02**

By default, Access activates the control wizards each time you select a group, toggle button, list, combo box, or button control in the form. To follow the steps outlined below, turn off control wizards by clicking the control wizards button in the control toolbox.

To create a combo box that holds a self-referential list, perform the following steps.

1. **Add a Combo Box control to the form whose** Control Source **is the field for which you want to generate a self-referential list.**

2. **Set the** Row Source Type **property for** Table/Query.

3. **In the** Row Source, **enter a SQL statement that selects the items you want to display in the list as a SQL query data set.**

   The statement takes the general form shown in the following code sample. The key element is the DISTINCT keyword. This keyword causes SQL to drop all the duplicate names from the list. In addition, you'll want to eliminate any null items from the list with IS NOT NULL.

```
SELECT DISTINCT field FROM table WHERE field IS NOT NULL;
```

More specifically, the following gives you a listing of the unique city names from the `City` field of the Businesses table. An added benefit of using the `DISTINCT` keyword is that the items are automatically sorted in ascending order because Access must sort the records in order to determine which records contain duplicate names.

```
SELECT DISTINCT city FROM businesses WHERE city IS NOT NULL;
```

List or box?

Using self-referentials at first seems to solve the problem of data entry for a field like `City`, that is likely to have duplicates. However, in practice, a form like the one in Figure 5-2 serves two functions — data entry and data display.

Using combo boxes with drop lists is very beneficial when you enter new records. However, once you establish the record and simply want to use the combo box for data display and occasional modifications, you may find that these records look better if the data is displayed in the text boxes.

More seriously, accidentally changing the data entered into a field when it is part of a combo box control is quite easy. An inexperienced user can open the list box and, without knowing it, change the contents of the field by choosing another item from the list. It's much less likely (though still possible) that the same user would accidentally change data in a text box that doesn't have a drop-down list attached to it.

In essence, you need two types of forms — data entry with lists, and data display with text boxes. However, such a solution often becomes too awkward. A more ideal solution involves a single form that displays text boxes when existing records are displayed but changes to combo boxes with self-referential lists when you add a new record to the table.

You can begin by creating a form that contains both types of controls for the `City` field, as shown in Figure 5-3. The first control is a text box control called `City Box`. The second is a combo box control called `City List`, which uses the SQL statement to display a list of the city names that were previously entered.

> **Form: Entry Form 03 a**

Hiding a control

Having two controls for the same field on the same form is bound to cause some confusion. The trick is to not allow them both to be visible at the same time. All controls on a form have a `Visible` property that you can set to True (show the control) or False (hide the control), either in the property sheet for the control or while the form is on display, using VBA. For

[City List] - combo box control

[City Box] - text box control

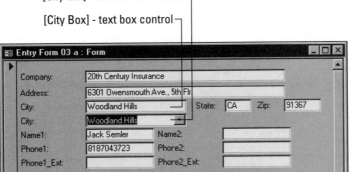

Figure 5-3:
A form that
contains a
text and
combo box
for the
same field.

example, if you want to hide the City Box control (the text box used for the City field), you execute the following statement in a procedure.

```
Me![City Box].Visible = False
```

You can also use the Visible property to determine the current state of a control on a form. The following code fragment displays a message box if the City Box control is hidden.

```
If Me![City Box].Visible = False
Msgbox "City Box exists, but is currently hidden"
End If
```

The form pictured in Figure 5-4 shows how you can create a form that alternates between a text box and a combo box for the same field, City. In this form, the Visible property for the City Box control is initially set in the control's property sheet as True. The opposite is true of the City List control whose Visible property is set to False in the property sheet.

A command button labeled *Toggle Box/List* appears on the form. Use this button to alternate between the two controls.

Form: Entry Form 03 b

On the On Click event listed in the button's property sheet, enter a procedure like the one shown below. Begin this procedure by checking the Visible property of the City Box control. If that property is true — that is, the control is visible — the procedure then inverts the relationship between the two controls by hiding City Box and showing City List.

Command Button hide/show control

[City List] Visible = False

[City Box] Visible = True

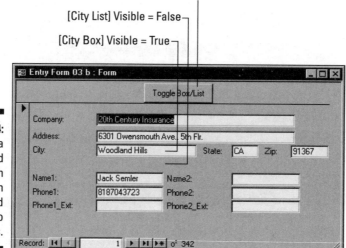

Figure 5-4:
Use a
command
to switch
between
text box and
combo
displays.

To reverse the process, click the button on the form and hide `City Box`:
`City List` becomes hidden and `City Box` is displayed.

```
Private Sub Command15_Click()
    If Me![City Box].Visible = True Then
        Me![City Box].Visible = False
        Me![City List].Visible = True
    Else
        Me![City Box].Visible = True
        Me![City List].Visible = False
    End If
End Sub
```

This approach allows a single form to display two different types of controls,
both of which can display or edit the same field.

Moving a control

The form shown in Figure 5-4 has one small but annoying quirk. Each time
you click the button and the visible properties of the controls become
reversed, the alternate control appears but not in the same location. Because the two controls were placed at different locations when the form was
designed, they remain at those same locations when they become visible.

In order for the form to appear normal to the user, both controls should appear at the exact same location when they are made visible. You can accomplish this in the design mode by dragging the controls so they overlap. However, this can be confusing since even in the design mode you aren't able to see both controls at the same time if one physically covers the other.

An alternate approach is to alter and then move the control as part of the procedure that makes each control visible. The following two properties determine the position of any control.

✔ Top. This is the distance between the top of the form section and the top of the control where zero is the topmost edge of the section. As this value increases, the control moves toward the bottom of the form section.

```
Me![City Box].Top = 1440
```

✔ Left. This is the distance from the left side of the form section where zero is the leftmost edge of the form. As this value increases, the control moves toward the right edge of the form.

```
Me![City Box].Left = 2160
```

Even though the property sheet usually expresses these settings in terms of inches, when you deal with the settings in VBA the unit of measurement is a twip.

A *twip* is a unit of measure that is equal to 1/1440th of an inch. To convert twips to inches simply enter the inch value, for example, 1.5, and then multiply it by 1440, which is the number of twips in one inch.

```
Me![City Box].Left = 1.5 * 1440
```

Forms can comprise three sections: the main section called *detail;* a form header section; and a form footer section.

In this case, the city controls should both appear at the same location — 1.0417 inches from the left and 0.625 inches from the top. Following is a modified version of the procedure that executes from the Toggle Box/List button. The procedure adds two *constant* values that represent the fixed location on the form to which the City List control should be moved before it's made visible. A *constant* is a value that's used by a procedure; however, unlike a variable that you can change during the execution of the program, *constants* cannot be modified. Because they cannot be changed, *constants* use up less memory and system resources than variables.

The Top and Left properties then use the constants to change the position of the City List controls before that control is made visible. Note that you don't need to change the position of the City Box control when it becomes visible because it's already located at the proper place.

```
Private Sub Command15_Click()
    Const CityLeft = 1.0417 * 1440
    Const CityTop = 0.625 * 1440
    If Me![City Box].Visible = True Then
        Me![City Box].Visible = False
        Me![City List].Top = CityTop
        Me![City List].Left = CityLeft
        Me![City List].Visible = True
    Else
        Me![City List].Visible = False
        Me![City Box].Visible = True
    End If
End Sub
```

Form: Entry Form 03 c

To see how this works, open form *Entry Form 03 c* on the CD and click on the Toggle Box/List button several times. You'll notice that when you click the button, the City control appears to change from a text box to a combo box and then back again. In reality the control type is not changing. The procedure is switching between two different controls that are simply displayed at the same location.

The With statement

If you look carefully at the code in the previous version of the Command15_Click procedure, you'll notice that there are three statements in a row that set properties for the same object, Me![City List].

```
Me![City List].Top = CityTop
Me![City List].Left = CityLeft
Me![City List].Visible = True
```

In order to simplify the coding of a series of statements that all operate on the same object, VBA provides the With…End With structure that takes the general form shown in the following code. The structure begins with a With statement that specifies the name of the object you need to modify. That's followed by one or more properties of that object that need to be changed. This eliminates the need to enter the object name for each property that needs to be changed. Further, it makes the code easier to read and understand since it shows clearly that all the property changes are being applied to the same object.

```
With object
    .Property1 = value1
    .Property2 = value2
    ...
End With
```

If you replace the three statements shown above with a With...End With structure, the code for Command15_Click will look like the following example.

```
Private Sub Command15_Click()
    Const CityLeft = 1.0417 * 1440
    Const CityTop = 0.625 * 1440
    If Me![City Box].Visible = True Then
        Me![City Box].Visible = False
        With Me![City List]
            .Top = CityTop
            .Left = CityLeft
            .Visible = True
        End With
    Else
        Me![City List].Visible = False
        Me![City Box].Visible = True
    End If
End Sub
```

Form: Entry Form 03 c1

With structures are always optional in VBA. You can always accomplish the same thing by using a series of statements that include the full name of the object and the property. Like indenting, it's used to streamline the entry and appearance of the code.

Changing for New Records Only

In preceding sections I describe a procedure that changes the control type for the City field from a text box to a combo box, and then back again each time you click on a button placed on the form. However, the original reason for having the two different controls was that one control (the text box) is more appropriate for existing records, while the other (the combo box) is best when you add a new record to the table.

Instead of manually selecting the style of control by clicking a button, you can automatically trigger that change each time you add a new record to the table. This eliminates the need for the command button and relieves you from having to remember to click it in order to get the combo box control to display when it's needed.

You can accomplish this change by associating the procedure that hides and displays controls with an event that's related to the entry of new records. Two events are associated with new records.

- ✔ `Before Insert`. You trigger this event when you enter (with the keyboard or mouse) the first character into a new record. Keep in mind that you *do not* trigger this event when you display a new blank record such as with the Edit⇨Goto⇨New Record command.

- ✔ `After Insert`. This event takes place when the data entered into the form is saved as a new record in the underlying table. This occurs when you move to a different record or press Ctrl+Enter.

To show and hide controls based on the entry of new records, the procedure used in the previous examples will actually be divided into two separate procedures, each executed by different events. The part of the procedure that hides the text box and shows the combo box is associated with the `Before Insert` event.

Keep in mind that the `Before Insert` and `After Insert` events belong to the `Form` object. To create an event procedure for these events, you must select the Form. To create a procedure for the `Before Insert` event, perform the following:

1. **Open the form (for example,** `Entry Form 03 d`**) in the Design mode.**
2. **Display the property sheet, View⇨Properties.**
3. **Select the** `Form` **object, Ctrl+R.**
4. **Click on the Events tab in the property sheet.**
5. **Click on the ... icon (the build icon) for the** `Before Insert` **property.**
6. **Double click on Code Builder.**

Access automatically assigns the name `Sub Form_BeforeInsert` to the procedure. In this case, the procedure reacts to the beginning of the entry of a new record by showing the combo box control automatically.

```
Private Sub Form_BeforeInsert(Cancel As Integer)
    Const CityLeft = 1.0417 * 1440
    Const CityTop = 0.625 * 1440
    Me![City Box].Visible = False
    With Me![City List]
```

```
        .Top = CityTop
        .Left = CityLeft
        .Visible = True
    End With
End Sub
```

| *Form: Entry Form 03 d* |

To see how this works, perform the following steps:

1. **Open the** Entry Form 03 d **form.**

2. **Select the Edit⇨Go To⇨New Record command from the menu bar.**

    The form shows a new, blank record. The City Box control (the text box) is what you see displayed. Recall that Access doesn't trigger the Before Insert event until you enter at least one character in one of the controls on the form.

3. **Type** t.

You trigger the Before Insert event as soon as you type the first character into the Company field. These procedural changes hide the City Box control and display the City List control in its place.

You may continue entering data on your own, or press Esc to discard the entry you started to make.

Using After Insert

At this point (if you've been following along), you have a procedure in place that automatically replaces a text box control with a combo box control as soon as the user begins to enter data into a new record. However, there's still a need for a second event-triggered procedure that returns the text box control when the user navigates to existing records.

You can do this by attaching a procedure to the After Insert event of the form. Recall that the After Insert event doesn't occur until Access saves the new record. This means that the user can edit the new record for as long as he or she likes, and the combo box controls remain displayed. You trigger the After Insert event as soon as you save the record (either by moving to a different record or pressing Ctrl+Enter).

Recall that the `After Insert` event is associated with the `Form` object. To create an `After Insert` procedure, follow these steps.

1. **Open the form (for example, `Entry Form 03 e`) in the Design mode.**

2. **Display the property sheet by choosing View⇨Properties.**

3. **Select the `Form` object by choosing Ctrl+R.**

4. **Click on the Events tab in the property sheet.**

5. **Click on the ... icon (the build icon) for the `After Insert` property.**

The following procedure hides the combo box and displays the text box control in its place.

```
Private Sub Form_AfterInsert()
    Me![Company].SetFocus
    Me![City List].Visible = False
    Me![City Box].Visible = True
End Sub
```

> **Form: Entry Form 03 e**

When you activate this form, the combo box control will appear whenever you begin entering data into a new record. Keep in mind that as soon as you type the first character into a new record the `Before Insert` event is triggered. When you save the new record or move to an existing record, the combo box disappears and the text box control becomes visible.

You now have a form that uses one set of controls for existing records and a different set of controls for new records.

Hiding and showing multiple fields

In addition to the `City` field, you may want to have combo box drop lists for other controls on the form likely to have duplicate records, such as the `State` and `Zip` fields. You can create combo box controls for these fields in a similar way as you did for the `City` field. Use the following SQL statement below as the `Row Source` for the control called `State List`.

```
SELECT DISTINCT state FROM businesses WHERE state IS NOT NULL;
```

Use the following SQL statement as the `Row Source` for the control called `Zip List`.

```
SELECT DISTINCT zip FROM businesses WHERE zip IS NOT NULL;
```

Table 5-1 shows the controls used in `Entry Form 03 f` for the `City`, `State`, and `Zip` fields. Note that there's a parallel structure in which each field has a text box and a combo box control bound to the same field. The text box controls are initially set as visible while the combo box controls are set as hidden.

Table 5-1   Duplicate Controls in Entry Form 03 f

Control Name	Type	Control Source	Visible Initially
City Box	Text Box	City	Yes
City List	Combo Box	City	No
State Box	Text Box	State	Yes
State List	Combo Box	State	No
Zip Box	Text Box	Zip	Yes
Zip List	Combo Box	Zip	No

The controls in this example can have any names. However, it's helpful to give names to controls that help you remember what each control is used for. In this example, the names form a pattern that makes it easy to remember their function. Remember that Access doesn't allow two controls with the same name on the same form. Access automatically gives forms generic names like *Text12*. To change the name of a control, click on the Other tab of the control's property sheet and change the `Name` property.

> **Form: Entry Form 03 f**

Now that you have three controls to alter, you need to modify the procedures to include the additional controls. The `Form_BeforeInsert` procedure now handles switches for the `City`, `State`, and `Zip` fields. The program includes constants for the locations of the controls. In the following example, they all share the same `Top` property value because they're all positioned in a row.

```
Private Sub Form_BeforeInsert(Cancel As Integer)
   Const CityLeft = 1.0417 * 1440
   Const StateLeft = 3.0833 * 1440
   Const ZipLeft = 3.9583 * 1440
   Const CSZTop = 0.625 * 1440
   Me![City Box].Visible = False
   Me![state Box].Visible = False
   Me![zip Box].Visible = False
   With Me![City List]
      .Top = CSZTop
```

(continued)

(continued)

```
        .Left = CityLeft
        .Visible = True
    End With
    With Me![state list]
        .Top = CSZTop
        .Left = StateLeft
        .Visible = True
    End With
    With Me![zip list]
        .Top = CSZTop
        .Left = ZipLeft
        .Visible = True
    End With
End Sub
```

You also expand the `Form_AfterInsert` procedure, as follows, to include the additional controls.

```
Private Sub Form_AfterInsert()
    Me![Company].SetFocus
    Me![City List].Visible = False
    Me![state list].Visible = False
    Me![zip list].Visible = False
    Me![City Box].Visible = True
    Me![state Box].Visible = True
    Me![zip Box].Visible = True
End Sub
```

With these changes, the form now replaces three text boxes with three combo boxes, as shown in Figure 5-5, each time you enter a new record. On the other hand, when you save the new record, the display returns the display of the text boxes.

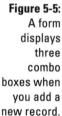

Figure 5-5:
A form
displays
three
combo
boxes when
you add a
new record.

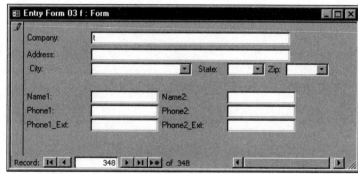

Updating lists

Controls, such as the combo boxes used in the previous examples, use recordsets as the Record Source. It's possible that the lists may be out of sync with their data source. The items appearing in a combo box or other control that displays a list of values are initialized the first time the list is displayed after you open the form. At the moment you initialize the list, its contents reflect the data stored in the tables which are the source for that list. However, it's possible that while the form is on display, changes take place to the tables that affect the items on the list.

Suppose you add a new record to the Businesses table for a city that hasn't been previously entered into the table, for example, Martinez. If you then add a second record for that city, you find that it hasn't been added to the combo box list. This is because Access doesn't automatically re-evaluate the contents of combo box (and other controls) after the list has initially displayed.

One way to solve this problem is to close the form and open it again. This forces Access to update the contents of any lists associated with form controls.

A better way to handle this problem is to use the Requery method to force Access to update the list for a specific control without forcing the user to close the entire form. The following statement causes Access to perform a query based on the Row Source property of the City List control. Here, the Row Source is a SQL statement that retrieves unique city names from the Businesses table.

```
Me![City List].Requery
```

Following is a modified version of the Form_AfterInsert procedure that automatically updates the combo box controls each time the user adds data to a new record. This ensures that new city, state, or zip entries are available on the combo box lists when you enter additional records.

```
Private Sub Form_AfterInsert()
    'Update lists for any new additions
    Me![City List].Requery
    Me![State List].Requery
    Me![Zip List].Requery
    'move the cursor to a control that
    'is always visible
    Me![Company].SetFocus
    'turn off lists /turn on boxes
    Me![City List].Visible = False
```

(continued)

(continued)

```
    Me![State List].Visible = False
    Me![Zip List].Visible = False
    Me![City Box].Visible = True
    Me![state Box].Visible = True
    Me![zip Box].Visible = True
End Sub
```

Form: Entry Form 03 g

A possibility still exists that the lists can get out of sync with their record sources. The previous example deals with new city, state, or zip entries made in new records. You can change the city, state, or zip entry for an existing entry by simply editing the contents of the text box controls used to display the data. In order to ensure that changes made to existing records also appear in the combo box drop lists, you should apply Requery methods after updating existing records.

You can do this in two ways:

- **After Record Updates.** Access triggers the After Update event for the form each time you add data to any control within a record and save those changes. You can use this to trigger the Requery methods. The advantage of this approach is that the event is triggered by any change to any control, so that a single procedure will cover changes you make to any control on the form. On the other hand, a change made to a control like Company, which is not related to any lists, would still cause a Requery. If the requery process is slow (due to large tables and/or slow hardware), you may find it annoying to requery the controls when it's not absolutely necessary. The code that follows updates the three combo boxes each time you make a change to an existing record.

```
Private Sub Form_AfterUpdate()
    Me![City List].Requery
    Me![State List].Requery
    Me![Zip List].Requery
End Sub
```

You can apply most methods and change most properties of a control even when the control is hidden. In this example, you can requery controls that are currently hidden.

Form: Entry Form 03 h

- **After Control Updates.** The alternative is to attach the Requery method to procedures triggered by the After Update events of individual controls. These events occur after you make a change to a specific control, for example, City Box. They won't be triggered if you make changes to other controls on the form. This approach allows you to limit the requery operation to only those times when you know for sure that a change has been made that affects the list for a specific control. This also minimizes the amount of time required to requery controls. On the other hand, this approach requires more programming. You will have to create separate procedures for each control on the form that may need to be requeried when changes are made to the form.

Following are the three procedures (each with a single statement) that implement control-level requeries for each field that's related to a combo box control. Note that the procedures are attached to the AfterUpdate events for the text box controls because these are the ones that are visible when the form displays existing records.

```
Private Sub City_Box_AfterUpdate(Cancel As Integer)
    Me![City List].Requery
End Sub
Private Sub State_Box_AfterUpdate(Cancel As Integer)
    Me![State List].Requery
End Sub
Private Sub Zip_Box_AfterUpdate(Cancel As Integer)
    Me![Zip List].Requery
End Sub
```

Form: Entry Form 03 i

Displaying Related Lists

In the previous section, a single form used several list boxes to enable users to make selections for fields like city, state, and zip when entering new records into a form. In that example, a SQL statement was used to define the items that should appear on the list. However, because each statement operated independently of the other, the choice available in the controls have no logical relationship to each other.

For example, suppose that while entering a new record, you select Los Angeles as the city name. When you move the State List control and display the list, you get a list of all the values that had been previously entered into that field, as you can see in Figure 5-6. While the list accurately summarizes the data previously entered into the Businesses table, it doesn't take into account the relationship that exists in reality between cities, states, and zip codes. The result is a combo box list, as shown in Figure 5-6, that presents the user with a list that contains invalid choices.

The goal of controls such as combo boxes is to speed up entries and eliminate mistakes. However, the list you see in Figure 5-6 could cause as many problems as it solves. It displays a list of state names, most of which would be incorrect choices. In addition, even if you know the right choice to make, you must still scroll through the list in order to find the correct state name.

Choice not logical based on previous choice

Figure 5-6:
Some
choices
shown in
the State
list are
logically
incorrect
with the
selected
city.

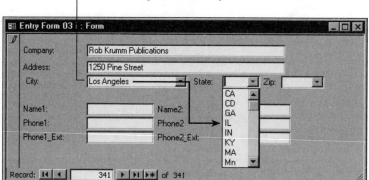

A better approach is to create lists that reflect the logical relationship between data items such as cities, states, and zip codes. While it's possible to enter this information in any order, the nature of the data suggests that you can create most records by entering the city followed by the state and then by the zip code. Further, once you know the name of the city, you can use a SQL statement to select only those state names in the table that are stored in records containing the selected city name. For example, if the city name is Los Angeles, the state list should be limited to CA. If the city name is Lafayette, you might get a longer list since that city name occurs in a number of states (for example, California, Indiana, and Pennsylvania). In any case, the goal is to limit the list to possible valid choices.

Following is the SQL statement used to generate the list of state names shown in Figure 5-6. This statement selects all unique state names from the Businesses table.

```
SELECT DISTINCT state FROM businesses
WHERE state IS NOT NULL;
```

It is logical to limit the list to states that actually have a city matching the value that you selected for the City field. The following statement limits the list to records that match Los Angeles as the city.

```
SELECT DISTINCT state
FROM businesses WHERE state IS NOT NULL
AND City = 'Los Angeles';
```

Of course, the city name will not always be Los Angeles. It will be the current contents of the City List control on the current form. How can you include that reference in a SQL statement? The answer is to use the Forms collection object. With this object you can refer to any open form and any control on any open form using the general form shown in the following code sample.

```
Forms![formname]![controlname]
```

The Forms collection includes only forms that are currently open. Forms in the database but not currently open are not included in the Forms collection.

Access does not recognize the Me object inside a SQL statement. For this technique to work properly you must use the Forms object to refer to an open form or a control on an open form.

In this example, you can find the control on the form Entry Form 04 a. The Forms object reference for the City List control will be the following:

```
Forms![Entry Form04 a]![City List]
```

You can insert that reference into the SQL statement so that the records selected by the control will match whatever city name already has been selected. Insert this statement into the Row Source property of the State List control, as shown in the following code. Note that you should enter the statement as a single line of text even though it is too wide to show as a single line in this book.

When you make a large entry into a property sheet item such as the Row Source property, you can open an editing window by using the Zoom command, Shift+F2.

```
SELECT DISTINCT state FROM businesses WHERE state IS NOT
    NULL AND City = Forms![Entry Form 04 a]![CityList];
```

You can use a similar statement to select zip codes based on the selected city and state. Enter the following statement in the Row Source property of the Zip List control. Note that this statement makes use of two Form object reference — one for the City List control and the other for the State List control.

```
SELECT DISTINCT zip FROM businesses WHERE city =
Forms![Entry Form 04 a]![City List] AND state =
Forms![Entry Form 04 a]![State List] AND zip IS NOT NULL
```

Using SQL statements like those shown as the Row Source property for a control means that Access must be forced to requery these controls whenever you make a change in a control referenced in the SQL statements. For example, both statements refer to the value of the City List control. This means that you must requery both controls each time City List is updated. The procedure, linked to the After Update event of the City List control, ensures that each time you select a new city name, the state and zip code lists are adjusted to contain only items that fit the criteria established in the following SQL statements.

```
Private Sub City_List_AfterUpdate()
   Me![State List].Requery
   Me![Zip List].Requery
End Sub
```

```
Private Sub State_List_AfterUpdate()
   Me![Zip List].Requery
End Sub
```

Figure 5-7 shows the effect of this approach on the data-entry process, and also shows the Entry Form 04 a form. The city name has been entered as Lafayette. When the list for the State List control is displayed, it shows only the states in which a city of that name exists based on the data previously entered into the table.

Figure 5-7:
Choices shown in the state list are logically consistent with the selected city.

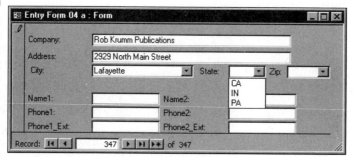

Form: Entry Form 04 a

The same technique works for lists that depend on more than one other control. Recall that the SQL statement for the Zip List control limits the list to records matching the currently selected city and state. Suppose the selected city is Redwood City and the state is CA. The Zip List control lists the two zip codes for that city and state that were previously entered into the Businesses table.

Referring to the current form

In the previous section, references to the values stored in controls on the form were inserted into the SQL statement by using the Forms object to refer to a specific open form. This approach has one drawback: If you change the name of the form, Access is unable to resolve the reference in the SQL statement.

For example, in the LIST.MDB file on this book's CD, I created the form Entry Form 04 b by using the Edit⇨Copy and Edit⇨Paste commands. When you attempt to display the State List combo box list, you get the dialog box shown in Figure 5-8. You see this dialog box because the SQL statement contains a reference to a specific form, for example, Entry Form 04 a, which is not part of the Forms collection at this time.

Form: Entry Form 04 b

Figure 5-8:
Access cannot resolve a reference to a form that is not open.

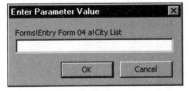

To avoid this problem you can replace the reference to the Forms object, for example, Forms![Entry Form 04 a]![City List], with the Screen object. The Screen object (see Table 5-2) provides a simple way to refer to the form, report, or control that currently has the focus.

Table 5-2	Screen Object Properties
Object	*Refers to*
ActiveForm	the currently active form
ActiveControl	the active control on the current form or report
ActiveReport	the currently displayed report form

You can modify the SQL statements used in State List and Zip List to refer to the Screen.ActiveForm object as shown in the following. The SQL statements are no longer linked to a specific form name but will execute properly regardless of the name of the form.

```
SELECT DISTINCT state FROM businesses WHERE state IS NOT
NULL AND City = Screen.ActiveForm![City List];
```

```
SELECT DISTINCT zip FROM businesses WHERE city =
Screen.ActiveForm![City List] AND state =
Screen.ActiveForm![State List] AND zip IS NOT NULL
```

> **Form: Entry Form 04 c**

Smart defaults

To make data entry more efficient, a standard feature built into Access includes the ability to designate default values for fields or controls. A *default value* is a value that Access automatically inserts into a field or control each time you add a new record to the table.

A drawback to the default value feature is that the value is typically set during the design of the table or form. The assumption is that you can decide before you enter any data into a record what value should be the default for a field. For example, if you do most of your business in California, you might set the default value for the State field to CA. Unless the geographic range of your business is quite small, you probably couldn't come up with a default zip code value.

On the other hand, situations exist where Access can infer the default values for some controls by checking out the value that the user enters in some other field or control on a form. For example, if you enter or select Los Angeles as the name of the city, the SQL statement used as the RowSource property of the State List control can generate a list that contains only one state name, for example, CA. Because that's the only name generated, it's useful to have the program automatically insert that as the State value. This is a *smart* default because it occurs only when the combo box list contains only one choice. Otherwise, no default is inserted.

To create this type of default entry you must define the RowSource SQL statement dynamically as part of a VBA procedure, rather than as a static property of the control entered at the time of the form's design. For example, the following code fragment shows how to define the RowSource property of a control in a procedure. The first statement assigns a SQL statement to RowSource property of the control. That's followed by a Requery method, which ensures that the control's list is updated.

```
Me![State List].RowSource = _
"SELECT DISTINCT state FROM businesses " _
& "WHERE state IS NOT NULL;"
Me![State List].Requery
```

If the SQL statement is complex, you may want to separate the text of the statement from the other statements by storing the text in a variable. The following code fragment shows that the text of the SQL statement is stored in the variable SQLStmt. Note that this statement integrates the value in the City List control into the SQL statement by using the concatenation operator (&) to combine literal text with the contents of a control. You then use the variable SQLStmt to set the RowSource property of the control.

```
Dim SQLStmt
SQLStmt = "SELECT DISTINCT state FROM businesses " _
& "WHERE state IS NOT NULL AND City = '" _
& Me![City List] & "';"
Me![State List].RowSource = SQLStmt
Me![State List].Requery
```

Pay careful attention to the apostrophe (') characters in the SQL statement. Apostrophes are used to insert quotations inside the text of the SQL statement. For example, the expression "City = 'Los Angeles'" in a SQL statement selects all the records for Los Angeles. If you substitute a reference to a control for the literal name you still need to include the apostrophes, for example, "City ='' "" & Me![City List] & ""' ' "

This approach may seem more complicated than setting the RowSource property on the property sheet as was done in Entry Form 04 c on the CD. The reason for using this method is that you can use the SQL statement assigned to the RowSource property again in the same procedure to determine the default value, if any, for the control. Recall that the goal is to determine how many records are included in the RowSource. If it turns out that the list contains only one item, then you should insert it as the default value.

You can determine the number of items in the list by using the same SQL statement previously assigned to the RowSource property to create a temporary recordset. The following statements use the variable SQLStmt to generate a recordset called R that matches the contents of the control's list.

```
Dim R As Recordset
Set R = CurrentDb.OpenRecordset(SQLStmt)
```

Once created, you can determine the number of records in the set by moving to the last record in the set. If the record count is still 1, then Access should insert that value as the default.

```
R.MoveLast
   If R.RecordCount = 1 Then
      Me![State List] = R![State]
   End If
```

If the entry in the `city` field is a new name (one not already entered in another record), the SQL statement returns an empty recordset (`RecordCount=0`). If you attempt to execute the `MoveLast` method on an empty record set, an error will occur. You can avoid this problem by checking the `RecordCount` property prior to the `MoveLast` method. An empty recordset always returns a record count of zero. The code for this is shown in bold in the following sample.

```
If R.RecordCount > 0 Then
   R.MoveLast
   If R.RecordCount = 1 Then
      Me![State List] = R![State]
   End If
Endif
```

When you put all these elements together, you arrive at the procedures `City_List_AfterUpdate` and `State_List_AfterUpdate`. These procedures automatically fill in the controls if the result of their SQL queries returns only a single item for the combo box list. Otherwise they leave the control blank and allow the user to make a selection from the list.

```
Private Sub City_List_AfterUpdate()
   Dim SQLStmt, R As Recordset
   SQLStmt = "SELECT DISTINCT state FROM businesses " _
      & "WHERE state IS NOT NULL AND City = '" _
& Me![City List] & " ';"
   Me![State List].RowSource = SQLStmt
   Me![State List].Requery
   Set R = CurrentDb.OpenRecordset(SQLStmt)
   If R.RecordCount > 0 Then
      R.MoveLast
      If R.RecordCount = 1 Then
         Me![State List] = R![State]
      End If
```

```
      End If
      SQLStmt = "SELECT DISTINCT zip FROM businesses " _
"WHERE  city = '" & Me![City List] & _
"' AND state = '" & Me![State List] & _
"' AND zip IS NOT NULL;"
      Me![Zip List].RowSource = SQLStmt
      Me![Zip List].Requery
      Set R = CurrentDb.OpenRecordset(SQLStmt)
      If R.RecordCount > 0 Then
         R.MoveLast
         If R.RecordCount = 1 Then
            Me![Zip List] = R![Zip]
         End If
      End If
End Sub
Private Sub State_List_AfterUpdate()
   Dim SQLStmt, R As Recordset
   SQLStmt = "SELECT DISTINCT zip FROM businesses " _
   WHERE  city = '" & Me![City List] & _
   "' AND state = '" & Me![State List] & _
   "' AND zip IS NOT NULL;"
   Me![Zip List].RowSource = SQLStmt
   Me![Zip List].Requery
   Set R = CurrentDb.OpenRecordset(SQLStmt)
   If R.RecordCount > 0 Then
      R.MoveLast
      If R.RecordCount = 1 Then
         Me![Zip List] = R![Zip]
      End If
   End If
End Sub
```

Figure 5-9 shows how `Entry Form 04 d` behaves. If you enter a name like `Dublin` into the `City List` control of a new record when you update the field (for example, press Tab to go to the next field), the program automatically inserts the state and zip code because they're the only matching values currently in the database. This is an example of how you can create forms that have smart defaults, as well as smart lists.

Form: Entry Form 04 d

Figure 5-9:
Because
only one
state and
zip code
exists for
Dublin, the
controls are
filled auto-
matically.

```
Entry Form 04 d : Form                                    _ □ ×

 Company:    Rob Krumm Publications

 Address:    1250 Pine Street

 City:       Dublin          ▼    State:  CA   ▼   Zip: 94568  ▼


 Name1:      [          ]          Name2:   [          ]
 Phone1:     [          ]          Phone2:   [          ]
 Phone1_Ext: [          ]          Phone2_Ext:[          ]


 Record: I◄ ◄       352  ► ►I ►*  of  352
```

Random Lists

Most of the time you direct your energy toward keeping your data in the proper order by using indexes and sorting. But there are times when you may want or need to list the records in a totally random order. For example, you may want to send out a customer satisfaction survey to a random list of customers to get an objective view of how well (or not so well!) your company is fulfilling expectations. Another example involves producing an exam with questions stored in a test database: You may want to randomly select the questions from the test database.

The Rnd function

You can execute random selection by using VBA programming because VBA, like most versions of BASIC, include the Rnd function. The Rnd function generates a series of pseudo-random numbers between zero and 1. If you enter the following statement into the Debug window, you get a number like the one shown. You can display the Debug window by pressing Ctrl+G.

```
? rnd
0.7055475
```

The Rnd function generates what is technically referred to as a *pseudo-random* number series. The term *pseudo* (meaning false) is applied to this function because, philosophically speaking, any series of numbers generated by a machine like a computer could not be a truly random sequence. A series of numbers is truly random if it can be determined that any of the numbers has an equal probability of appearing in the series, such as tossing a coin that's equally weighted on both sides. However, since all computer processes are the result of strictly defined algorithms, these sequences don't fit the accepted definition of true randomness.

To attempt to produce a unique series of numbers, you must use the Randomize statement before you use Rnd. Randomize uses the system's clock to generate a unique starting point — called the *seed* — for the subsequent number series produced by the Rnd function.

To generate numbers that are more frequently greater than 1, multiply the random number by some standard value, for example, 10.

```
? rnd*10,rnd*10,rnd*10
  0.4535276      4.140327      8.626193
```

As you can see from the preceding code, this method doesn't always produce numbers greater than 1.

In many cases you want to limit the random numbers to discrete values such as integers. This can be done by using the Int() function to truncate the decimal portion of the number. The following example generates integers between 0 and 9 only.

```
? Int(rnd*10),Int(rnd*10),Int(rnd*10)
  7              3                    9
```

As a rule, you can generate a series of random integers within a specified range by using the following formula, which uses both Int() and Rnd.

```
Int((top - bottom + 1) * Rnd + bottom)
```

For example, to generate a random number between 50 and 100, you enter an expression like the following:

```
? Int((100-50+1)*rnd+50)
  94
```

The procedure shown in the following code sample demonstrates the principle of random selection by generating a series of random numbers (here, 1,000,000) between a specific range (for example, 1 to 100). The program calculates the actual average of the random numbers generated by the loop, then displays the theoretical random average that is the mid-point of the range of numbers and the variation between the two.

```
Sub TestRandom()
    Randomize 'seeds a unqiue series
    Dim Total, k, RNum
    Dim Top, Bottom, Repeats
    Top = 100
    Bottom = 1
```

(continued)

(continued)

```
    Repeats = 1000000
    For k = 1 To Repeats
        RNum = Int((Top - Bottom + 1) * Rnd + Bottom)
        Total = Total + RNum
    Next
    Debug.Print "Actual Average", Total / Repeats
    Debug.Print "Theoretical Average", (Top-Bottom+1) / 2
    Debug.Print "Variance",Format(((Total/Repeats)-((Top- _
        Bottom + 1)/2))/((Top-Bottom+1)/2), "percent")
End Sub
```

The result of the program displayed in the Debug window shows that the average of the random numbers is typically within 1 percent of the ideal random distribution. Decreasing the repetitions tends to increase the variance from the ideal.

```
Actual Average          50.438184
Theoretical Average     50
Variance                0.88%
```

Adding random numbers to a table

To randomly list or select records in a table, you need to add a field (a long integer data type) to the table. You use this field to store the random values which are, in turn, used to sort or select records. The Employees and Businesses tables in the Lists.mdb database on the CD already have this field defined. The `RandomList1` procedure seeks to generate a random order for the records in the Employees table by filling the `Seq` field with random numbers.

The range of the random numbers begins at 1 and goes up to the total number of records in the table. You can determine the total number of records in a table by using the `RecordCount` property. Note that in order to ensure that this property returns the correct value, the `MoveLast` method must be used to force Access to find the end of the recordset. The `MoveFirst` method then returns the pointer to the beginning of the recordset. The `Employees Random` query simply lists the names in order by the field that contains the random numbers, for example, `Seq`.

```
Sub RandomList1()
    Dim D As Database, R As Recordset
    Dim Top, Bottom
    Set D = CurrentDb
    Set R = D.OpenRecordset("Employees")
```

```
    Randomize 'seeds a new random series
    R.MoveLast: R.MoveFirst 'gets the proper recordcount
Top = 1
    Bottom = R.RecordCount
    Do Until R.EOF
        R.Edit
        R![Seq] = Int((Top - Bottom + 1) * Rnd + Bottom)
        R.Update
        R.MoveNext
    Loop
    R.Close
    DoCmd.OpenQuery "Employees Random"
End Sub
```

The result of `RandomList1()` is shown in Figure 5-10. While the result does contain a significant degree of randomness, you may notice that the values in the Seq field tend to repeat. The reason is that in using the numbers directly generated by the Rnd function you have not eliminated the possibility of duplicate values. In fact, if the recordset is small, it is likely that many records are assigned the same random number. The following section shows you how to avoid duplicating values when using random numbers.

First Name	Last Name	Seq
Xavier	Martin	3
Steven	Buchanan	3
Margaret	Peacock	5
Tim	Smith	6
Laurent	Pereira	6
Caroline	Patterson	7
Robert	King	9
Justin	Brid	9
Janet	Leverling	9
Andrew	Fuller	10
Michael	Suyama	13
Anne	Dodsworth	13
Albert	Hellstern	13
Nancy	Davolio	14
Laura	Callahan	14
*		0

Record: I◄ ◄ 1 ► ►I ►* of 15

Figuer 5-10: Records listed in a random order.

REMEMBER

Keep in mind that because these procedures use random numbers, your output will be in a different order than the one shown in this book.

Making random numbers unique

Ideally you would like Access to assign to each record a unique number in the range of 1 to X (with *X* being the total number of records in your recordset). How can you get the random number generator to produce a list without duplicates?

> **Module: Random**
> **Procedure: RandomList2**

You can find the solution by using the random numbers generated by the Rnd function indirectly. Instead of storing the random numbers in the Seq field, the numbers are used to create a random movement through the recordset. This approach is illustrated in RandomList2 on the CD.

In the example that follows, the random number generated by the Rnd function is used as the argument for the Move method of a recordset to move randomly to one of the records. Each time you run this procedure, Access randomly selects one of the records in the Employees table and the name of that person is displayed in a message box. In this way, you can use the Rnd function to randomly select a record from any recordset.

```
Sub RandomList2()
    Dim D As Database, R As Recordset
    Dim Top, Bottom
    Set D = CurrentDb
    Set R = D.OpenRecordset("Employees")
    Randomize 'seeds a new random series
    R.MoveLast: R.MoveFirst 'gets the proper recordcount
Top = 0
    Bottom = R.RecordCount - 1
R.Move Int((Top - Bottom + 1) * Rnd + Bottom)
    MsgBox R![Last Name] & ", " & R![First Name]
End Sub
```

However, the problem of generating a randomly sorted list requires some additional tricks. The technique shown in RandomList2 is a clue as to the approach that's needed. In RandomList2, Access randomly selects a single name from the table each time the code runs. But suppose each time a name is selected, that record is removed from the list of available records. The next time you execute the procedure a different name is selected at random from the remaining records and then removed from the running.

Using this approach you never get a duplicate name because the list of possible selections is narrowed to eliminate any of the names already selected before the next selection is made. As this process is repeated, eventually all the records from the original table will have been selected at one time or another. This approach ensures that each record is selected only once (no duplicates) but that the order in which they are selected varies randomly each time you start with a new set of records. This is exactly the result required to generate random listings of a set of records.

The next task is to translate this general concept into VBA techniques. The trick is to create a procedure whereby the recordset from which the random selection is made automatically removes all the previously selected records. You can accomplish this by using a query definition to select the records based on the value in the Seq field. Begin with the assumption that all the records have a zero value in the Seq field. You can ensure this is the case by executing an UPDATE query that sets all the Seq fields to zero. The following statements create a temporary query definition (" ") which performs the update when executed. Note that when you create a query definition with an empty string (" ") as the name, Access creates a temporary query that is erased when the procedure ends.

```
Set Q = D.CreateQueryDef("")
Q.SQL = "UPDATE Employees SET seq=0;"
Q.Execute
```

The next step is to define the available recordset as all the records in the table that have a zero value in the Seq field. The following example creates a recordset *R* that contains only records that have a zero Seq value.

```
Q.SQL = "Select Seq From Employees Where seq = 0;"
Set R = Q.OpenRecordset()
```

At this point, *R* contains all the records in the Employees recordset. But that isn't always going to be the case. Using the Move method and Rnd function as they were used in RandomList2 to select a record at random, you can then change the value of the Seq field to a non-zero value. One approach is to consecutively number each of the records that Access selects randomly — that is, make the first record 1, the second 2, and so on.

```
R.Edit
R![Seq] = K 'give it a sequence number
R.Update
```

The critical operation comes next. You apply the Requery method to the recordset *R*. Recall that when a recordset is requeried, the contents of the recordset adjust to any changes made since the recordset was defined. In this case, the record into which the value was inserted in the Seq field is eliminated from the recordset because it no longer has a zero in the Seq field. This means that the size of the recordset is now one record smaller than it had been. For example, if there were 15 names in the recordset, the randomly selected name is now taken out of the recordset leaving 14 names available for the next random selection.

```
R.Requery
```

To randomly select all the records, the process is repeated for a number of cycles equal to the number of records in the original recordset. The result is that the Seq field now contains a series of numbers (for example, 1 to 15 for a 15-record table) that are scrambled in a random order. RandomList3 shows how this technique is implemented. Note the following points:

- ✔ A For...Next loop is used instead of Do...Loop because the procedure modifies the size of the recordset along the way. The For...Next loop ensures that the random selection repeats for all the records in the table.

- ✔ A MoveFirst method is applied at the start of cycle to ensure that the random movement starts from the top of the recordset.

- ✔ The value of the Bottom variable, which controls the range of random numbers generated in the program, is decreased by one each cycle. This is necessary to ensure that the program does not try to move beyond the last record in the recordset. This ensures that the Bottom value is always in sync with the size of the recordset.

```
Sub RandomList3()
    Dim D As Database, R As Recordset, Q As QueryDef
    Dim Top, Bottom, K
    Set D = CurrentDb
    Randomize
    'Fill the Seq Field with zeros
    Set Q = D.CreateQueryDef("")
    Q.SQL = "Update Employees SET seq=0;"
    Q.Execute
    Q.SQL = "Select Seq From Employees Where seq = 0;"
    Set R = Q.OpenRecordset()
    R.MoveLast: R.MoveFirst 'set recordcount
Top = 0
    Bottom = R.RecordCount - 1
    For K = 1 To R.RecordCount
        R.MoveFirst
        'move to a random record
        R.Move Int((Top - Bottom + 1) * Rnd + Bottom)
        R.Edit
        R![Seq] = K 'give it a sequence number
        R.Update
        R.Requery 'remove all non-zero records
        Bottom = Bottom - 1 ' adjust random range
```

```
     Next
     R.Close
     DoCmd.OpenQuery "Employees Random"
  End Sub
```

ON THE CD

> **Module: Random**
> **Procedure:RandomList3**

You can see the result of RandomList3 when the Employees Random query is opened in Figure 5-11. The records are listed in order by the Seq value. However, since the Seq values have been entered in a random order, the records appear in a random order. Each time you execute the RandomList3 procedure the names are scrambled into a (different) random order.

Figure 5-11: Records assigned unique random numbers.

First Name	Last Name	Seq
Anne	Dodsworth	1
Laurent	Pereira	2
Caroline	Patterson	3
Robert	King	4
Michael	Suyama	5
Andrew	Fuller	6
Justin	Brid	7
Steven	Buchanan	8
Margaret	Peacock	9
Nancy	Davolio	10
Tim	Smith	11
Janet	Leverling	12
Laura	Callahan	13
Xavier	Martin	14
Albert	Hellstern	15
		0

Employees Random : Select Query

Record: 1 of 15

Making a random selection

Random selection is similar to random sorting with the exception that only some of the records in the underlying table are included in the random sorting. For example, the Businesses table contains 333 records. Suppose you want to make a random selection of 10 percent of those records. The only change you need to make is to limit the number of cycles executed in the loop to 10 percent of the total records in the table. This is accomplished in the For statement by setting the upper value to 10 percent of the RecordCount property. The Int() function is used to ensure that the number of cycles is a whole number.

```
For K = 1 To Int(R.RecordCount * 0.1)
```

The full code for the random selection procedure is found in the LISTS.MDB database in the location described below. Run `RandomList4` to generate the random data set.

> *Module: Random*
> *Procedure: RandmList4*
> *Query: Businesses Random*

Chapter 6

Data and Forms

● ●

In This Chapter

▶ Navigating forms logically

▶ Linking related lists of items

▶ Finding related items within a form

▶ Using subforms

● ●

*I*n Access 97, *forms* are the primary point of contact between the person using the database and the database tables that actually contain the data. With the help of Access 97 VBA procedures to add intelligence to your forms, you discover in this chapter a number of techniques for building forms and sets of forms that are easy for users to work with, even if the corresponding tables are large and complex.

> **Database Folder: Chapter 6**
> **Database File: NAVFRM.MDB**

To begin this chapter, open the database for Chapter 6, NAVFRM.MDB. After the database opens, click the Forms tab to see a list of the forms discussed in this chapter.

Logical Record Navigation

After a form appears on-screen, Access 97, by default, displays the *navigation* buttons at the bottom of the form window, as shown in Figure 6-1. These buttons move you to the first, preceding, next, or last record. You can also enter a record number into the text box in the navigation bar to move to that specific record.

These methods of navigating through records have one thing in common: They represent physical characteristics of the record set. Moving to the first, last, next, or preceding record doesn't take into account the logical nature of the records — that is, the key values stored in various fields that represent the meaning of the records. In the form shown in Figure 6-1, for example, the capacity to move to a record by part number or product type

Figure 6-1:
Standard
navigation
buttons that
Access 97
displays on
all forms.

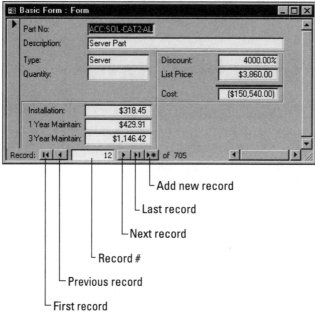

would be more useful than simply flipping from record to record. Programmers call this type of navigation *logical navigation* because the *content* of the records, rather than their physical sequence, is the basis for navigation.

Finding by value

The most basic type of logical navigation involves locating records by the value of a particular field. Using the `Parts` table shown in Figure 6-1 as an example, you can select a record based on its `Part No` field by combining a list-type control (either a List or a Combo Box control) with an event procedure.

To accomplish this task, the first step you must take is to create an unbound control — in this example, a combo box. This control displays the data (for example, part numbers) that you want to use as the logical criterion for switching records. The form shown in Figure 6-2 displays a combo box called *FindIt* that uses the following SQL statement as its `Record Source` to generate a list of all the part numbers in the table. Keep in mind that the `FindIt` control isn't bound to any of the fields in the table — that is, the `Control Source` property is blank.

```
SELECT [Part No] FROM Parts ORDER BY [Part No];
```

SELECT [Part No]
FROM Parts
ORDER BY [Part No]

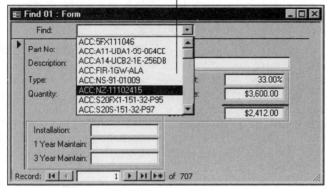

Figure 6-2:
The combo
box, FindIt,
displays a
list of all
the part
numbers in
the table.

Form: Find 01

Be mindful that you don't want to bind the combo box control shown in
Figure 6-2 to the Part No field. If you did, it would change information in the
table each time you made a selection. The purpose of this control is to
provide a way for users to locate an existing record. After users make a
selection, the value that they select triggers an event procedure that
changes the record displayed in the form to match the part number selected
from the list. This process is called smart navigation because the program
locates the next record to display based on some logical criterion — for
example, the part number — instead of simply showing the records in the
order in which they were originally entered.

You want to associate the event procedure that locates the next record with
the AfterUpdate event of the FindIt control so that, each time the user
makes a selection from this combo box list, the form displays the record
that corresponds to that part number.

The form's RecordsetClone

To write the event procedure for the FindIt control, you need to become
familiar with the following two concepts:

  ✔ The RecordsetClone property. As you create a form, you can bind that
    form to a table by entering the name of the table (or query) in the
    RecordSource property of the form. Binding occurs automatically if
    you use the Form Wizard. The records you specify in the
    RecordSource property represent the Recordset of the form. A clone
    Recordset is an object that is a copy of the record defined for the

form, and is available to any event procedures you create for the form. The RecordsetClone property provides a means by which event procedures can access the same set of records displayed in the form without disturbing the record currently on display. In this example, you can search the cloned Recordset for the record that matches the one selected from the FindIt combo box.

✔ Bookmarks. Access 97 doesn't directly support the idea of record numbers because Recordsets in Access are subject to dynamic changes. Access 97 does, however, provide a way to uniquely identify each record in a Recordset: Each record has a Bookmark property that represents a string that Access 97 generates, and this Bookmark property is unique for each record in the Recordset. In most cases, you don't display the bookmark string. Instead, you simply refer to the Bookmark property of a record if you want to identify one record within a Recordset.

Access 97 doesn't store bookmarks as part of a table or a form. Instead, the program generates a new set of marks each time Access creates a Recordset. This process occurs if you open a table, query, form, or report.

The one exception is when you create a cloned Recordset, such as by using the RecordsetClone property. The bookmarks in a cloned Recordset are identical to the bookmarks in the original Recordset.

Suppose that the record currently displayed in the form is record #3. Figure 6-3 shows how these two concepts work together to create a search procedure that locates the next record to display.

The first step is to search the RecordsetClone of the form to locate the record you want to display. Suppose, for example, that you know the record you want to display contains a part number, ACC:SS-S5-12. Because you can manipulate the clone without disturbing the record displayed in the form, you can search the cloned Recordset and locate the record with the desired part number — for example, record #7.

After you locate the desired record in the clone, you can force Access 97 to display that record in the current form by synchronizing the Bookmark property of the Form object with the current bookmark in the clone. (A cloned Recordset has a set of bookmarks identical to the Recordset from which it was cloned.)

In Figure 6-3, the form starts out by displaying record #3. A search of the cloned Recordset locates the desired record — #7. Synchronizing the form with the clones causes Access 97 to change the form's display from record #3 to record #7.

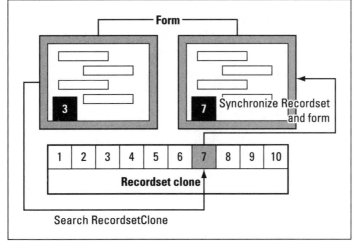

Figure 6-3:
Recordset-
Clone and
Bookmarks
combine to
create
logical
navigation.

To create a procedure that changes the displayed record, you begin by creating a `Recordset` type object that is a clone of the `Recordset` assigned to the current form, as shown in the following example:

```
Dim R As Recordset
Set R = Me.RecordsetClone
```

If you want to view this code, open the form `Form 01` in the design mode. Then open the form's code module by choosing View⇨Code.

`Recordset` objects have all the characteristics of a table or a query. In this example, you search the `Recordset` for a record with a `Part No` field that contains the part number the user selected in the `FindIt` combo box control. You can accomplish this task by using the `FindFirst` method, as shown in the following example:

```
Recordset.FindFirst WhereClause
```

The `WhereClause` argument is a logical expression similar to the kind that you use in a SQL statement's `WHERE` clause to select a record. The only difference is that you omit the keyword `WHERE`. The following example searches the clone `Recordset` for the first record containing a `Part No` field that matches the current value in the `FindIt` control:

```
R.FindFirst "[Part No] = '" & Me![FindIt] & "'"
```

Notice that, because `Part No` is a text field, the expression must include apostrophes to act as quotations inside the expression. The following example uses `Chr(34)` to insert the quotations. You can use either approach.

```
R.FindFirst "[Part No]=" & Chr(34)& Me![FindIt] & Chr(34)
```

The final step is to synchronize the record in the clone with the record currently appearing in the form. You synchronize these records by setting the form's `Bookmark` to the current `Bookmark` of the cloned `Recordset`, as shown in the following example:

```
Me.Bookmark = R.Bookmark
```

After you put all these elements together, you arrive at the procedure shown in the following example, which you should assign to the `AfterUpdate` event of the `FindIt` control. You use the last statement to clear the selection from the `FindIt` control, because the selection is no longer needed and may confuse the user if it remains on the form.

```
Private Sub FindIt_AfterUpdate()
    Dim R As Recordset
    Set R = Me.RecordsetClone
    R.FindFirst "[Part No] = " & Chr(34) _
        & Me![FindIt] & Chr(34)
    Me.Bookmark = R.Bookmark
    Me![FindIt] = Null
End Sub
```

You can try out this procedure and form by opening the form `Form 01` in the database for this chapter. If you're in the Design mode, you can activate the form by choosing View⇨Form View from the menu bar.

> **Form: Find 01**
> **Procedure: FindIt_AfterUpdate**

After you open `Form 01`, you can find any part by selecting the part number from the combo box in the form's header section.

Selecting from Other Lists

The examples in the preceding section show the basic mechanics involved in creating a control/procedure combination that enables you to logically navigate through the records on a form. Technically, the part numbers listed in the `FindIt` combo box make good search criteria (because each part number identifies a unique record). These numbers may not be the easiest for the user to employ in a search, however, because the numbers themselves don't provide much practical information about the part.

Access provides combo box properties that enable you to display more meaningful lists. The user can use these lists to make a selection without changing the control's behavior or the event procedure that locates and displays the records. Figure 6-4, for example, shows a modified version of the FindIt control that displays the part type, its description, and its list price — but not the part number.

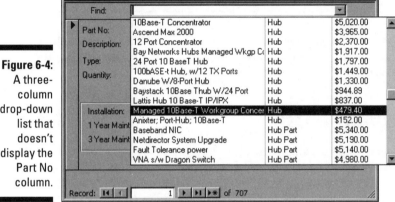

Figure 6-4:
A three-column drop-down list that doesn't display the Part No column.

The expanded list shown in Figure 6-4 can provide the user with more meaningful information from which to make a selection. At the same time, you need to ensure that the value of the control provides your procedure with the actual Part No associated with the selected item. The first step is to alter the RowSource SQL statement to return columns in addition to Part No. The following example returns four columns (Part No, Description, Type, and List Price) and sorts the items by type and list price. (The list price sort is a descending sort.)

```
SELECT [Part No] , [Description], [Type], [List Price] FROM
          Parts ORDER BY [Type], [List Price] DESC;
```

The RowSource statement returns four columns, but only three appear in the drop-down list. How do you accomplish this feat? The answer lies in the values you assign to the control's properties, as listed in Table 6-1. The trick is in the Column Widths property found on the Format tab of the control's property sheet. To hide the Part No column, you must set the width for that column to **0"**. Now, although the column is part of the logical Recordset that the control displays, the user doesn't see the column because its width is zero.

Table 6-1	Properties of the FindIt Combo Box	
Property	**Setting**	**Tab**
Column Count	4	Format
Column Heads	no	Format
Column Widths	0"; 2"; 1"; 1"	Format
List Rows	15	Format
List Width	4"	Format
Bound Column	1	Data
Limit To List	Yes	Data

By using this approach, you can present users with a list that employs a field such as Part No to uniquely identify records but doesn't display the field on-screen.

Limiting the list

In the abstract, using a single list as a method of locating records is all that you need to do to provide Access 97 with the capability to logically locate records. In practice, however, drop-down lists that include an entire table may become too long and cumbersome for anyone to use comfortably.

One possible solution is to create a form that includes controls to limit the number of items appearing in a combo list, based on some logical criteria. Suppose, for example, that you want to limit the items appearing in the FindIt control's list to specific product types — that is, to routers, servers, DSUs, and so on.

Figure 6-5 shows one possible configuration that you can use to keep the number of items in a combo box list to a reasonable amount. In this example, you use a bar of toggle buttons to select the list contents based on specific product types. After the user clicks a toggle button, an event procedure executes to alter the contents of the combo box list so that only the selected type of item appears. The button bar also contains an All button that enables you to view all the records in the FindIt list.

> **Form: Find 03**

In Form 03, I placed the toggle buttons in a *group frame control* called TypeFrame. Frame controls group together two or more check boxes, radio buttons, or toggle buttons, so that they operate as if they were a single control. If check boxes or buttons are grouped together in a frame control, the value obtained by user interaction with any of the controls in the group is assigned to the Frame control.

Figure 6-5:
Toggle
buttons
control the
items that
appear in a
combo box
list.

The AfterUpdate event procedure of the TypeFrame control modifies the RowSource property of the FindIt control so that the SQL statement that generates the list in the combo box corresponds to the selected button.

Group Frame controls return numeric values based on which button in the group you click. Access 97 assigns the buttons in TypeFrame the values 1 through 5, in the same order in which the buttons appear. The procedure in the following example uses a Select Case structure to determine the SQL statement that the program assigns to the RowSource property of FindIt.

Because most of the text of the SQL statement is identical in each case, each Case provides only the name of a specific product type — for example, "Router" or "DSU" — that the program assigns to a variable called WClause, which is short for WHERE *clause*. After the Select Case structure, the program combines the WClause text with the SQLText text to form a complete statement. The only exception is the last case, which is the All button. Because this option includes all the records, you don't need a WHERE clause. You adjust SQLText here to omit the WHERE keyword and set the WClause text to an empty string, "".

```
Select Case Me![TypeFrame]
   Case 1
      WClause = Chr(34) & "Router" & Chr(34)
   Case 2
      WClause = Chr(34) & "DSU" & Chr(34)
   Case 3
      WClause = Chr(34) & "Server" & Chr(34)
   Case 4
      WClause = Chr(34) & "Hub" & Chr(34)
   Case 5
      SQLText = "SELECT [Part No],[Description]," _
      & "[List Price]FROM Parts"
      WClause = ""
End Select
```

After you assemble the SQL statement, you can insert the statement into the RowSource property of the FindIt control. You then need to apply the Requery method to the FindIt control to generate a new list based on the revised SQL statement. If the Requery method isn't included, Access 97 doesn't update the list. The following code changes the RowSource property, requeries the control, and sets the background color of the control:

```
With Me![FindIt]
     .RowSource = SQLText & WClause
     .Requery
     .BackColor = RGB(255, 255, 255)
  End With
```

The BackColor property statement isn't essential to the procedure in this example in that the statement doesn't affect the data or the control list. In this case, the button simply sets the background color to white, which is the default color. (In the RGB color system, 255 for the red, green, and blue colors results in white.)

You need to include this statement because the form also includes an Enter event procedure for the TypeFrame control. The procedure shown in the following example turns the FindIt combo box background to red as soon as the user enters the TypeFrame box:

```
Private Sub TypeFrame_Enter()
   Me![FindIt].BackColor = 255
End Sub
```

Okay, why bother to change the color of the FindIt control to black if the AfterUpdate event procedure turns the background from black to white immediately afterward?

Although the color change is brief, it provides the user with feedback to indicate that clicking the toggle button actually affects the contents of the combo box. After the procedure runs, the TypeFrame box flashes red for a moment every time the user makes a selection. You don't need this type of feedback to make the procedures work logically, but the flashing color provides users with a visual clue to confirm that they're selecting a new list.

The following example lists the full AfterUpdate procedure:

```
Private Sub TypeFrame_AfterUpdate()
   Dim SQLText, WClause
   SQLText = "SELECT [Part No],[Description]," & _
   "[List Price]FROM Parts WHERE Type = "
   Select Case Me![TypeFrame]
     Case 1
```

```
            WClause = Chr(34) & "Router" & Chr(34)
        Case 2
            WClause = Chr(34) & "DSU" & Chr(34)
        Case 3
            WClause = Chr(34) & "Server" & Chr(34)
        Case 4
            WClause = Chr(34) & "Hub" & Chr(34)
        Case 5
            SQLText = "SELECT [Part No],[Description]," _
            & "[List Price]FROM Parts"
            WClause = ""
    End Select
    With Me![FindIt]
        .RowSource = SQLText & WClause
        .Requery
        .BackColor = RGB(255, 255, 255)
    End With
End Sub
```

The preceding code example contains statements with SQL statements included as text. The lines that define the variable SQLText are usually too wide to fit on a single line. Because the text of a SQL statement is usually quite long, I don't have sufficient room between the margins of a book to display the lines as they'd appear on your computer screen. You can't simply insert a line continuation character (_) inside a text item, because Access 97 would simply think that the character was part of the text. To break the lines correctly, you must break the text into several segments, all of which you enclose in " " and combine by using the & operator. Some of the code examples on the CD show these segments as single line statements. If you're copying the code lines from the book, you can enter these lines exactly as they appear or combine separate lines into a single long line to save time.

Figure 6-6 shows the results of this coordination between two controls. The combo box lists only those items that match the button you select.

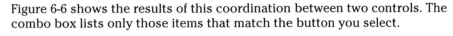

Form: Find 03

Setting default values

By default, the combo box control selects all the product types in the table. Because the group frame and toggle buttons aren't bound to a field, you need to explicitly set a default value so that the All button is automatically selected when the form first appears.

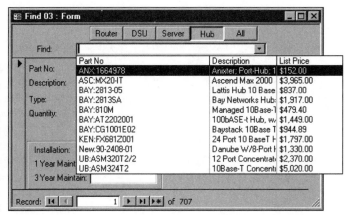

Figure 6-6:
The combo
box lists
only items
that match
the toggle
button
selection.

The event procedure that you can use to set such initial conditions on a form is the Load event of the Form object, as shown in the following example:

```
Private Sub Form_Load()
    Me![TypeFrame] = 5
End Sub
```

Three form events take place whenever a form opens: Open, Load, and Current. The Open event takes place after a form opens but before you can access any records in the underlying table. You can access information about the permanent structure of the form — for example, the number of controls on the form, or the width or height of the controls. You can't refer to the value of a control or set its default value at this time. If you want to perform data-related actions, you must wait until the Load event, which occurs after the form fills with data. Use Load to perform one-time-only operations on the first record that appears. Use Current if you want to apply the operations to every record that appears, including the first one.

Automatically opening the list

In the preceding example, two controls worked together to provide a way to restrict the contents of a list box. In that form, users click a toggle button to select the type of products they want listed in the combo box. They then open the combo box list, which is now limited to a subset of the records in the table.

You can eliminate any need for a user to click a second time if you add some additional methods to the AfterUpdate event procedure of the TypeFrame control. Adding the SetFocus method, as in the following example, moves the focus to the `FindIt` control. Adding the `Dropdown` method makes the list open just as if the user had clicked the list arrow or pressed the Alt+↓ key combination.

```
With Me![FindIt]
    .RowSource = SQLText & WClause
    .Requery
    .BackColor = RGB(255, 255, 255)
    .SetFocus 'move focus to Findit
    .Dropdown 'open the list box
End With
```

Form: Find 04

Linking two list controls

The form `Find 04` uses a set of toggle buttons to control the number of items that the `FindIt` combo box list displays. The form's buttons, however, include only a few of the possible categories of products you can store in the table. The `Type` field of the `Parts` table actually contains 14 types of products. An alternative to using the toggle button group is to use another list control — either a list box or a combo box — that lists all the possible types. Figure 6-7 shows in the upper-left corner of the form a list box that you can use to select the product type. That selection triggers an event procedure that modifies the contents of the `FindIt` combo box so that `FindIt` lists only items that match the selected product type.

Figure 6-7:
The combo box now lists only items matching the selected product type.

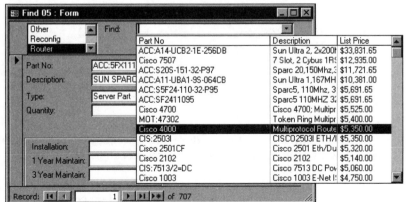

Form: Find 05

You define the contents of this list box, ProductTypeList, by using the SQL statement shown in the following example. (The DISTINCT keyword produces a list of unique values from the specified field.)

```
SELECT DISTINCT [Type] FROM parts;
```

You can define the relationship between the two list controls, ProductType-List and FindIt, by using the SyncLists procedure shown in the following example. In some ways, this procedure is simpler (requires fewer lines of code) than the one you used for the toggle button example. The reason for this is that the value from the list box control ProductTypeList, which specifies the product type, doesn't require a Select Case structure. The value of ProductTypeList is the actual name of the product type, so you can insert that value directly into the SQL statement. You use the Const (constant) statement to define two blocks of text, SQL1 and SQL2, that are the same for all the product types. You define only WClause as a variable, because its value changes, depending on what item the user selects in the ProductTypeList control. Using Const eliminates any need to declare the names SQL1 and SQL2 in the Dim statement, because the values of a constant never change.

```
Sub SyncLists()
    Dim WClause
    Const SQL1 = "SELECT [Part No] , [Description]," _
        & "[List Price] FROM Parts "
    Const SQL2 = " ORDER BY [List Price] DESC;"
    WClause = " WHERE [Type] = " & Chr(34) & _
        Me![ProductTypeList] & Chr(34)
    With Me![FindIt]
        .RowSource = SQL1 & WClause & SQL2
        .Requery
        .SetFocus
        .Dropdown
    End With
End Sub
```

Notice that you don't directly enter the procedure you use to update the FindIt list into an event procedure. In Form 05, that procedure needs the following two different event procedures to call it:

- ProductTypeList AfterUpdate. This event triggers every time the user changes the selected item in the list box control ProductType-List. The following statement shows how this event procedure can call SyncLists:

```
Private Sub ProductTypeList_AfterUpdate()
    SyncLists
End Sub
```

✔ Form_Load. This event takes place after the form displays its first record.

In this example, the first record poses a problem. When the form first loads, unbound controls do not have an initial value. For the form to operate correctly, you need to set a default value for the list controls. What should be the default value of the list box control?

Why not simply choose the first item on the list as the default? Sound simple?

Well, that course turns out not to be quite as simple as it sounds. Recall that the list box is an unbound control; it doesn't have an initial value at the time the form first loads. If the control were a group frame, which always has a numeric value, you could simply assign the control the same numeric value each time the form loads.

Unfortunately, with a list box control, you can't be sure what the first item on the list may be.

To solve this problem, I must take you on a brief detour to find out about user-defined functions because such functions are integral to completing this code.

User-defined functions

All the procedures described in earlier chapters of this book are Sub type procedures — mainly the event procedures you use inside forms. Another category of VBA procedure is the Function. Function procedures are identical to Sub procedures, with the following two exceptions:

✔ **Implicit calling.** If a program calls a Sub procedure — that is, it executes that procedure from within another procedure — you enter the name of the procedure at the beginning of a statement. This process is known as an *explicit call* because the statement directly indicates what procedure to execute. The following statement is an example of an explicit call. The name of the Sub procedure, GetFirstInList, appears at the beginning of the statement followed by the Me![ProductType-List] argument.

```
GetFirstInList Me![ProductTypeList]
```

On the other hand, you enter Function procedure names as part of an expression. In the following example, GetFirstInList is the name of a Function procedure. This procedure appears as part of the expression that defines the value of `FirstType`. This process is known as an *implicit call*; the execution of the procedure is implied because it's part of an expression that you use to determine the value of an object, property, or variable.

```
FirstType = GetFirstInList(Me![ProductTypeList])
```

✔ **Return values.** A `Function` procedure can, but doesn't need to, return a value. The preceding statement uses the `GetFirstInList` function to provide a value for `FirstType`.

Here, the function you want is one that determines the first item in the list of a `List` or `Combo Box` control. The function requires one argument, which is a control-type object. The function uses the `RowSource` property (which contains an SQL statement) to create a `Recordset` with the same contents as the control.

```
Function GetFirstInList(ListCtrl As Control)
    Dim R As Recordset
    Set R = CurrentDb.OpenRecordset(ListCtrl.RowSource)
    GetFirstInList = R(0)' returns a value
End Function
```

| *Module: User Functions* |

In a `Function` procedure, a statement that assigns a value to the name of the `Function` is what determines the value that returns. In the `GetFirst-InList` function, the statement assigns the value of the first field in the `Recordset R` as the value of the function.

```
GetFirstInList = R(0)' returns a value
```

Notice the use of the index number to refer to the field in the `Recordset`. `Recordsets`, like tables, are a collection of fields. The first field is index number zero. Thus the first field in any `Recordset` is `R(0)`. By using the index form of object reference, you can use this procedure with any `Recordset` because the procedure doesn't explicitly refer to a field name.

Because this function may be useful with a variety of forms, you should store it in a standard module, for example, *User Functions,* rather than inside the form's module. Procedures, both `Sub` and `Function`, stored in standard modules are by default *public* procedures. A public procedure is available to be called from any other procedure in the database, regardless of whether it's stored in a standard, form, or report module. If you choose to write the procedure in the form module, its function would be identical, but it would be a private procedure — that is, only procedures in the same form module forms could call that procedure.

The Recordset I use in this example isn't a cloned Recordset. Although they both use the same SQL statement to define their record sets, each record set is generated independently of the other. Using the same SQL statement ensures that both sets contain the same data, but they may not have identical record bookmarks. Cloned Recordsets share identical record bookmarks with the source Recordset.

After you create the function to find the first item in the list, you can use that function to set the default value for the list box control inside the Form_Load event procedure, as shown in the following example. The procedure also calls the SyncLists procedure to set the initial values for the FindIt control.

```
Private Sub Form_Load()
    Me![ProductTypeList] = _
    GetFirstInList(Me![ProductTypeList])
    SyncLists
End Sub
```

Updating the label

A small addition to the procedure that can help users keep track of what sort of list is currently selected involves updating the label on the FindIt control. This label shows the currently selected product type. The statement in boldface type in the following example synchronizes the label with the contents of the combo box.

```
Sub SyncLists()
    Dim WClause
    Const SQL1 = "SELECT [Part No] , [Description]," _
        & "[List Price] FROM Parts "
    Const SQL2 = " ORDER BY [List Price] DESC;"
    WClause = " WHERE [Type] = " & Chr(34) & _
        Me![ProductTypeList] & Chr(34)
    With Me![FindIt]
        .RowSource = SQL1 & WClause & SQL2
        .Requery
        .SetFocus
        .Dropdown
    End With
    Me![Label18].Caption = [ProductTypeList]
End Sub
```

You can observe the results of these modifications as you interact with form Find 05 a, as shown in Figure 6-8. Notice that the label on the FindIt combo box changes to match the type of product listed.

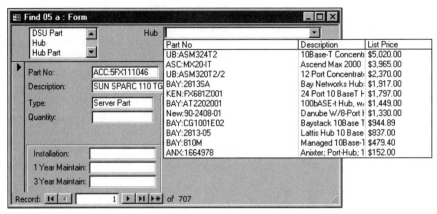

Figure 6-8:
The combo
box lists
only parts
that match
the value in
the list box
— in this
example,
Hub.

Form: Find 05 a

Smart Navigation

All forms enable you to move to the next and previous record by using the navigation buttons, the Go To menu commands, or the Ctrl+PgDn and Ctrl+PgUp shortcut keys.

A variation on the idea is *smart navigation,* which advances the form to the next or previous record based on some logical criterion. Using the set of forms discussed in this chapter as an example, suppose that you want to create a pair of smart navigation buttons that advance to the next or previous record of the same product type.

A way to accomplish this is to set a *filter* on the form's records. If you set a filter, however, you limit the form's display to only those records that match the specified criterion.

The purpose of a smart navigation button is to locate the matching records whenever necessary, while still leaving the normal navigation buttons capable of browsing through the records regardless of type.

To create a set of buttons that move through the records finding the next and previous records that match, you use the same basic technique employed in previous forms in this chapter. You search through a clone of the form's Recordset to locate the desired records and then synchronize the form to the clone by using the Bookmark property.

The only difference here is the starting point of the search. If you create a cloned `Recordset`, which record is the first active record? The following statement, for example, creates a `Recordset` clone and then displays the `Part No` from the current record in a message box:

```
Dim R As Recordset
Set R = Me.RecordsetClone
Msgbox R![Part No]
```

The part number that appears is that of the first record in the form's `Recordset` — for example, *ACC:5FX111046*. You have no reason to assume that the record appearing in the form is the same as the current record in the cloned `Recordset`. Of course, you have no way of knowing which record is the next or previous record unless you've synchronized the clone and the form record. You can accomplish this task by reversing the bookmark technique. The following statement synchronizes the clone with the form by assigning the form's bookmark to the cloned `Recordset`:

```
R.Bookmark = Me.Bookmark
```

After you position the `Recordsets` to the same record, you can use the `FindNext` or `FindPrevious` methods to search the clone for either the next or previous record that meets the specified criterion — for example, the same product type.

The `NavByType` procedure uses this approach in the following example. This procedure requires an argument called `Direction` that you set to B to search backward through the `Recordset`, or to F, to search forward. This argument enables you to write one procedure to handle both the next and previous searches.

```
Sub NavByType(Direction)
    Dim R As Recordset
    Set R = Me.RecordsetClone
    R.Bookmark = Me.Bookmark ' sync clone with form
    If Direction = "B" Then 'forward
        R.FindPrevious "[Type] = '" & Me![Type] & "'"
    Else 'backward
        R.FindNext "[Type] = '" & Me![Type] & "'"
    End If
    If R.NoMatch Then 'can not find any
        MsgBox "No More Matches"
    Else ' sync form with clone
        Me.Bookmark = R.Bookmark
    End If
End Sub
```

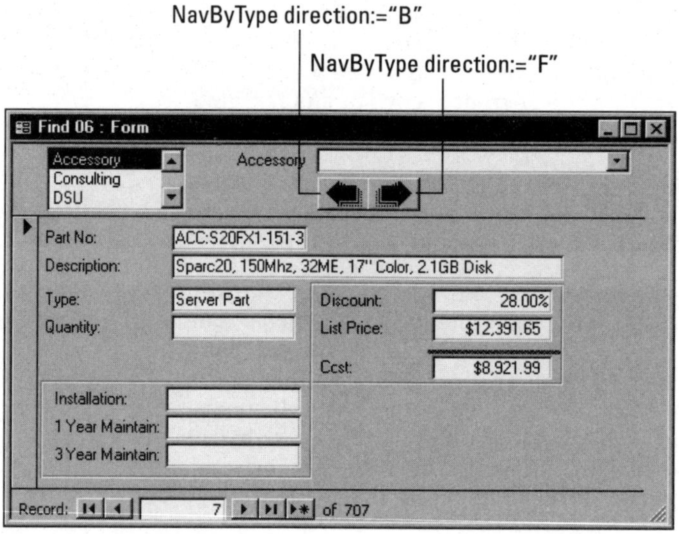

NavByType direction:="B"

NavByType direction:="F"

Figure 6-9:
Smart
navigation
buttons
now appear
on the form.

Notice the use of the `NoMatch` property of the cloned `Recordset` to determine whether the search for matching records is successful. Following a `Find` method (`FindFirst`, `FindLast`, `FindNext`, or `FindPrevious`), Access 97 assigns a `False` value to the `NoMatch` property if the search finds a matching record or a `True` value if the search fails to locate a matching record. This assignment may seem counterintuitive because you normally associate true with something positive, such as success. Just keep in mind that, in Access 97, if `NoMatch` is `True`, the operation *failed*.

```
Private Sub Command32_Click()
    NavByType Direction:="F"
End Sub
Private Sub PrevRec_Click()
    NavByType Direction:="B"
End Sub
```

You see the result of these additions in Figure 6-9, where the buttons with the arrow icons now execute the `NavByType` procedure each time you click them.

Form: Find 06

Tips and labels

The arrow command buttons shown in Figure 6-9 use icons to indicate the direction in which they search. But the icons alone may not clearly tell the user exactly what these buttons do. Access 97 provides the following two ways to clarify the function of a button:

✔ ControlTipText. Access 97 supports the capability to assign pop-up tips next to the controls that appear on a form. This feature is similar to the tool-tips function, added to the Microsoft Office 95 applications, that displays tips for all the icons on the application's toolbars. You can add or modify the tip text for a control by using the ControlTipText property of the control object. In the example shown in Figure 6-10, the Form_Current procedure adjusts the text of the tip for the arrow buttons each time you display a new record.

```
Private Sub Form_Current()
    Me![NextRec].ControlTipText = "Next " & Me![Type]
    Me![PrevRec].ControlTipText = "Previous " _
        & Me![Type]
End Sub
```

Form: Find 06 a

✔ Caption. Although control tips are useful, many users don't take advantage of these tips because they're not aware that your forms use this feature. You can make the information more explicit by displaying a caption in place of the icon in the button and using the Form_Current procedure to update the caption for each new record you display. This approach also appears in Figure 6-10.

```
Private Sub Form_Current()
    Me![NextRec].ControlTipText = "Next " & Me![Type]
    Me![PrevRec].ControlTipText = "Previous " _
        & Me![Type]
End Subw
```

Form: Find 06 b

Displaying record numbers

Access 97 records don't have fixed record numbers. Access 97 dynamically calculates a record's number value and displays that record number along with the total number of records in the form's Recordset as part of the *navigation bar* that appears at the bottom of the form.

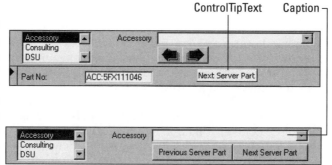

Figure 6-10:
You can use
tips or
captions (or
both) to
explain
button
functions.

If you choose to turn off the navigation bar display or want to move the record-number display to some other part of the form, you can use VBA to create a record-number-type display in any text box or label control on a form. (Placing the record number display at the top of the form, for example, makes the display more visible to users who aren't familiar with the meaning of the navigation bar.)

At first glance, this doesn't seem to be much of a programming challenge. The techniques involved in this example, however, demonstrate the general solution to a number of problems involving automatic generation of numbering sequences — for both forms and reports. Keep in mind that Access 97 doesn't have a built-in feature that automatically numbers items in forms or reports.

Figure 6-11 shows a form that doesn't display the standard navigation bar at the bottom of the form window. (The form's Navigation Buttons property is set to No.) Instead, a series of controls at the top of the form displays the record numbers and provides first, previous, next, and last record movement.

Figure 6-11:
User-
defined
controls
create a
navigation
bar at the
top of the
form.

Form: Record Number

Interestingly, the easiest part of the user-defined navigation bar shown in Figure 6-11 is the code that supports the navigation buttons. Each button uses the same GoToRecord method of the DoCmd object (which I discuss in Chapter 1). The only difference is the built-in constant that the code uses as the Record argument.

```
Private Sub Command20_Click()
    DoCmd.GoToRecord Record:=acFirst
End Sub
Private Sub Command21_Click()
    DoCmd.GoToRecord Record:=acPrevious
End Sub
Private Sub Command22_Click()
    DoCmd.GoToRecord Record:=acNext
End Sub
Private Sub Command23_Click()
    DoCmd.GoToRecord Record:=acLast
End Sub
```

Surprisingly, the more complex problem is how to generate the record-number display. Why? The answer involves the limitations the program imposes on *local* variables. Look at the Form_Load procedure in the following example. This procedure uses RecordsetClone to create a clone of the form's Recordset. You can then obtain the total number of records that the form can display from the RecordCount property of the cloned Recordset. The variable TotalRecords stores that value.

To get an accurate record count from the RecordCount property, you must force Access 97 to read through the entire Recordset by using the MoveLast method. Otherwise, the RecordCount property simply returns 1 as its value, regardless of the true size of the Recordset.

```
Private Sub Form_Load()
    Dim TotalRecords
    Set Records = Me.RecordsetClone
    Records.MoveLast
    TotalRecords = Records.RecordCount
End Sub
```

It seems logical enough that you refer to the value stored in the variable TotalRecords to display the total number of records in another procedure. The Form_Current in the following statement, for example, inserts the value into the caption of a label control called RecNum:

```
Private Sub Form_Current()
    Me![RecNum].Caption = TotalRecords
End Sub
```

Unfortunately, if you try to run this code as shown, you get an error. Why? Local variables are temporary storage areas. They exist only as long as the procedure in which they were created is running. After the procedure reaches the End Sub statement, Access 97 destroys all the local variables. If you attempt to use that local variable in a different procedure, you are, in effect, referring to an object that Access 97 has already destroyed.

The solution? Access 97 VBA supports the following four types of variables:

- ✔ **Local/procedure level.** You can access local variables only from within the procedure in which they are defined by the Dim statement. Local variables are the default variable type in Access 97. If you do not specify what type of variable you are creating, Access 97 assumes the variable to be local. Local variables are destroyed after the procedure in which they are created terminates.

```
Private Sub Form_Load()
    Dim TotalRecords 'Local/Procedure Level
End Sub
```

- ✔ **Static.** Static variables are preserved in memory after the procedure in which they are defined terminates. After you create a static variable, that variable continues to exist until the entire module in which it occurs closes. This type of variable, therefore, remains available until you close the form. Static variables enable you to run a procedure several times and start out each run with the same variables and data that you had at the end of the last run. Notice that these variables are available only to the procedure in which they were first created. If you create a static variable in the Form_Current procedure, that variable is available only if you execute Form_Current again. Other procedures cannot access the variable.

```
Private Sub Form_Load()
    Static TotalRecords 'Local/Procedure Level
End Sub
```

- ✔ **Module level.** Access 97 creates a module-level variable whenever you use the Dim statement in the opening section of the module (called the *declarations section*). Module-level variables are available to all procedures in the module. These variables enable you to create values in one procedure that subsequent procedures in the same module can use or modify. A module-level variable that you create in a form module is available to all the procedures executed on that form.

```
Option Compare Database
Option Explicit
Dim TotalRecords
```

✔ **Public.** Public variables are the broadest type of variable. If you create one in a module's declarations section, the variable becomes available to procedures in any module within the database.

```
Option Compare Database
Option Explicit
Public TotalRecords
```

In this case, you need to employ two module-level variables. One you name Records; it is a clone of the form's Recordset. The other, TotalRecords, maintains the total number of records in the form's Recordset. Notice that you enter the code in the following example in the declarations section of the form's code module.

```
Option Compare Database
Option Explicit
Dim Records As Recordset
Dim TotalRecords
```

The first in the module to use these variables is the Form_Load procedure, which creates the cloned Recordset and captures the record total in a variable. You need no Dim statements in this procedure, because you already defined the variables at the module level. The procedure that follows can use the module-level variable TotalRecords without a Dim statement:

```
Private Sub Form_Load()
    Set Records = Me.RecordsetClone
    Records.MoveLast
    TotalRecords = Records.RecordCount
End Sub
```

The next procedure involved in this program is Form_Current. The appearance of a different record causes this procedure to trigger; therefore, this procedure is the one that must update the record counter. This procedure uses the following two properties, not previously mentioned:

✔ NewRecord. This property enables you to determine whether the form is displaying an existing record or a new record. The property is True if a new record is on-screen. This property changes prior to the Before Insert event, which triggers only after the user enters a character into the new record. This property is a property of the Form object.

✔ AbsolutePosition. This property returns the record number of the current record in a Recordset in which the first record is number 0, the second is 1, and so on. This property is a property of a Recordset object.

The Form_Current procedure can keep an accurate record-number display by performing several actions. First, the NewRecord property determines whether a form is showing an existing or a new record. If the record is new, New Record appears. If the record is an existing one, the Bookmark properties synchronize the cloned Recordset with the form. The Absolute-Position property of the cloned Recordset is then equivalent to the number of the record appearing in the form. Notice that the record number is always the AbsolutPosition property plus 1, because Absolute-Position begins with 0 as the position of the first record.

```
Private Sub Form_Current()
   If Not Me.NewRecord Then
      Records.Bookmark = Me.Bookmark
      Me![RecNum].Caption = "Record " & _
         Records.AbsolutePosition + 1 & " of " & _
         TotalRecords
   Else
      Me![RecNum].Caption = "New Record"
   End If
End Sub
```

The only other code you need to add is the code that accounts for the addition of new records to the Recordset. In the following example, you divide the changes into two procedures. The BeforeInsert procedure, which takes place after you enter the first character of the new record but before you save it, changes the display to show that a new record number is *pending*. The AfterInsert procedure, which occurs after you save the new record, updates the overall record total and then the record number display.

```
Private Sub Form_BeforeInsert(Cancel As Integer)
   Me![RecNum].Caption = TotalRecords + 1 & " pending..."
End Sub
Private Sub Form_AfterInsert()
   Records.MoveLast
   TotalRecords = Records.RecordCount
End Sub
```

Form: Record Number

Finding related items

List and combo box controls, by design, enable you to fill a given control with a data item by selecting the item from a list instead of manually entering the item in a text box. Each list, however, can bind or insert only one item of data into a given control. If you make one item selection, however, you often need to insert a number of other related items of information along with the selected item.

Look at the layout of the form shown in Figure 6-12. This form displays information from the Orders table. Each order must have a customer name, an address, and phone number information. Fortunately, the database includes a Customers table that contains just this data for all past customers.

You can speed up the entry of invoice information if you can select the customer from a list of customers that the Customers table stores. But that isn't all. After you select a customer, you also need to insert into the order form, as a block of related data items, the address and phone information that the Customers table stores for that customer. The form's combo and list box controls, however, can bind, or insert, only one column of data from their source. You need to develop a procedure that somehow uses the customer selection to also copy the address and phone information from the Customers table into the order form.

Figure 6-12:
Your
selection in
the
Customer
list must fill
in the
address
block
information
as well.

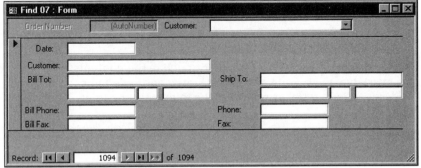

Form: Find 07

The first step is to create a combo box that lists all the customer information in the Customers table. The RowSource property contains the SQL statement shown in the following example. The statement creates a two-column list: ID and Name. If you set the Bound Column property to 1, the control's value is the ID number of the selected customer.

Although this item is only one of the data items you need, the ID number is the key item to creating a procedure that retrieves the rest of the data from the Customers table.

```
Select [ID], [Name] from customers Order by [Name];
```

Using a Recordset variable

Earlier sections of this chapter describe a special type of variable called a RecordsetClone. This cloned Recordset contains a set of records and fields that are identical to those appearing on the form. Use the clone to search for records and to manipulate the form by synchronizing the records into the two Recordsets. Utilizing Bookmark properties helps synchronize the records.

Here, the problem is a bit different. The form's Recordset consists of data in the Orders table. the Recordset you need to search, however, is one that contains data from the Customers table. The Recordset variable you need to create, therefore, isn't a clone of the form's Recordset but one defined by another criterion.

Specifically, you want to perform a query that retrieves the record in the Customers table that matches the selected customer ID. The SQL statement in the following example retrieves the data in the Customers table for the records that match the value in the [Customer ID] control on the current form.

```
"SELECT * FROM [Customers] WHERE [ID]="& Me![Customer ID]
```

You can use this SQL statement to define the contents of a Recordset variable. First, you use the Dim statement to define a variable of a Recordset type, as shown in the following example:

```
Dim CustInfo As Recordset
```

To fill a Recordset variable with a specific set of records, you use the OpenRecordset method. OpenRecordset is a method of the database object — in this case, the current database, CurrentDB. The Set statement in the following example assigns a set of records, as defined by the SQL statement text, to the Recordset variable. (Notice that, to shorten the line, I abbreviated the SQL statement text.) Keep in mind that, because you can have only one customer in the Customers table for each customer ID, the Recordset variable always contains just a single record.

```
Set CustInfo = CurrentDb.OpenRecordset("SELECT * FROM …")
```

After you create the Recordset variable, you can refer to the fields in the Recordset as fields within the variable. The following statement, for example, fills the Customer control on the active form with the Name field from the Recordset variable:

```
Me![Customer] = CustInfo![Name]
```

If you put all these elements together, they result in a procedure similar to the one shown in the following example, which triggers each time the user makes a selection in the Link_To_Customer combo box:

```
Private Sub Link_To_Customer_AfterUpdate()
    Dim CustInfo As Recordset, SQLText
    SQLText = "SELECT * FROM [Customers] WHERE " _
    & "[ID] = " & Me![Customer ID]
    Set CustInfo = CurrentDb.OpenRecordset(SQLText)
    Me![Customer] = CustInfo![Name]
    Me![Bill Street] = CustInfo![Street]
    Me![Bill City] = CustInfo![City]
    Me![Bill State] = CustInfo![State]
    Me![Bill Zip] = CustInfo![Zip]
    Me![Bill Phone] = CustInfo![Phone]
    Me![Bill Fax] = CustInfo![Fax]
End Sub
```

You can see the effect of this procedure in Figure 6-13. After the user makes a customer selection from the list, Access 97 also copies the customer's address and phone information into the corresponding controls on the form.

> **Form: Find 07**

Copying a block of controls

In many cases, the *ship-to* address of an order or invoice is the same as its *bill-to* address. To facilitate filling in the ship-to addresses, you may want to create a Copy button, as pictured in Figure 6-14, that copies this information automatically.

You assign the following procedure to the Copy button. After you click the button, the procedure copies the data in the corresponding bill-to and ship-to controls.

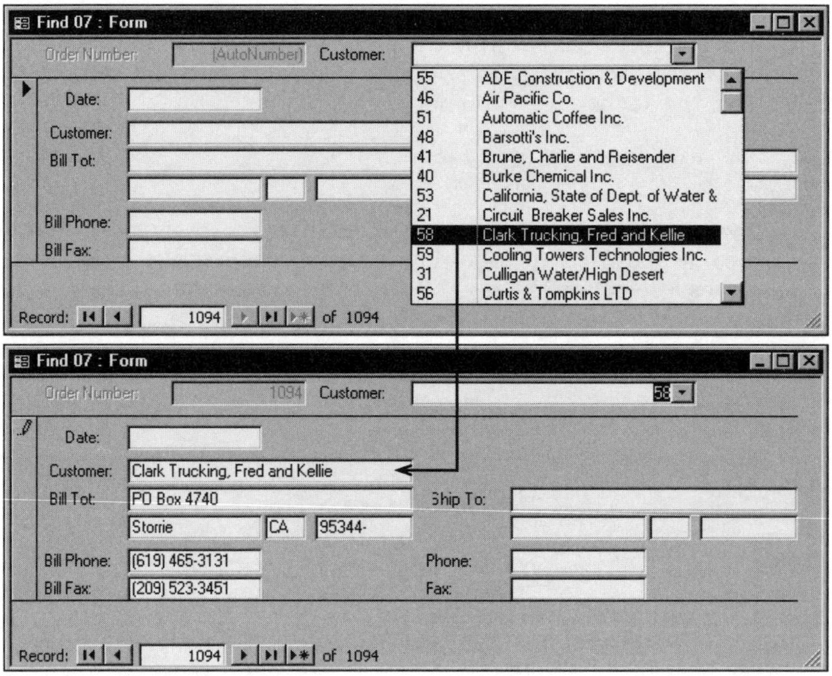

Figure 6-13:
Access 97
inserts
address
and phone
data after
you select
a customer
ID.

```
Private Sub Command44_Click()
    Me![Ship Street] = Me![Bill Street]
    Me![Ship City] = Me![Bill City]
    Me![Ship State] = Me![Bill State]
    Me![Ship Zip] = Me![Bill Zip]
    Me![Ship Phone] = Me![Bill Phone]
    Me![Ship Fax] = Me![Bill Fax]
End Sub
```

ON THE CD

Form: Find 07 b

Subforms

Most order or invoice forms, such as the one shown in Figure 6-15, involve
the use of a *subform*. Such a subform displays the details of the order in a
one-to-many relationship to the record appearing in the main form. In this
example, the subform contains the part number, description, quantity, unit
price, and extended price for each line item you associate with the order.
This data is stored in a table called Order Details.

Figure 6-14:
The Copy
button
transfers
bill-to
address
data to
ship-to
address
controls.

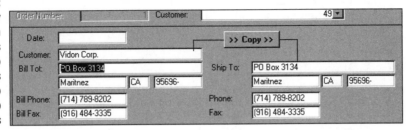

> **Form: Find 07 a**
> **Form: Nav Sub 01**

The records in the subform also require a Recordset search to fill in the
information you need to complete a line-item entry. In the subform shown in
Figure 6-15, a combo box control provides the user with a list of available
parts from the Parts table. You can use the following SQL statement as the
RowsSource property of the combo box control:

```
SELECT [Part No], [Description],[List Price] FROM Parts
       ORDER BY [Type];
```

Figure 6-15:
Subforms
require a
procedure
that
inserts the
description
and list
price after
you select
a part
number.

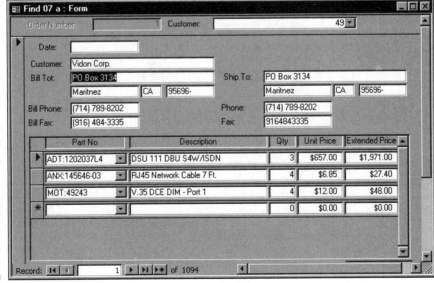

As with the address block in the main form, after the user selects a part number, a procedure needs to trigger to search the Parts table for the corresponding description and list price so that the program can automatically insert these values into the corresponding controls on the subform.

The Part_No_AfterUpdate procedure shown in the following example executes each time the user selects a part from the combo box in the subform control. This procedure is similar to the one you use in the main form to obtain the address and phone number information. As in that procedure, you use the key value — in this case, the Part No — to define a SQL statement that retrieves the entire record associated with that part number. You use the SQL statement to create a Recordset variable, Parts, that contains the data fields you need to fill in the description and unit price controls.

```
Private Sub Part_No_AfterUpdate()
   Dim Parts As Recordset, SQLText
   SQLText = "SELECT * FROM Parts WHERE " & _
   "[Part No] = '" & Me![Part No] & "';"
   Set Parts = CurrentDb.OpenRecordset(SQLText)
   Me![Description] = Parts![Description]
   Me![Unit Price] = Parts![List Price]
   CalcExtended 'recalc extended total
End Sub
```

The following procedure calculates the extended price of the line item by calling the CalcExtended procedure:

```
Sub CalcExtended()
   Me![Extended Price] = Me![Unit Price] * Me![Quantity]
End Sub
```

Two other event procedures in the subform, Quantity_AfterUpdate and Unit_Price_AfterUpdate, also call the CalcExtended procedure to ensure that the extended price automatically reflects any changes in the quantity or unit price controls.

```
Private Sub Quantity_AfterUpdate()
   CalcExtended
End Sub
Private Sub Unit_Price_AfterUpdate()
   CalcExtended
End Sub
```

Running a subform setup

If you embed a form in another form so that the embedded form operates as a subform, you cannot change that subform's properties while you're working in the Design mode of the main form. Instead, you must open a separate Design window for the subform and make sure that you save any changes in that window before you open the main form. This process often gets a bit awkward, because you can best judge the appearance of the subform only if you display it as a subform instead of in its own form window.

You may, for example, want to turn off one or both of the scroll bars on the subform after you see how it looks as part of the main form. Unfortunately, if you select the wrong setting, you must go back to the Design window for the subform, open that window, make any changes, save the changes, and then display the main form to see whether you like the results.

One way to get around this problem is to control the form settings of the subform by using a SetUpSubForm procedure that executes each time you display your main form. This setup enables you to make changes to the appearance of the subform without needing to open a separate Design window.

The key to working with subforms is the use of the Form property of the Subform control. Suppose, for example, that the form Find 07 b is currently on-screen and you open the Debug window to enter commands. The name of the Subform control within Find 07 b is Order Details. If you want information about the Subform control, you specify a property of the control. The following example returns the name of the form that appears in the Subform control:

```
? forms![find 07 b]![order details].sourceobject
Nav Sub 01
```

If, however, you want information about the form within the Subform control, such as information about its fields or properties, you use the Form property to refer to the form within the Subform control. The following command returns the number of controls in the subform's form:

```
? forms![find 07 b]![order details].form.count

10
```

The following example returns the record source of the subform showing that the records in the subform come from the Order Details table:

```
? forms![find 07 b]![order details].form.recordsource
Order Details
```

To refer to the contents of a field in the subform, you use a reference similar to the one shown in the following example, which returns the value of the Part No field in the subform:

```
? forms![find 07 b]![order details].form("Part no")
ADT:1202037L4
```

The SetUpSubForm procedure in the following example sets a number of Form properties on the subform:

```
Sub SetUpSubForm(Ctrl As Control)
    With Ctrl.Form
        .NavigationButtons = False
        .ScrollBars = 2
        .DividingLines = False
        .RecordSelectors = False
    End With
End Sub
```

The Form_Load event procedure calls this procedure to ensure that it configures the subform each time the main form loads.

```
Private Sub Form_Load()
    SetUpSubForm Me![Order Details]
End Sub
```

> **Form: Find 07 b**
> **Form: Nav Sub 01**

Summarizing the subform

If you store the line-item details on a subform within a main form, you often want to place summary information on the main form — such as the total of all the items that the subform details list, as shown in Figure 6-16.

> **From: Find 08**

You can calculate totals based on the contents of the subform by using a cloned Recordset. The trick here is that you make the clone from the Recordset of the subform, not from the main form. The following example uses the Form property of the Subform control to create a clone of the Recordset that appears in the subform:

```
Dim R As Recordset
Set R = Me![order details].Form.RecordsetClone
```

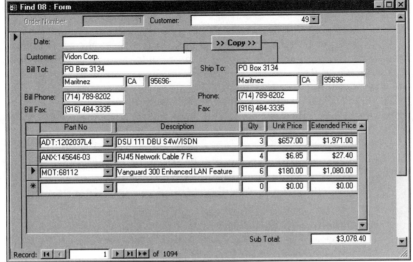

Figure 6-16:
The main
form
displays the
totals of the
subform's
extended
prices.

After you create that Recordset variable, you can scan through the
Recordset and add all the extended prices to arrive at the total. You can
then insert the total into the SubTotal control on the main form. The
CalcTotal procedure performs this operation on the Order Details
subform control, as shown in the following example:

```
Sub CalcTotal()
   Dim R As Recordset, subtotal
   Set R = Me![order details].Form.RecordsetClone
   R.MoveFirst
   Do Until R.EOF
      subtotal = subtotal + R![Extended Price]
      R.MoveNext
   Loop
   Me![Sub Total] = subtotal
End Sub
```

The Exit event of the Order Details subform control calls the CalcTotal
procedure. Every time the user moves out of the subform, therefore, Access 97
recalculates the total. Performing the calculation in the On Exit procedure
makes sense because the only time you want the program to recalculate the
total is after you change one or more of the details in the subform.

```
Private Sub Order_Details_Exit(Cancel As Integer)
   CalcTotal
End Sub
```

Null Values in Calculations

To complete the operations needed for the form shown in the preceding section, you need to make a few more calculations at the bottom of the form, which add items such as tax and shipping to the subtotal for the line items, as shown in Figure 6-17.

The items at the bottom of this form fall into the following two categories:

✔ **User input.** The Tax Rate and Shipping values require user input. These controls are normal controls into which you can enter data. The AfterUpdate event for these controls, however, needs to trigger a procedure that recalculates the other items that depend on these values.

✔ **Calculated.** These controls contain values that you don't want to directly edit, because their values derive from the values in other controls. You need to lock these controls — that is, set their Locked property to Yes — and your form's procedures should insert the values.

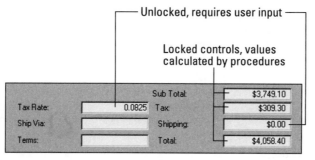

Figure 6-17:
The tax and toal section contains both locked and unlocked controls.

Unlocked, requires user input

Locked controls, values calculated by procedures

	Sub Total:	$3,749.10
Tax Rate: 0.0825	Tax:	$309.30
Ship Via:	Shipping:	$0.00
Terms:	Total:	$4,058.40

From: Find 09

You can create a procedure that updates the values in the Tax and Total controls whenever a user update necessitates recalculation of the tax and total controls. The Summarize procedure shown in the following example performs these calculations as needed:

```
Sub Summarize()
    Me![Tax] = Me![Tax Rate] * Me![Sub Total]
    Me![Total] = Me![Sub Total] + Me![Tax] + _
        Me![Shipping]
End Sub
```

Summarize, however, contains a problem that may not be obvious. Not all the orders require an entry for either Tax Rate or Shipping. If you make no entry in those fields, the value of the field or a control bound to that field is a Null value. So what? In Access 97, a Null value is very different from a value of zero. Take a look at the following statement, which calculates the amount of tax:

```
Me![Tax] = Me![Tax Rate] * Me![Sub Total]
```

But suppose that the Tax Rate control contains a Null. In Access 97, if any of the values in an expression are Null values, the *entire* expression is null. The Tax field, therefore, contains a Null, not a zero.

```
Me![Tax] = Null * 3000 = Null
```

But the damage doesn't stop there, because the next statement in the procedure uses the value of Tax to determine the value of Total. Following the rule about Null values, Access 97 determines that Total is also Null.

```
Me![Total] = Me![Sub Total] + Me![Tax] + _
      Me![Shipping]
```

This effect is known as the *propagation of Nulls.* The effect takes place if one expression in a series of dependent calculations generates a Null rather than a zero; the Null value then cascades through the entire sequence.

One solution is to add If statements and use the IsNull() function to test for Null values in key fields. Another is to force zeros into the fields as default values. If you prefer the unused fields to remain Null, you can use a new function that Access 97 provides that performs this task: Nz() (that is, *nonzero*). You use this function to convert nonzero values such as Nulls to zero values. The modified version of the Summarize procedure in the following example uses Nz() to protect the procedure from the unwanted propagation of Nulls. Nz() protects by converting Tax and Shipping to zero values for the purpose of the calculation without actually inserting zeros into the fields. Notice that Nz() has no effect on the value of a field or a control if that object contains something other than a Null.

```
Sub Summarize()
   Me![Tax] = Me![Tax Rate] * Me![Sub Total]
   Me![Total] = Me![Sub Total] + Nz(Me![Tax]) + _
      Nz(Me![Shipping])
End Sub
```

The last step is to add a call to the Summarize procedure to any event procedures that trigger after a change to one of the key controls.

```
Private Sub Order_Details_Exit(Cancel As Integer)
   CalcTotal
   Summarize
End Sub
```

```
Private Sub Shipping_AfterUpdate()
   Summarize
End Sub
```

```
Private Sub Tax_Rate_AfterUpdate()
   Summarize
End Sub
```

The form Find 09 now accurately calculates the financial data in the Orders and Order Details tables.

Part III
Controlling the Dialog

The 5th Wave — By Rich Tennant

"All through High School he wouldn't talk to anyone - hardly said a word. Now he's graduating from an Ivy League college with an advanced degree in communications."

In this part . . .

Any Windows user knows that one of the most important and useful elements in the entire Windows system is the dialog box. The dialog box grabs the attention of the user by presenting him or her with a set of options and choices that define how some activity (such as printing a report) should be carried out.

When you design an application you probably want to create your own custom dialog boxes to make your program as easy to use as those Windows programs you like so much. One problem: Access VBA doesn't provide dialog boxes. The chapters in Part III explain how to use Access VBA with normal Access forms to create forms that look, feel, and behave like dialog boxes.

Chapter 7

Making Your Own Dialog Boxes

● ●

In This Chapter

▶ Exploring interactive boxes

▶ Using input boxes for text input

▶ Forms as dialog boxes

▶ Multiple selections in one dialog box

▶ Setting default dates

● ●

*P*roviding users with lists of information from which they can select items is one way to increase the productivity of your Access 97 forms. At a certain point, however, you begin to realize that list and combo box controls can go only so far.

The alternative is to use dialog boxes. In Access 97, a *dialog box* is really a form that you specifically configure so that it looks and feels more like a dialog box than a data-entry form. In this chapter, you discover how you can use forms as dialog boxes and how you can enhance your applications by using these dialog box forms.

> **Database Folder: Chapter 6**
> **Database File: DIAGBOX.MDB**

If you want to use the examples on the CD, open the database file DIAGBOX.MDB, and then click the Forms tab. This tab lists the forms I discuss in this chapter.

Interactive Boxes

Although most of this chapter deals with using Access 97 forms as dialog boxes, you need to remain aware that Access 97 features two basic, built-in, dialog-box-type functions. Although these displays don't offer you the broad flexibility that form-based dialog boxes provide, they're handy if you want simple input without spending a lot of design and programming time:

- ✔ MsgBox( ). This function displays a message box, as you can see in Figure 7-1. Message boxes contain up to 1,024 characters of text and between one and three buttons. A message box returns user responses as numeric code that indicates which button the user clicked.

- ✔ InputBox( ). This function displays a dialog box that contains a single input box into which the user can make an entry, as illustrated in Figure 7-2. The entry can consist of any text up to about 63,000 characters. The function returns the user's input as the value of the function.

Figure 7-1:
A MsgBox-
style
dialog box.

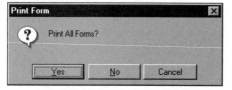

Figure 7-2:
An
InputBox-
style
dialog box.

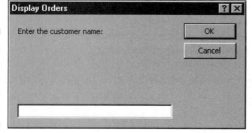

Using MsgBox as a dialog box

The MsgBox( ) function is useful if the user can express the required response by clicking one of two or three buttons — for example, Yes, No, or Cancel; or Abort, Retry, or Ignore. Suppose, for example, that you want to place a Print button on a form. By default, Access 97 prints a copy of each record in the form unless you select the current record and choose to print only that form. If you want to provide the user with the option of printing the current form or all forms, you may want to create two separate buttons.

An alternative is to link the button to a procedure that displays a message box that asks users what type of printing operation they want to perform, as shown in Figure 7-3.

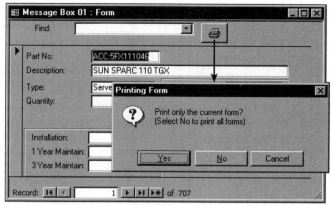

Figure 7-3:
A MsgBox()
that you
use to
determine
the type of
printing to
perform.

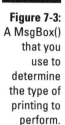

> ### Form: Message Box 01

The two procedures shown in the following examples implement the two
approaches to printing forms. The first uses the PrintOut method by itself
to print all the records in the form. The second, PrintCurrentForm, first
uses the RunCommand method to perform the equivalent of the Edit⇨Select
Record menu command. The procedure then prints the selected record
using the PrintOut method. The procedure limits the scope of the printing
to the selected record by using the PrintRange argument. The built-in
constant specifies the current selection as the print range.

```
Sub PrintAllForms()
    DoCmd.PrintOut
End Sub
```

```
Sub PrintCurrentForm()
    DoCmd.RunCommand Command:=acCmdSelectRecord
    DoCmd.PrintOut PrintRange:=acSelection
    Me![Part No].SetFocus ' deselects record
End Sub
```

The Command22_Click procedure uses the MsgBox() function, and the
procedure thus triggers after the user clicks the button. The message box
recognizes Chr(10) as an instruction to create a new line of text. The
message box text will appear on two lines. The value of the second argument
determines the style of the dialog box; the options for this argument appear
in Table 7-1. You can enter either the numeric value, the constant name, or
any combination. The constant names help the user to understand the
options that are chosen, but these names also make the statement longer. If
you omit this argument, the function defaults to an OK button and no icon.
The third argument sets the dialog box's title bar text.

```
Private Sub Command22_Click()
   Dim UserSelection
   UserSelection = _
     MsgBox("Print only the current form?" _
     & Chr(10) & "(Select No to print all forms)", _
   vbYesNoCancel + vbQuestion, "Printing Form")
   Select Case UserSelection
      Case 6 'if Yes is clicked
         PrintCurrentForm
      Case 7 'if No is clicked
         PrintAllForms
      Case 2 'if Cancel is clicked
         'no action /print canceled
   End Select
End Sub
```

Notice that the arguments for the message box style are cumulative. In this case, `vbYesNoCancel + vbQuestion` specifies three buttons (Yes, No, and Cancel) and a question mark (?) icon. The `Select Case` structure then evaluates the user's selection based on a numeric value that the function returns.

Table 7-1	Arguments for the MsgBox Style	
Value	*Constant*	*Description*
1	VbOKCancel	OK and Cancel buttons
2	VbAbortRetryIgnore	Abort, Retry, and Ignore buttons
3	VbYesNoCancel	Yes, No, and Cancel buttons
4	VbYesNo	Yes and No buttons
5	VbRetryCancel	Retry and Cancel buttons
16	VbCritical	Red X icon
32	VbQuestion	? icon
48	VbExclamation	Stop sign icon
64	VbInformation	! icon
256	VbDefaultButton2	Second button default
512	VbDefaultButton3	Third button default
768	VbDefaultButton4	Fourth button default
4096	VbSystemModal	Suspend all until finished

Interestingly, you don't strictly need to capture the user's input in a variable. You can directly insert the MsgBox() function as the expression for the Select Case statement. (This works with an If statement as well.) This approach, seen in the version of Command22_Click that appears in the following example, eliminates the use of the variable UserSelection and thus reduces the size of the procedure by two statements. This approach works because placing a function (either built-in or user-defined) within an expression forces Access 97 to execute that function. Although most functions simply return a value, MsgBox() also affects the user interface by displaying a dialog box prior to returning that value.

```
Private Sub Command22_Click()
    Select Case MsgBox("Print only the current form?" _
    & Chr(10) & "(Select No to print all forms)", _
    vbYesNoCancel + vbQuestion, "Printing Form")
        Case 6
            PrintCurrentForm
        Case 7
            PrintAllForms
        Case 2
            'no action /print canceled
    End Select
End Sub
```

> **Form: Message Box 01**

Using InputBox for text input

You use the InputBox() function if the user's response must be a specific date, number, or text item rather than simply a button click. Suppose, for example, that you want to create a button on a form that prints out a report. This report would list all the items in the Parts table of a specific product type — say, *Router* or *Server.* This task requires an input-box-style dialog box, as shown in Figure 7-4, because the type of product must be a text entry that the user makes.

> **Form: InputBox 01**
> **Report: Parts Report 01**

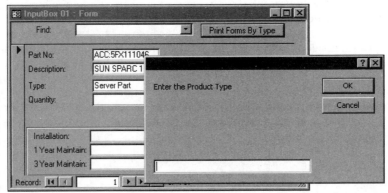

Figure 7-4:
An input
box that you
create to
accept user
input.

The code for this type of dialog box is quite simple. In `Command25_Click`, which follows, you define a variable, `PrintType`, that Access 97 uses to store the text the user enters after the `InputBox()` function displays the dialog box. Access 97 then uses the value that the user enters to create a criterion expression for the `WhereCondition` argument of the `OpenReport` method. This argument has the effect of limiting the printed `Recordset` in the reports to only those records that match the `WhereCondition` argument — for example `Type ="Router"`.

```
Private Sub Command25_Click()
    Dim PrintType
    PrintType = InputBox("Enter the Product Type")
    'Print a report
    DoCmd.OpenReport ReportName:="Parts Report 1", _
        WhereCondition:="[Type] = '" & PrintType & "'"
End Sub
```

Checking the InputBox entry

In the preceding example, the program uses the entry that the user makes to formulate a `WHERE` clause type expression — for example, `Type ="Router"` — that the `OpenReport` method uses as its `WhereCondition` argument. If the user enters **Router**, the report includes only those records that contain `Router` in the `Type` field.

But what's to prevent the user from making an entry for which no matching records exist in the `Parts` table — *Computer,* for example, or *CD-ROM?* The answer is, of course, nothing. If the user makes an invalid entry, he or she receives a report that doesn't contain any records. Although this type of result isn't a disaster, you're much better off if you set up your procedure to check whether the user's input represents a valid product type before printing a report.

How can you perform such a check? (A *valid entry,* by the way, is one for which you have at least one record of that type in the source table — for example, `Parts`.) You answer that question by creating a `Recordset` variable, which you base on the user's input, to determine whether the source table contains at least one matching record. If there's a match, the procedure can print the report. If not, a message appears informing the user that the entry is invalid.

The `IsAValidType` function shown in the following code example performs this test. The function requires one argument, `PType`, which is the product type that the user enters. The procedure will use the value of `PType` to define a `Recordset`-type variable called `R` by limiting the contents of `R` to only those records with a `Type` field that matches `PType`.

After the procedure creates the `Recordset` variable, the procedure evaluates the contents of that variable by checking the `RecordCount` property. If the count equals zero, the function returns a `False` value. If not, the function returns a `True` value. The value that the function returns is the value the procedure assigns to `IsAValidType`, because `IsAValidType` is the name of the function.

```
Function IsAValidType(PType)
   Dim R As Recordset
   Set R=CurrentDb.OpenRecordset("SELECT * FROM" & _
   " Parts WHERE Type = '" & PType & "';")
   If R.RecordCount = 0 Then
      IsAValidType = False
   Else
      IsAValidType = True
   End If
End Function
```

You may recall from previous chapters that the `RecordCount` property isn't accurate until you apply a `MoveLast` method to the `Recordset`. In the `IsAValidType` procedure, however, you don't need to apply `MoveLast` because you don't care how many records the `Recordset` includes, as long as you have at least one record. After you first create a `Recordset` variable by using the `Set` statement, the `RecordCount` property is either zero (an empty `Recordset`) or one (a `Recordset` with at least one record). Because that's all the information you require, you don't need the `MoveLast` method in the procedure `IsAValidType`.

You can then integrate the `IsAValidType` function with the `Command25_Click` code to validate the user's entry before the report prints. If the entry is invalid, a message box appears to warn the user that no report will print.

```
Private Sub Command25_Click()
    Dim PrintType
    PrintType = InputBox("Enter the Product Type")
    If IsAValidType(PrintType) Then
        DoCmd.OpenReport ReportName:="Parts Report 1" _
        ,WhereCondition:="[Type] = '" & PrintType & "'"
    Else
        MsgBox PrintType & " not a valid product type." _
        ,vbCritical
    End If
End Sub
```

> **Form: InputBox 01 a**
> **Report: Parts Report 01**

Notice the way that `Command25_Click` uses the `IsAValidType` function. The goal of the `If` statement is to determine whether the value that the `IsAValidType` function returns is true or false. In VBA, however, you can omit the `= True` portion of the statement. If you place any value between the `If` and `Then` statements, VBA treats that value as if you were comparing the value to a `True` value. Both statements that follow are functionally equivalent:

```
If IsAValidType(PrintType) = True Then
```

```
If IsAValidType(PrintType) Then
```

Conversely, you can test for `False` values by using the `Not` operator. The two examples that follow are functionally equivalent:

```
If IsAValidType(PrintType) = False Then
```

```
If Not IsAValidType(PrintType) Then
```

VBA also evaluates numeric values as `True` or `False`. A numeric value is the equivalent of `False` if its value is exactly zero. VBA treats any other value as `True`. This enables you to simplify the `IsAValidType` function because that function is supposed to return a `False` value if the `RecordCount` property is zero and a `True` if the property is anything other than zero. The following example directly assigns the `RecordCount` property as the function value, eliminating the need to use an `If` structure:

```
Function IsAValidType(PType)
   Dim R As Recordset
   Set R=CurrentDb.OpenRecordset("SELECT * FROM" & _
   " Parts WHERE Type = '" & PType & "';")
   IsAValidType = R.RecordCount
End Function
```

Using this shortcut may seem confusing at first, because the statement
IsAValidType = R.RecordCount appears to imply that the IsAValidType
function is to return a numeric value, not a True or False value. You can
clarify the purpose of the function by assigning the function a specific data
type by using the As keyword. In the following example, the phrase As
Boolean ensures that whatever value Access 97 assigns to the function
returns as either an explicit True or False value:

```
Function IsAValidType(PType)As Boolean
   Dim R As Recordset
   Set R=CurrentDb.OpenRecordset("SELECT * FROM Parts" & _
   " WHERE Type = '" & PType & "';")
   IsAValidType = R.RecordCount
End Function
```

> **Form: InputBox 01 b**
> **Report: Parts Report 01**

Forms as Dialog Boxes

The use of the InputBox() function in the preceding section provides a
good illustration of the limits of InputBox() as a user-interface element.

- **Single input.** The InputBox() function enables the user to input only a
  single item of information. In many cases, however, you may need the
  user to specify more than one option or value.

- **Text box only.** Although the routine that checks the validity of the
  input is useful, a better course is to present the user with a list of valid
  product types to ensure that whatever selection the user makes is
  valid. The InputBox() function, however, limits the user to a text-box
  entry only.

- **Closes after input.** The InputBox() function automatically closes the
  window when the user completes the entry of the value. In some cases,
  however, having the input dialog box remain on-screen until the user
  explicitly elects to close the dialog box is more useful. A user may, for
  example, want to print two or three different reports from one dialog
  box before closing the dialog box.

The solution to all these problems is to replace the built-in dialog functions with a custom-designed form that operates as a dialog box, similar to the form you see in Figure 7-5.

Figure 7-5:
A dialog
box form
displays
several
controls.

> *Form: Dialog 01*
> *Module: User Functions*
> *Report: Parts Report 01*

A list box control called ProductType is at the heart of this form. This control supplies a list of the valid product types by using the following SQL statement to retrieve a list of the unique values in the Type field of the Parts table:

```
SELECT DISTINCT [Type] FROM Parts;
```

You use the PrintButton control to actually print the report by using the PrintButton_Click procedure shown in the following example. This procedure uses the current value of ProductType to generate a WHERE clause expression (the WClause variable) that you use as the WhereCondition argument in the OpenReport method. The current value of the ProductType control limits the report's Recordset.

```
Private Sub PrintButton_Click()
    Dim WClause
    WClause = "[Type] = '" & [ProductType] & "'"
    DoCmd.OpenReport Reportname:="Parts Report 1", _
    WhereCondition:=WClause
End Sub
```

You may recall the GetFirstInList function from Chapter 6, which you use to obtain a default value for the contents of a list or combo box control. You use this function again with this form to set the default for the ProductType list box to the first item in the list, as shown in the following example:

```
Private Sub Form_Load()
    [ProductType] = _
    GetFirstInList(ListCtrl:=[ProductType])
End Sub
```

Another procedure in this form attaches to the CloseForm button. The CloseForm_Click procedure closes the currently open form by applying the Close method of the DoCmd object. The button is necessary because the dialog box form will remain open after the procedure prints each report. Users can choose to print as many reports as they want from the same dialog box. Users click the CloseForm button only after they have printed all the reports they want to print.

```
Private Sub CloseForm_Click()
    DoCmd.Close
End Sub
```

The last procedure in this form is the Form_Open procedure. This procedure calls another procedure, SetupDialog. The SetupDialog procedure is stored in a standard module called User Functions. The purpose of SetupDialog is to set a group of properties for the form that provides the form with a dialog box-like appearance. You can set up these properties directly in the form's property sheet during the design phase. Unfortunately, the default values of the new form are the opposite of the values that you want to have in a dialog-type form. For example, the NavigationButtons property is Yes by default. In a dialog box form it should be No. Manually editing the settings on a property sheet can be quite tedious and time-consuming. A faster way is to call the SetupDialog procedure from the OnLoad procedure of the form. This procedure will set up a new dialog box form programmatically instead of requiring you to manually change the settings in each form's property sheet.

```
Private Sub Form_Open(Cancel As Integer)
    SetupDialog FormWindow:=Me
End Sub
```

```
Sub SetupDialog(FormWindow As Form)
    With FormWindow
        .ScrollBars = 0 'no bars
        .RecordSelectors = False
        .NavigationButtons = False
        .DividingLines = False
    End With
End Sub
```

Preview or print?

The default operational mode for the OpenReport method is to send the report directly to the printer. A more useful method, however, is to include a set of option buttons that enable the user to send output either to the screen preview display or directly to the printer, as you can see in Figure 7-6.

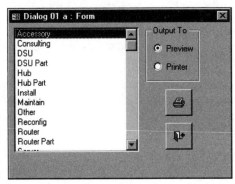

Figure 7-6: Option buttons enable the user to control the output location of the report.

> *Form: Dialog 01 a*
> *Module: User Functions*
> *Report: Parts Report 01*

The values of the OpenReport method's View argument control the output location of the report, as Table 7-2 describes.

Table 7-2	OpenReport View Argument Values	
Value	*Constant*	*Meaning*
0	acViewNormal	Send directly to printer
1	acViewDesign	Open in the design mode
2	acViewPreview	Display the print preview window

Here, you want to use the option buttons in the Output To area of the dialog box shown in Figure 7-6 to select either acViewPreview(2) or acView-Normal(0). By default, Access 97 assigned the Value property of the option buttons the values 1, 2, 3, and so on, as you added each button to the group. But these values are only the default values. The buttons don't need to show consecutive values, nor does the first button need to display a value of 1. The only restriction is that two buttons can't have the same value.

In the next example (Sub Command2_Click), the first option button displays the label Preview, which means that the Value property of this button must be set to **2** and the other button to **0**, as shown in Table 7-3.

Table 7-3	Option Button Values
Control Name	*Value Property*
Option6	2
Option8	0

Because the values you assign to the controls correspond to the values of the acViewPreview and acViewNormal constants, you can avoid building an If structure to evaluate the user's selection. Instead, you can insert the value of the group frame control, OutputTo, in which the buttons reside, directly into the DoCmd.OpenReport statement as the View argument, which appears in **bold** in the following example:

```
Private Sub Command2_Click()
    Dim WClause
    WClause = "[Type] = '" & [ProductType] & "'"
    DoCmd.OpenReport Reportname:="Parts Report 1", _
    WhereCondition:=WClause, View:=Me![OutputTo]
End Sub
```

The user can now direct the output to the screen or printer by clicking the corresponding option button.

Opening the dialog box from a form

After you create a dialog box to handle the printing of a report, users can open that dialog box from any form so that they can print the report. Adding a button that opens the dialog box form enables the user to do so.

> *Form: Parts 01*
> *Form: Dialog 01 b*
> *Module: User Functions*
> *Report: Parts Report 01*

In the following example, the procedure that you assign to the click event for the button uses the OpenForm method to open the dialog box form — in this example, Dialog 01 b:

```
Private Sub Command25_Click()
    DoCmd.OpenForm FormName:="Dialog 01 b", _
    View:=acNormal, WindowMode:=acDialog
End Sub
```

If you use the OpenForm method to open the dialog box form, the most critical argument you need to include is WindowMode, as shown in Table 7-4. In the preceding example, you use the acDialog value to create a *modal window*. The term *modal* refers to the effect that opening a form has on focus. In Windows programs, the active window has focus, which means that pressing a key or clicking inside that window affects only that window. Only one window at a time can have focus. All other open windows are without focus, that is, inactive.

If you open a form normally, by using acWindowNormal, the focus shifts to the new form window, but users can select any other open window by clicking the window or by using the menu commands or shortcut keys (Ctrl+F6 switches to the next window in Access 97). If you use the acDialog option, however, users can't change the focus to any other window in the application until they close the window containing the focus. (Users can switch to a different application window.) Modal windows force users to deal with the current window before moving to anything else.

Table 7-4   OpenForm WindowMode Arguments

Value	Constant	Meaning
acDialog	3	Modal window
acHidden	1	Open but not visible
acIcon	2	Displayed as a form icon
acWindowNormal	0	Nonmodal window

In this example, the decision to use a modal-style window is most likely the best because the user probably wants to print the required reports and go on to work with other windows. Using a modal window is not critical, however, because the function of this dialog box isn't affected by opening or closing other dialog boxes. If one form depends on another form being open, the use of modal windows can help you prevent users from closing the wrong windows at the wrong time.

Multiple Selections in One Dialog Box

The example in the preceding section illustrates how you can use a dialog box to control the contents of a report by taking advantage of the WhereCondition argument of the OpenReport method. If you use this argument, the Recordset for the report automatically filters to include only the records that satisfy the WhereCondition argument. Without this technique, you'd need to create individual report forms and matching query forms for each variation of a report you want to print.

Consider the Orders table in Chapter 6. Suppose that you want to print selected reports for a range of dates, for a particular customer, or for a range of values based on the order total. Furthermore, you want to mix and match the criteria — that is, all the orders of more than $5,000 from November 15 through December 15, 1996, or all the orders for Dressel Enterprises for the first quarter of 1996.

The following dialog-box examples illustrate how a single dialog box can fulfill a wide number of reporting functions. The best part of this approach is that users don't feel as though they're working with a very simple set of options. Your programming makes all the complicated adjustments, giving users the results they desire quickly and easily.

Figure 7-7 shows a dialog box form with two different types of criteria that you can use to define the records to include in a report. The dialog box requires three user inputs: the starting date, the end date, and the name of the customer.

Figure 7-7: A dialog box that enables users to enter date and customer criteria for report printing.

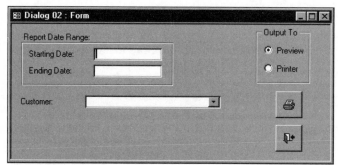

ON THE CD

Form: Dialog 02

The dialog box pictured in Figure 7-7 requires three user inputs: the starting date in a control called Start, the end date in a control called End, and the name of the customer in a control called Customer. The values you enter into these three controls form the basis of a WHERE clause that you use to select the records for the report. The following example is a typical WHERE clause of this type. The Between operator specifies a range of values — in this example, dates. Notice that # symbols enclose the date values. The pound (or number) symbol is part of the Access 97 convention for writing date values in a statement.

```
[Date] Between #1/1/96# AND #1/31/96#" AND [Customer] =
"Air Pacific Co."
```

The use of the # to enclose date values is a VBA and Visual Basic convention, as well as an Access 97 convention. You can use this operator in other VBA applications, too, such as Excel 7.0 and later versions. Most SQL-based client/server databases, such as Microsoft SQL Server, however, don't recognize this operator. If you're passing a date directly to a SQL server, you need to enter the date as text — for example, '2/2/96', not #2/2/96#. Read more about working with SQL Server in Chapter 13.

The VBA statement shown in the following example creates a WHERE clause along the lines of the example by inserting the values from the three controls (Start, End, and Customer) into the statement at the appropriate positions:

```
WClause = "[Date] Between #" & _
    Me![Start] & "# AND #" & _
    Me![End] & "# AND [Customer] = '" & _
    Me![Customer] & "'"
```

The following procedure uses the data you enter into the dialog box form to create a WHERE clause that the program then inserts as the WhereCondition argument of the OpenReport method:

```
Private Sub PrintButton_Click()
    Dim WClause
    Const RName = "Orders 01"
    WClause = "[Date] Between #" & _
        Me![Start] & "# AND #" & _
        Me![End] & "# AND [Customer] = '" & _
        Me![Customer] & "'"
    DoCmd.OpenReport _
        Reportname:=RName, _
        WhereCondition:=WClause, _
        View:=Me![OutputTo]
End Sub
```

Setting default dates

One of the most common criteria applied to any set of records is a *range of dates*. In most cases, the range of dates involves monthly periods, such as January 1 to January 31, or February 1 to February (?). What's the last day in February this year? Is it a leap year or not? Silly questions? Do you find yourself saying "Thirty days hath September . . ." a lot? These are exactly the kinds of questions that make what appears to be an easy-to-use dialog box not quite as easy to use as it seems (refer to Figure 7-7).

The fact is that most people don't keep a perpetual calendar in their heads — nor should you waste more time and effort trying to do so, because all the calendar information you need is already built into the computer. The trick is to get this information working for you when you need it.

Because most reporting is based on monthly periods, the critical dates for any report specification are the first and last days of a given month. If today is 12/11/96, for example, and you want to print a report, the dates 12/1/96 to 12/31/96 or 11/1/96 to 11/31/96 (oops!) are probably the ones you want to enter into the dialog box.

Given any date, how would you get Access 97 to automatically return the beginning and end dates of that month? Table 7-5 lists some of the built-in functions that Access 97 provides for making calendar-related calculations.

Table 7-5   Useful Functions for Date Calculations

Function	Returns
Date	The current date in the computer's clock/calendar
DateSerial	A date based on numbers for year, month, and day
Month	Extracts the number of the month from a date
Year	Extracts the number of the year from a date
DateAdd	Returns a date that's a specific period of time (month, week, and so on) from a given date
DateDiff	Returns the number of time units (month, week, and so on) between two dates

To get the first day of a month if you start with any given day in the month, you first need to separate the month and year values from the date, as follows:

```
Mnth = Month(Date)
Yr = Year(Date)
```

You can use the `DateSerial` function to combine those values with the day value of 1 to get the first day of the month, as follows:

```
DateSerial(Yr, Mnth, 1)
```

That was easy enough. But what about the last day of the month? That number varies with each month and, in the case of February, the year as well. The solution is to realize that the last day of any month is the day before the first day of the next month. If the current month is 1/97, for example, the last day of the month is 2/1/97 minus one day. The following expression performs exactly that calculation:

```
DateSerial(Yr, Mnth + 1, 1) - 1
```

You can put this logic together by using some standard VBA programming structures to create a user-defined function that returns the start or end of the month based on any date. The following example demonstrates two functions, `StartofMonthlyPeriod` and `EndofMonthlyPeriod`, that make these calculations. Each function requires a single argument, which is a date value for any day within the period.

```
Function StartofMonthlyPeriod(Keydate)
    Dim Mnth, Yr
    Mnth = Month(Keydate)
    Yr = Year(Keydate)
    MonthlyPeriod = DateSerial(Yr, Mnth, 1)
End Function
```

```
Function EndofMonthlyPeriod(Keydate)
    Dim Mnth, Yr
    Mnth = Month(Keydate)
    Yr = Year(Keydate)
    MonthlyPeriod = DateSerial(Yr, Mnth+1, 1)-1
End Function
```

If you examine these two procedures, you can see that they're similar in content. You could combine the two into a single function, `MonthlyPeriod`, listed next, that can return either the start or end of period dates. The function requires a second argument, `StartofMonth`, which should be `True` to calculate the start or `False` to calculate the end of the period.

```
Function MonthlyPeriod(Keydate, StartofMonth As Boolean)
    Dim Mnth, Yr
    Mnth = Month(Keydate)
    Yr = Year(Keydate)
    If StartofMonth Then
```

```
        MonthlyPeriod = DateSerial(Yr, Mnth, 1)
    Else
        MonthlyPeriod = DateAdd("m",1,_
            DateSerial(Yr, Mnth, 1))- 1
    End If
End Function
```

> **Module: List Functions**
> **Procedure: MonthlyPeriod**

Notice that you store the code for the MonthlyPeriod procedure in a
standard module, not in a form module. Procedures stored in standard
modules are by default public procedures. Public procedures can be called
from any form, report, or other procedure. Because this calculation is such a
useful one, many subsequent programs use it.

After you create the MonthlyPeriod procedure, you can use this procedure
to set default values for the controls in a dialog box form to the start and
end of the current period, as shown in Figure 7-8. In Form_Load, shown in
the following block of code, the current period is defined as the month of
the current date. The Form_Load procedure uses the MonthlyPeriod function to fill the Start and End controls with the default values:

```
Private Sub Form_Load()
    SetupDialog FormWindow:=Me 'setup window
    Me![Start] = MonthlyPeriod(Keydate:=Date, _
        StartofMonth:=True)
    Me![End] = MonthlyPeriod(Keydate:=Date, _
        StartofMonth:=False)
End Sub
```

Figure 7-8:
The current
start and
end of
month
appear as
default
dates.

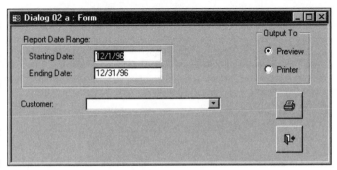

> **Form: Dialog 02 a**

In most businesses, you're usually generating reports after the fact — for example, you print your November reports in December. You can modify the example so that the default dates are for the previous month rather than the current month. If you run the following modified code in December, for example, the default dates become 11/1/?? to 11/30/??:

```
Me![Start] = MonthlyPeriod(Keydate:= _
    DateAdd("m", -1, Date), _
    StartofMonth:=True)
Me![End] = MonthlyPeriod(Keydate:= _
    DateAdd("m", -1, Date), _
    StartofMonth:=False)
```

Form: Dialog 02 a last Month

Incrementing the periods

If setting the initial values to a specific month's beginning and end dates is useful, providing a means by which you can move the dates forward or backward to other financial periods is even better. Figure 7-9 shows two arrow buttons that you can add to the form to change the pair of dates on a monthly basis.

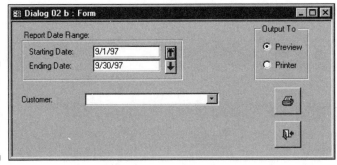

Figure 7-9:
Use Arrow
buttons to
change the
date values.

Form: Dialog 02 b

The first step in adding these buttons is to place into a separate procedure the statements that alter the dates in the Start and End controls because you must use these commands several times to adjust the Start and End controls. The procedure, shown in the following example, requires a single argument, called Pointer, which is a date value.

```
Sub SetDates(Pointer)
   Me![Start] = MonthlyPeriod(Keydate:=Pointer, _
      StartofMonth:=True)
   Me![End] = MonthlyPeriod(Keydate:=Pointer, _
      StartofMonth:=False)
End Sub
```

You use the SetDates procedure in three different event procedures on this form, as shown in the following code. The first is in the Form_Load procedure, which uses the Date function as the argument to set the initial value of the date controls. The event procedures that you link to the arrow buttons also call the SetDates procedure. These event procedures use the DateAdd function to increase or decrease the date in the Start control by a month each time someone clicks one of the buttons (see Table 7-6). Notice that the SetDates procedure changes both the Start and End controls.

```
Private Sub Form_Load()
   SetupDialog FormWindow:=Me
   SetDates Date
End Sub
```

```
Private Sub NextPeriod_Click()
   SetDates DateAdd("m", 1, Me![Start])
End Sub
```

```
Private Sub PreviousPeriod_Click()
   SetDates DateAdd("m", -1, Me![Start])
End Sub
```

Table 7-6	DateAdd Arguments
Argument	_Meaning_
time unit	A text entry that specifies the unit of time for which you make the calculation: yyyy for year, q for quarter, m for month, y for day of year, d for day, w for weekday, ww for week, h for hour, n for minute, s for second.
units	The number of time units you add to the base date. A positive number of units advances the date forward in time. A negative unit value moves backward in time.
base date	The initial date from which you make the calculation.

The dialog box procedures you explored in this chapter illustrate how the same basic elements that make up normal Access 97 forms — for example, text boxes, buttons, and button groups — can, with the addition of some programming code, become custom-designed dialog boxes that help users become more productive. For example, when you combine a dialog box form with a report form, the result is equivalent to a dozen or more specific reports.

Chapter 8

Using Functions to Fill Lists

● ●

In This Chapter

▶ Understanding user-defined RowSourceType functions

▶ Expanding Recordset lists with options

▶ Displaying the actual date range

▶ Creating multicolumn lists

● ●

> **Database Folder: Chapter 8**
> **Database File: ROWFUNC.MDB**

*T*o begin this chapter, load the database for Chapter 8, DIAGBOX.MDB. When the database is open, click on the Forms tab. This is where you can find the forms discussed in this chapter.

The chapter covers creating Access VBA functions that generate lists for list and combo box controls. The programming techniques required to create these lists are a bit more complex than the procedures you have written up to now. However, the functions you read about in this chapter allow you to enhance your applications in ways that are not possible with ordinary list and combo boxes. Be patient. The results will be worth it.

User-Defined RowSourceType Functions

Combo and list box controls typically display lists of information based on data stored in one or more tables. For example, in the form Dialog 01 that I discuss in Chapter 7, the results of a SQL query fill the Customer combo box list. The SQL query, such as the following one, constitutes the RowSource property of the combo box control:

```
SELECT DISTINCT [Type] FROM Parts;
```

If you use the RowSource property, you assume that the items you want to display on the list exist in one of the tables in the database. If a table doesn't contain the data, a SQL statement will not be able to include that item in the list.

But the list you want isn't always composed of data that you can directly retrieve from the existing tables. A good example of this type of information is a list of monthly periods similar to those shown in Figure 8-1. A list of first days of the months for 1996 consists of values that none of the tables actually stores. The tables may contain dates entered by the users, but those dates don't make up a list of the first days of the month.

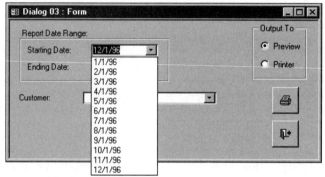

Figure 8-1:
A list of values not stored in any table.

Form: Dialog 03

Of course, one way to get a list of the first days of each month over some period of time is simply to enter a fixed list of items into the RowSource property. Enter **"1/1/96;2/1/96;3/1/96..."** to check this out. However, this approach locks your program into a fixed set of dates that you can update only by editing the control's property sheet. If you take this approach, the list doesn't automatically update after the year changes to 1997.

The solution lies in the third method that Access 97 supports for filling a list or combo box control. This third method is a RowSourceType *function*. This method enables you to fill in the contents of the list by using a VBA function of your own design. RowSourceType functions provide the flexibility to overcome the problem of filling a list with a series of dates or other types of data that you can't draw from an existing table.

Filling a list with dates

The first RowSourceType function example addresses the list of dates displayed in Figure 8-1. Because RowSourceType functions interact with built-in Access features (such as list and combo box controls), you must always create the functions using the same basic structure illustrated in the next example of code.

The function uses five arguments that Access automatically passes to the function, as you can see in Table 8-1, and nine different action codes that correspond to the tasks required to create a list. Each action (except for acLBEnd and acLBClose) returns a value to the control that helps define the list's contents. You can see a list of those action codes in Table 8-2.

Unlike most functions that event procedures execute, the RowSourceType function is executed repeatedly if someone displays a form containing a control that uses one of these functions. The list's content determines the number of times that Access 97 calls the function. Access 97 uses the action argument to specify which operation is to take place each time the program calls the function. Access 97 calls the acLBInitialize action, for example, only once, but calls the acLBGetValue action once for each row in the list. The procedure uses a Select Case structure to assign specific statements to each type of action, if necessary, for creating the list.

As with all functions, Access 97 returns the value assigned to the variable that has the same name as the function. In the outline shown in the following example, ???? refers to the name of the function.

```
Function ????(C As Control, ID, Row, Col, Action)
    Select Case Action
        Case acLBInitialize
            ???? =
        Case acLBOpen
            ???? =
        Case acLBGetRowCount
            ???? =
        Case acLBGetColumnCount
            ???? =
        Case acLBGetColumnWidth
            ???? =
        Case acLBGetValue
            ???? =
        Case acLBGetFormat
            ???? =
        Case acLBEnd
        Case acLBClose
    End Select
End Function
```

Table 8-1	Arguments for RowSourceType Functions
Argument	**Usage**
C	The control object for which the list is generated.
ID	A unique value that identifies the control being filled, in case you want to use the same function for several lists. You typically use the built-in Timer function to generate this number.
Row	The row number, starting at 0, of the row in the list being filled. If not filling a row, the value is −1.
Col	The column number of the column being filled. If not filling a column, the value is −1.
Action	A numeric code that indicates what operation is to be executed.

Table 8-2	Action Values
Constant	**Usage**
acLBInitialize	Set initial values
acLBOpen	Assign an ID
acLBGetRowCount	Set the number of rows
acLBGetColumnCount	Set the number of columns
acLBGetColumnWidth	Set the column width
acLBGetValue	Insert one item in the list
acLBGetFormat	Format the inserted item
acLBEnd	List complete; clean up if needed
acLBClose	Not used
acLBInitialize	1 set initial values
acLBOpen	Assign an ID
acLBGetRowCount	Set the upper limit on the number of rows
acLBGetColumnCount	Set the number of columns
acLBGetColumnWidth	Set the column width
acLBGetValue	Insert one item in the list
acLBGetFormat	Format the inserted item
acLBEnd	List complete; clean up if necessary
acLBClose	Not used

The first action that Access initiates when it begins to fill a list is `acLBInitialize`, which occurs once at the beginning of the process that fills the list. You use this action to create any values that you may need later in the process and to determine whether to fill the list. If this action returns `False` (zero or null), Access 97 immediately terminates the list-filling process and the control displays an empty list. If a `True` value (anything other than zero or Null) returns, the process continues with the next action.

```
acLBInitialize
    StartofMonths = True
```

The `acLBOpen` action is next. Its purpose is to secure a unique ID number. In most cases, you use the `Timer` function to supply this value.

```
acLBOpen
    StartofMonths = Timer
```

You use the third action, `acLBGetRowCount`, to set the number of rows in the list. In the following example, that value is 12 for the 12 months in a calendar year. The `acLBGetColumnCount` action sets the number of columns, in this case, 1.

```
acLBGetRowCount
    StartofMonths = 12
acLBGetColumnCount
    StartofMonths = 1
```

The next action, `acLBGetValue`, is an action that Access repeats for each of the rows in the list. After this action takes place, Access 97 assigns the `Row` and `Col` argument values so that you can determine which item on the list is being filled. The first time this action takes place, for example, `Row` equals 0 and `Col` equals 0, meaning that the item is the first item in the first column. Notice that these values begin with 0 as the first number rather than with 1.

In this specific case, the value that `StartofMonths` assigns to the row is a date calculated by the `DateSerial` function. You use the `Date` function to supply the year. The `Row` argument plus 1 (because `Row` is zero-based) determines the month. The day argument is always 1.

```
acLBGetValue
    StartofMonths = DateSerial(Year(Date), Row + 1, 1)
```

You can see the full function in the example that follows. Although you can store this function in the form's module, a better idea is to store the function in a standard module that a number of different forms can use.

```
Function StartofMonths(C As Control, ID, Row, _
    Col, Action)
    Select Case Action
        Case acLBInitialize
            StartofMonths = True
        Case acLBOpen
            StartofMonths = Timer
        Case acLBGetRowCount
            StartofMonths = 12
        Case acLBGetColumnCount
            StartofMonths = 1
        Case acLBGetColumnWidth
            StartofMonths = -1
        Case acLBGetValue
            StartofMonths = _
                DateSerial(Year(Date), Row + 1, 1)
        Case acLBGetFormat
        Case acLBEnd
        Case acLBClose
    End Select
End Function
```

> **Module: List Functions**
> **Function: StartofMonths**

To use this function to fill a list, you must specify the name of the function in the RowSourceType of the control. Note that the RowSource should be blank. In the following example, the set length of the list is 12 to match the 12 items that are to appear:

```
RowSourceType     StartofMonths
RowSource
ColumnCount    1
ColumnHeads    False
ColumnWidths    Auto
BoundColumn    1
ListRows    12
ListWidth
AfterUpdate    [Event Procedure]
```

After the form opens, the RowSourceType function automatically fills the list with a beginning date for each month in the current year. Note that the function automatically adjusts to a new calendar year when the computer's clock moves to 1997.

Formatting list items

The list that the `StartofMonths RowSourceType` function creates displays the actual dates of the first of the month values. It makes more sense for the list to display the month and year, such as *Mar 96*.

Form: Dialog 03 a

You can apply numeric or date formatting to the items using the `acLBGet-Format` action. This action executes once for each row and column in the list. The following example shows the `acLBGetFormat` action used to apply the format string `mmm yy` to the date value defined by the `acLBGetValue` action.

```
Case acLBGetValue
   StartofMonths01 = _
      DateSerial(Year(Date), Row + 1, 1)
Case acLBGetFormat
   StartofMonths01 = "mmm yy"
```

You can see the entire `StartofMonths01` function in the following example. When you use this function as the `RowSourceType` property, the list that the function produces displays the date as a three-letter month and two-digit year (for example, *Jun 97*).

```
Function StartofMonths01(C As Control, ID, _
   Row, Col, Action)
   Select Case Action
      Case acLBInitialize
         StartofMonths01 = True
      Case acLBOpen
         StartofMonths01 = Timer
      Case acLBGetRowCount
         StartofMonths01 = 12
      Case acLBGetColumnCount
         StartofMonths01 = 1
      Case acLBGetColumnWidth
         StartofMonths01 = -1
      Case acLBGetValue
         StartofMonths01 = DateSerial(Year(Date), _
         Row + 1, 1)
      Case acLBGetFormat
         StartofMonths01 = "mmm yy"
      Case acLBEnd
```

(continued)

(continued)

```
        Case acLBClose
    End Select
End Function
SQLText = "SELECT [Customer], Count(Orders.[Order Number])
```

> **Form: Dialog 03 a**
> **Module: List Functions**
> **Function: StartofMonths01**

Adding options to Recordset lists

You can provide users the ability to choose a value by means of a combo or list box, such as the list of customers in Figure 8-2. Such a selection eliminates the possibility that a user would incorrectly enter a customer name. However, along with these benefits comes a limitation: You have no way to select an option (such as *All*) to indicate that the report should include all the customers rather than a particular customer.

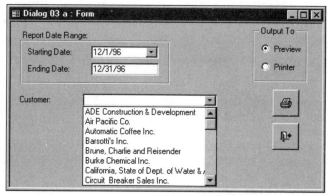

Figure 8-2:
A list composed of Recordset data that omits the All option.

Here's one way to add an option, such as *All* or *None,* to a list of items you draw from a table, such as the customer list. Use a `RowSourceType` function to fill in the list with the data that a table or query supplies, as well as special options such as *All*.

This type of `RowSourceType` function uses a SQL statement to create a `Recordset` from which most of the list items come. To make room for special items like *All*, however, you need to make the size of the list larger than the size of `Recordset`. If, for example, 50 unique customer names are in the `Orders` table, the `RowSourceType` function must have a list size of 51 so you can insert `<All>` into the list.

One technique you can use in RowSourceType functions is to create *static variables*. A static variable, unlike a local variable, retains its value after the procedure concludes. The next time the procedure runs, therefore, the value of the variable picks up from where it left off at the end of the previous run. Because a RowSourceType function calls repeatedly during the process of filling the list, static variables provide a connection between each run of the procedure.

In the following example, you can declare the Recordset variable that you use to provide the customer names as static. After you define the Recordset, its records are available each time Access 97 calls the function to fill another row.

```
Static Names As Recordset
```

Your first step is to assign to the static Recordset variable Names a Recordset that includes all the customer names. You can do so by using the acLBInitializeusing action with the OpenRecordset method. Keep in mind that, because you define the variable Names as a static variable, the variable remains available to subsequent actions that this function performs.

```
Case acLBInitialize
    SQLText = _
        "SELECT DISTINCT Customer FROM Orders;"
    Set Names = CurrentDb.OpenRecordset( _
        SQLText, dbOpenSnapshot)
```

The acLBGetRowCount action requires the use of the Recordset object. In the following example, the RecordCount property provides the value to determine the length of the list. At first, this setup may not seem correct. After all, isn't the purpose of this function to create a list that's longer than the Recordset? Setting the list to a length of RecordCount +1 would seem to make more sense. You must remember, however, that the row count that RowTypeSource functions uses is zero-based. So if you have a list of 50 customers, the row numbers are 0 to 49. This still leaves row 50 for <All>.

```
Case acLBGetRowCount
    Names.MoveLast
    CompanyNames = Names.RecordCount
```

The acLBGetValue action fills the actual list. You use the Row argument to determine the item to add to the list. First, if the Row argument is zero, Access 97 inserts <All> into the list. For any other value, the source of the list item is the recordset Names. The tricky part is to determine which records to use for which row of the list. You solve the problem by first moving the `MoveFirst` method to the beginning of the `Recordset` each time a nonzero row number passes to the function. Then you use the `Move` method to move to a specific record. If the `Row` argument is 10, for example, the `Move` method moves 10 records from the start — that is, it moves to the 11th record, which then goes into the list. This process continues until you fill all the rows.

```
Case acLBGetValue
    If Row = 0 Then
        CompanyNames = "<All>"
    Else
        'use row number to locate records
        Names.MoveFirst
        Names.Move Row
        CompanyNames = Names![Customer]
    End If
```

The entire `CompanyNames` function appears in the following example:

```
Function CompanyNames(C As Control, ID, Row, Col, Action)
    Static Names As Recordset
    Dim SQLText
    Select Case Action
        Case acLBInitialize
            SQLText = _
            "SELECT DISTINCT Customer FROM Orders;"
            Set Names = CurrentDb.OpenRecordset( _
            SQLText, dbOpenSnapshot)
            CompanyNames = True
        Case acLBOpen
            CompanyNames = Timer
        Case acLBGetRowCount
            Names.MoveLast
            CompanyNames = Names.RecordCount
            Names.MoveFirst
        Case acLBGetColumnCount
            CompanyNames = 1
        Case acLBGetColumnWidth
            CompanyNames = -1
        Case acLBGetValue
            If Row = 0 Then
                CompanyNames = "<All>"
```

```
        Else
            Names.MoveFirst
            Names.Move Row
            CompanyNames = Names![Customer]
        End If
    Case acLBGetFormat
    Case acLBEnd
    Case acLBClose
  End Select
End Function
```

Now that the list contains an <All> option, you need to alter the
PrintButton_Click procedure in case you want to print all the customers
in a single report. The following code employs an If structure that handles
this problem by checking to see whether the user selects either <All> or a
specific customer. The arguments for the two types of reports display two
differences: The WHERE clause for <All> omits the Customer criterion
because you want to include all customers. The report form you use for
each one also is different. The Order with Subtotals report groups
records by customer. If users select <All>, they not only get more records,
but also implicitly choose a different report form — one that's more appropriate to the amount of data they intend to print.

```
If Me![Customer] = "<All>" Then
    WClause = "[Date] Between #" & _
        Me![Start] & "# AND #" & _
        Me![End] & "#"
    RName = "Order with Subtotals"
  Else
    WClause = "[Date] Between #" & _
        Me![Start] & "# AND #" & _
        Me![End] & "# AND [Customer] = '" & _
        Me![Customer] & "'"
    RName = "Orders 01"
  End If
```

After you put all these elements together, you can select <All> from the
customer list and print a summary report for the specified dates. You can
also choose individual customers for reports.

> *Form: Dialog 03 b*
> *Report: Order with Subtotals, Orders 01*
> *Module: List Function*
> *Function: CompanyNames*

Showing the actual date range

In the examples in previous sections that involve calculating date lists, I arbitrarily fixed the range of dates at 12 months for the current calendar year. A more accurate approach is to query the data and determine the total number of months. This approach ensures that you have a list of dates that actually covers the range of dates existing in the data tables.

The date list open in Figure 8-3 shows a series of monthly periods that correspond to the total range of dates included in the records in the Orders table.

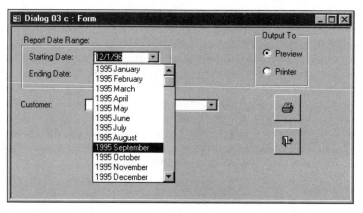

Figure 8-3:
The calendar periods cover the actual range of dates in the Orders table.

> *Form: Dialog 03 c*
> *Module: List Function*
> *Function: ListPeriods*

The ListPeriods procedure uses two static variables that contain the earliest and latest dates from the Orders table. In the following example, the Recordset isn't a static variable because you need to use the variable only once in the procedure to calculate the date range.

```
Function ListPeriods(C As Control, ID, Row, Col, Action)
    Dim DateRange As Recordset, SQLText
    Static StartRange, EndRange
```

As the following example shows, you obtain the actual date range with a SQL statement with aggregate sum functions to calculate the MAX() and MIN() dates in the Orders table:

```
SELECT MIN([Date])As D1, MAX([Date]) AS D2 FROM [Orders]
```

The following procedure obtains those dates by using the SQL statement to generate a Recordset with the summary values. The procedure then assigns those values to the static variables StartRange and EndRange so that they will be available for subsequent calculations.

```
Select Case Action
    Case acLBInitialize
        SQLText = "Select Min([Date]) _
            As D1, Max([Date]) " _
        & " As D2 From [Orders];"
        Set DateRange = _
        CurrentDb.OpenRecordset(SQLText)
        StartRange = MonthlyPeriod(_
            DateRange![D1], True)
        EndRange = MonthlyPeriod(_
            DateRange![D2], True)
        ListPeriods = True
```

You use the two values to calculate the size of the list by using the DateDiff function to calculate the number of months between the two dates. The size of the range is one larger than the value that DateDiff calculates. DateDiff calculates the number of months from 1/1/96 to 6/1/96 as five. As far as you're concerned, however, those dates indicate a range of six months, not five.

```
Case acLBGetRowCount
        ListPeriods = DateDiff(_
            "m", StartRange, EndRange) + 1
```

The acLBGetValue action, shown in the following code, calculates the actual dates by using the Row argument as the number of units in the DateAdd function. The acLBGetFormat action applies the appropriate formatting to the value that the acLBGetValue action adds.

```
Case acLBGetValue
        ListPeriods = DateAdd("m", Row, StartRange)
    Case acLBGetFormat
        ListPeriods = "yyyy mmmm"
```

Multicolumn Lists

In previous sections, all the RowSourceList functions are single-column displays. Although most lists are single-column, in this section you create a multicolumn list like the one in Figure 8-4. This example uses a RowSourceList function so that the list still includes an <All> option. The data in the list shown in Figure 8-4 contains summary information about the customers. Here, the number of orders and the total sales amount for each customer are displayed as part of the list.

Figure 8-4:
A multi-column list that includes summary information.

Form: Dialog 03 c
Module: List Function
Function: CompanyDetails

The key to this procedure is a SQL statement that produces a summary of the sales for each customer. In the following example, the assumption is that you calculate the amount of sales by performing a link between the Orders and Order Details tables. This link is called a JOIN in SQL and ensures that you correctly calculate the total sales. The following SQL statement joins two tables, Orders and Order Details, on a common field called Order Number.

```
SELECT [Customer], Count(Orders.[Order Number]) AS Orders,
Sum([Extended Price]) AS Sales FROM Orders INNER JOIN
[Order Details] ON Orders.[Order Number] = [Order
Details].[Order Number] GROUP BY Customer;"
```

The following code shows this SQL statement written as a text item stored in the variable SQLText. Note that the SQL statement is broken up into a series of short text items concatenated with & operators due to the limitations of printing this book. You could choose to write the entire statement as one long line of text.

```
Case acLBInitialize
    SQLText = "SELECT [Customer], " & _
    "Count(Orders.[Order Number]) AS Orders,"& _
    " Sum([Extended Price]) AS Sales " & _
    "FROM Orders INNER JOIN [Order Details] " & _
    "ON Orders.[Order Number] = " & _
    "[Order Details].[Order Number] " & _
    "GROUP BY Customer;"
    Set ListInfo =CurrentDb.OpenRecordset( _
        SQLText, dbOpenSnapshot)
    CompanyDetails = True
```

The CompanyDetails procedure uses this statement to create a static recordset variable, ListInfo. This recordset has three columns. To create a multiple-column list, the acLBGetColumnCount action, which follows, uses ListInfo.Fields.Count to set the number of columns in the list to match the number of columns in the recordset. The RecordCount property sets the number of items. Recall that by using the actual RecordCount you have an empty item that can be used for the <All> option.

```
Case acLBGetRowCount
        ListInfo.MoveLast
        CompanyDetails = ListInfo.RecordCount
    Case acLBGetColumnCount
        CompanyDetails = ListInfo.Fields.Count
```

You assign the values to the list in the acLBGetValue action by using the same technique you use for the single-column customer list. The only difference is the use of the reference ListInfo(Col) to fill in the list item. This statement takes advantage of the Access 97 program's capability to refer to a field in a recordset by index number rather than by name. If the Col value is 0, for example, the reference ListInfo(0) inserts the first field in the Recordset. If Col changes to 1, field 1 goes into column 1 and so on until the reference fills all the columns. This trick saves you from needing to write a Select Case structure to insert the fields into different columns.

```
Case acLBGetValue
        If Row = 0 Then
            If Col = 0 Then
                CompanyDetails = "<All>"
            End If
        Else
            'use row number to locate records
            ListInfo.MoveFirst
            ListInfo.Move Row
            CompanyDetails = ListInfo(Col)
        End If
```

The `acLBGetFormat` action applies a whole number format to column 1 and a currency format to column 2. Column 0 gets no formatting because that column contains the customer name.

```
Case acLBGetFormat
    Select Case Col
        Case 1
            CompanyDetails = "###,###"
        Case 2
            CompanyDetails = "Currency"
    End Select
```

The entire `CompanyDetails` function appears in the following example. After you execute the function from the `RowSourceType` property of the combo box control, it produces the list shown in Figure 8-4.

```
Function CompanyDetails(C As Control, ID, _
    Row, Col, Action)
    Static ListInfo As Recordset
    Dim SQLText
    Select Case Action
        Case acLBInitialize
            SQLText = "SELECT [Customer], " & _
            "Count(Orders.[Order Number]) AS Orders,"& _
            " Sum([Extended Price]) AS Sales " & _
            "FROM Orders INNER JOIN [Order Details] " & _
            "ON Orders.[Order Number] = " & _
            "[Order Details].[Order Number] " & _
            "GROUP BY Customer;"
            Set ListInfo =CurrentDb.OpenRecordset( _
                SQLText, dbOpenSnapshot)
            CompanyDetails = True
        Case acLBOpen
            CompanyDetails = Timer
        Case acLBGetRowCount
            ListInfo.MoveLast
            CompanyDetails = ListInfo.RecordCount
        Case acLBGetColumnCount
            CompanyDetails = ListInfo.Fields.Count
        Case acLBGetColumnWidth
            CompanyDetails = -1
        Case acLBGetValue
            If Row = 0 Then
                If Col = 0 Then
                    CompanyDetails = "<All>"
                End If
```

```
            Else
                'use row number to locate records
                ListInfo.MoveFirst
                ListInfo.Move Row
                CompanyDetails = ListInfo(Col)
            End If
        Case acLBGetFormat
            Select Case Col
                Case 1
                    CompanyDetails = "####,####"
                Case 2
                    CompanyDetails = "Currency"
            End Select
        Case acLBEnd
        Case acLBClose
    End Select
End Function
```

Copying SQL statements

You may wonder how you'd come up with the complicated SQL statement used in the preceding example. Access provides a shortcut for getting SQL statements for VBA programs with the SQL display feature of the query design grid. The SQL button toggles the query between the grid display and the SQL text display.

Figure 8-5 shows a query grid layout. The list box control pictured in Figure 8-4 uses the recordset generated by that function to produce the multiple-column list.

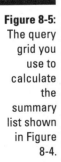

Figure 8-5: The query grid you use to calculate the summary list shown in Figure 8-4.

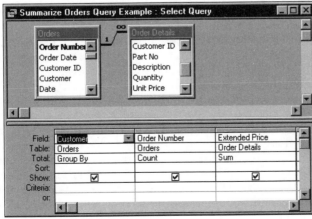

Figure 8-6:
The SQL
view of the
query
shown in
Figure 8-5.

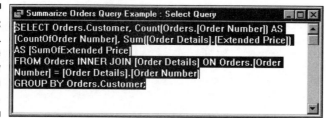

```
Summarize Orders Query Example : Select Query
SELECT Orders.Customer, Count(Orders.[Order Number]) AS
[CountOfOrder Number], Sum([Order Details].[Extended Price])
AS [SumOfExtended Price]
FROM Orders INNER JOIN [Order Details] ON Orders.[Order
Number] = [Order Details].[Order Number]
GROUP BY Orders.Customer;
```

You can get a copy of the SQL text behind that query grid by using the
View⇨SQL View command. Access 97 displays and highlights the SQL text,
as shown in Figure 8-6.

You can copy that text into your module by using the Copy and Paste
commands. Notice, however, that the text does not paste into the module as
a valid string. You need to delete any line endings and enclose the entire
statement in double-quotation marks (""). If the SQL statement itself contains double-quote marks (""), change them to apostrophes (') so that
Access sees only a single set of double quotations: one at the beginning and
one at the end of the SQL text.

Adding column headings

You can also create a multicolumned list that includes column headings. See
the function CompanyDetailsH in the List Functions module.

> **Form: Dialog 03 d**
> **Module: List Function**
> **Function: CompanyDetailsH**

As I mentioned at the start of this chapter, programming RowSourceType
functions is more rigorous than ordinary Access programming, primarily
due to the predetermined structure of the functions. In addition, unlike
most procedures that perform a complete task each time they are called,
the RowSourceType function is called multiple times to complete its task
of filling a list. When you plan a RowSourceType function, you must take
into consideration which values can be treated as local variables (not
preserved between calls) and which must be defined as static variables
(preserved between calls).

The procedures in this chapter illustrate how a list is generated directly by
calculation or when combined with sets of records defined by a SQL statement. You also saw how a multiple-column list can be generated with a
RowSourceType function. These examples illustrate the power and flexibility of RowSourceType functions to enhance the design of your application's
user interfaces by adding lists that otherwise would not be available.

Chapter 9

Printing, Reports, and Output

· ·

▶ Calculating report headings

▶ Numbering records

▶ Summary tables on reports

▶ Multiple selections

▶ Fast form letters

▶ E-mail, HTML, and other output

· ·

*I*n this chapter, I move into the wonderful world of printing, reports, and output. Without these three, you don't get the most out of programming with Access (and you'll soon find out why).

> **Database Folder: Chapter 9**
> **Database File: REPORTS.MDB**

To begin this chapter, load the database for Chapter 9, REPORTS.MDB. Click the Forms tab in the database window. The forms I discuss in this chapter appear in that file.

Calculating Report Headings

One of the primary benefits of using a dialog box-type form, such as the one shown in Figure 9-1, is that you can use a single report form to generate any number of individual reports. The selections the user makes in the dialog box limit the records that the report includes. The records are limited by the WhereCondition argument of the OpenReport action, which applies a SQL WHERE clause to the form's Recordset.

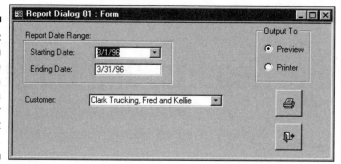

Figure 9-1:
This form
has the
information
that needs
to appear
as report
headings.

One problem, however, becomes obvious after you begin to print different reports from the dialog box. Although the dialog box criteria control the contents of the form, the headings on the printed report don't include that information. Most report headings are entered directly into the report it form as fixed-text labels. When a dialog box is employed to print a report, the customer and the date range information change dynamically every time you print a report. You need to find a way for the report to dynamically adjust the heading of the report so that it reflects the current set of criteria entered in the dialog box.

Reports, like forms, contain a certain set of properties that the report stores as you design and save it. Event procedures built into the report can, however, dynamically alter these properties.

Because reports are for display only (in contrast to the interactive nature of forms), the number and type of events that can occur on a report are fewer and simpler than those of forms. The following five events occur as you print a report:

- ✔ Format. This event takes place as Access 97 is formatting the layout of a report section. You can use the Format event to make changes to the report that affect the layout, such as showing or hiding a control or changing the size or location of a control.

- ✔ No Data. This event occurs if you bind the report to an empty Recordset. You can use this event to cancel the printing of a report if the Recordset contains no data.

- ✔ Page. This event takes place after Access 97 formats all the sections on the page but before you print the page. You can use this event to add items to the page, such as a border, which is drawn by using the Line, Circle, and PSet methods.

✓ Print. This event takes place after Access 97 formats the report section but before you actually print it. During this event, you can perform only those types of operations that don't affect the layout of the section. You can change the value or the font of a control during the Print event, for example, but you can't change the width of the control or change its visible property. To change layout properties, use the Format event.

✓ Retreat. In some cases, you must return to a section that Access 97 has already formatted to make adjustments to changes that other formatting options may cause. You can use the KeepTogether property, for example, to ensure that an entire group prints on the same page. Access 97 may need to remove part of a group from a page if the program finds that it can't fit the entire group on the same page. After Access 97 reaches the end of a page, therefore, you may need to reformat the entire page, minus the group that doesn't fit.

Keep in mind that pagination events (such as page headers and footers) may trigger some of the events on a report, whereas other events relate to the data in the Recordset (such as group headers and footers and other details).

In the following example, the contents of the report header section are what concern you. In the Report 10 No Sub report form, two label controls (Main Heading and Content Limits) contain generic contents, as shown in Figure 9-2.

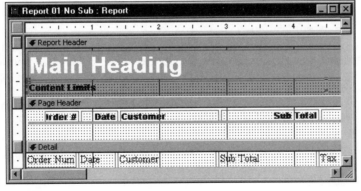

Figure 9-2:
Labels with generic contents go on the report header.

The trick is to attach a procedure to the print event of the report header that copies the values from a dialog box and inserts the values into the report headings. This way, the report always displays the customer and date information that you use to select the records. The following procedure accomplishes this by using references to controls on the Report Dialog 01 form to set the captions for the label controls:

```
Private Sub ReportHeader_Print(Cancel As Integer,
          PrintCount As Integer)
   Dim frmSetup As Form
   Set frmSetup = Forms![Report Dialog 01]
   Me![Main Heading].Caption = "Orders for " _
       & frmSetup![Customer]
   Me![Content Limits].Caption = "Dates: " & _
       frmSetup![Start] & " through " & _
       frmSetup![End]
End Sub
```

Figure 9-3 shows that the procedure inserts the name and dates into the report. Content Limits identifies the criteria you use to select the records.

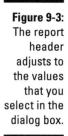

Figure 9-3:
The report header adjusts to the values that you select in the dialog box.

Orders

Orders for Town Country Fencing

Dates: 11/1/96 through 11/30/96

Order #	Date Customer	Sub Total	Tax
349 11/25/96 Town & Country Fenci		$1,546.85	$127.62
Totals:		$1,546.85	$127.62

Page: 1

If the user selects to print <All>, Access 97 selects the report containing subtotals for each product category because the report will contain records of all product types. TheReportHeader_Format procedure for that report is shown in the following example. This procedure draws the dates from the dialog box but simply displays Orders - All Customers as the main heading.

```
Private Sub ReportHeader_Format(Cancel As Integer, _
   FormatCount As Integer)
   Dim frmSetup As Form
   Set frmSetup = Forms![Report Dialog 01]
   Me![Main Heading].Caption = "Orders - All Customers"
   Me![Content Limits].Caption = "Dates: " & _
       frmSetup![Start] & " through " & _
       frmSetup![End]
End Sub
```

Form: Report Dialog 01
Report: Report 01 No Sub
Report: Report 01 with Sub

Using the report with the dialog box

The primary reason for creating a report linked to a dialog box is that you can print the report based on the dialog box settings. You may, however, want or need to open the report at various times while the dialog box is not open. The code shown in the examples in the preceding section (ReportHeader_Format and ReportHeader_Print) results in an error if you attempt to open the report while the linked dialog box — in this case, Report 01 Dialog — isn't open.

To solve this problem and create a report that you can use with or without the dialog box, you can alter the code that you use to fill the report's headings so that the report adjusts to the presence or absence of the dialog box. The key is to create a function that determines whether a given form is open. The Forms object in Access 97 refers to a collection that contains all the open forms in the current database. Keep in mind that forms appearing on the Forms tab of that database window aren't part of the Forms collection — only forms that are open either as a window or as an icon are in the Forms collection.

You can enumerate the members of this collection by using the object name (or its index number) or the For Each statement. The For Each structure in the following example shows you how to enumerate all the forms currently open in the active Access database:

```
Dim F As Form
For Each F In Forms
    statements...
Next
```

You can check for the existence of a specific open form by comparing the names of the forms in the Forms collection to the name of the form in which you're interested, as shown in the following example:

```
F.Name = "Report Dialog 01"
```

The IsFormOpen function in the following example uses the Forms collection to determine whether the form name that passes to the function as a parameter is open. The function is designated as a *Boolean function*, which means that the function returns either a True or a False value.

```
Function IsFormOpen(NameofForm As String) _
   As Boolean
   Dim F As Form
   For Each F In Forms
      If F.Name = NameofForm Then
          IsFormOpen = True
          Exit Function
      End If
   Next
   IsFormOpen = False
End Function
```

The ReportHeader_Print procedure shown in the following example is modified from the version in the preceding section so that it uses the IsFormOpen to check for the dialog box. If the dialog box is open, the program uses its settings. If not, the procedure inserts standard values into the report headings. Notice that you use the DMin() and DMax() functions to obtain the overall date range from the Orders table so that the dates print in the report header.

```
Private Sub ReportHeader_Print(Cancel As Integer, _
         PrintCount As Integer)
   If IsFormOpen("Report Dialog 01") Then
      Dim frmSetup As Form
      Set frmSetup = Forms![Report Dialog 01]
      Me![Main Heading].Caption = "Orders for " _
         & frmSetup![Customer]
      Me![Content Limits].Caption = "Dates: " & _
         frmSetup![Start] & " through " & _
         frmSetup![End]
   Else
      Me![Main Heading].Caption = "Orders Report"
      Me![Content Limits].Caption = "Dates: " & _
         DMin("[Date]", "Orders") & " through " & _
         DMax("[Date]", "Orders")
   End If
End Sub
```

Form: Report Dialog 01 a
Module: Report Functions
Procedure: IsFormOpen
Report: Report 01 No Sub a
Report: Report 01 with Sub a

Numbering records

Access 97 doesn't automatically number the records that appear in the detail section of a report. Numbering each item, however, often enhances the appearance of a report that lists a number of records in its detail section, as shown in Figure 9-4. Numbering helps the reader see how many items the report includes and provides a handy reference point if referring to a particular item — for example, "Why is item #23 so high?"

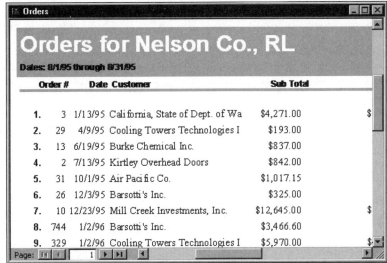

Figure 9-4: The records that the report's detail section lists are numbered consecutively.

To create the numbering scheme shown in Figure 9-4, you need to add an unbound label control to the detail section of the report form. In the next example (Detail_Print), RNum is that control. The trick is to add a procedure to the report that automatically fills this control with consecutive numbers as the records in the detail section print. The event to use is the OnPrint event of the detail section of the report.

The Detail_Print procedure in the following example shows you how to print consecutive line numbers. The key is the use of a Static variable called RCount. Recall that a static variable is one that's not destroyed after the procedure ends. Instead, the variable remains in memory until the module that contains it closes. In this case, the variable remains available for the entire report. The value of RCount continues to increase each time you add a new record to the report, which creates the consecutive numbering scheme shown in Figure 9-4.

```
Private Sub Detail_Print(Cancel As Integer, _
    PrintCount As Integer)
    Static RCount As Integer
    RCount = RCount + 1
    Me![RNum].Caption = RCount & "."
End Sub
```

This technique is meant only for adding numbering to printed reports. If you display the report in a Preview window, you can throw off the numbering scheme by moving back and forth between pages. This problem occurs because, in Preview mode, you can move randomly among the pages in a report. Depending on the size of the report and how you move among its pages, Access 97 occasionally needs to reformat and print pages. This operation can cause the record count to get out of sync with the number of records. If the numbers do get out of sync, cancel the preview and print the form again to get back to the correct number sequencing.

If a report contains a group subtotal, you can use this technique to number the items in each group consecutively. Figure 9-5 shows how a such a report may appear. In this case, you need to use a *module-level variable* rather than a static variable to hold the record count. The difference between the two variable types follows:

- **Static.** You create this type of variable by using the Static keyword. The variable is preserved while the module remains open but only the procedure that created the variable can use the variable.

- **Module level.** You create this type of variable by using the Dim statement in the declarations section of the module. As with static variables, the value of a module-level variable is preserved as long as the module remains open. Unlike with static variables, however, any procedure in the same module can use module-level variables.

In the following example, a module-level variable is necessary because two procedures need to modify and access the value in the RCount variable:

```
Option Compare Database
Option Explicit
Dim RCount As Integer
```

The first procedure, Detail_Print, increments the value of RCount each time a new record prints, as follows:

```
Private Sub Detail_Print(Cancel As Integer, PrintCount As
            Integer)
    RCount = RCount + 1
    Me![RNum].Caption = RCount & "."
End Sub
```

Orders - All Customers

Dates: 12/1/96 through 12/31/96

		Order #	Date	Sub Total	
ADE Construction & Development					
	1.	640	12/16/96	$240.00	
Totals for ADE Construction & Development				$240.00	
Air Pacific Co.					
	1.	43	12/6/96	$120.00	$7
	2.	975	12/8/96	$759.00	$45
Totals for Air Pacific Co.				$879.00	$52
Automatic Coffee Inc.					
	1.	862	12/18/96	$462.00	$32
Totals for Automatic Coffee Inc.				$462.00	$32

Page: 1

Figure 9-5:
The records in each group are numbered consecutively.

The second procedure is `GroupHeader0_Print`, which occurs each time a new group prints. In Figure 9-5, each customer is a group. The `GroupHeader0_Print` procedure resets the value of `RCount` to 0 so that each group is numbered independently of the other groups, as follows:

```
Private Sub GroupHeader0_Print(Cancel As Integer _
    , PrintCount As Integer)
    RCount = 0
End Sub
```

ON THE CD

> *Form: Report Dialog 02*
> *Report: Report 02 No Sub*
> *Report: Report*

Summary Tables on Reports

The reports shown in the preceding section list information about orders for various customers between a selected range of dates. You use the report *footer section* to generate summary information about the data on the reports, such as totals for numeric columns and the extended price.

In some cases, however, you may want to add a *summary table* to a report, consisting of information beyond a simple summarization of the data in the report's columns. If you print invoices, for example, you may want to include an aged accounts receivable table at the end of the form. Using the example of an orders summary, you may want to include a table at the end of this report that shows the amount of sales in each major sales category — for example, Routers, DSU, Server, Hubs, and Others. Figure 9-6 shows an example of this type of summary, which prints as part of the report footer.

Creating a summary such as the one shown in Figure 9-6 involves several interesting problems. The summary requires information from tables that aren't a part of the Recordset you use to generate the report. The report shown in the figure uses only the data from Orders. To summarize the sales by product type, you need to first locate all the order details for each order on the report so that you can obtain the part numbers. Then you must use the part numbers to look up the part type for that part number in the Parts table.

This process sounds like a lot of work, but you can handle it by using a SQL statement such as the one shown in the following example, which includes a JOIN between the Order Details and Parts tables. If this SQL statement seems a bit much, keep in mind that writing out the SQL text seldom is necessary. Instead, you can use an Access 97 query form, such as the one shown in Figure 9-7, to lay out the links and column specifications. After you have the query choose View⇨SQLView to view the SQL text. You can then copy this text into the module. Keep in mind that you need to edit the copied SQL text to correctly format it as a VBA statement.

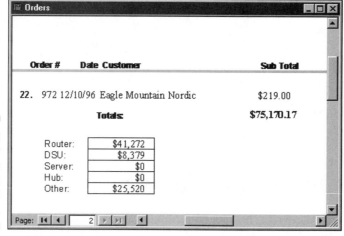

Figure 9-6:
A summary table appearing at the end of a report.

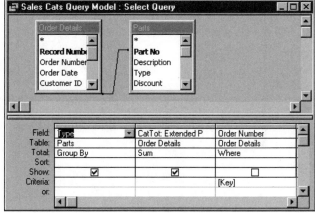

Figure 9-7:
A query
form from
which you
can copy
the desired
SQL
statement
text.

The SQL following statement summarizes sales in any order by product type:

```
SELECT Type, Sum([Extended Price]) FROM [Order Details]
         INNER JOIN Parts ON [Order Details].[Part No] =
         Parts.[Part No] WHERE [Order Number]=1000 GROUP
         BY Type;"
```

You can place this SQL operation into a procedure such as the one in the
following example, called AnalyzeOrder, which can summarize the product
types for any order:

```
Sub AnalyzeOrder(OrderNumber, Summary())
   Dim Q As QueryDef, R As Recordset
   Dim SQLText
   SQLText = "PARAMETERS Key Value;" & _
   "SELECT Type, Sum([Extended Price]) As CatTot " & _
   "FROM [Order Details] INNER JOIN Parts " & _
   "ON [Order Details].[Part No] = Parts.[Part No] " & _
   "WHERE [Order Number]=[Key]" & _
   "GROUP BY Type;"
   Set Q = CurrentDb.CreateQueryDef("")
   Q.SQL = SQLText
   Q.Parameters(0) = OrderNumber
   Set R = Q.OpenRecordset()
   Do Until R.EOF
      Select Case R![Type]
         Case "Router"
             Summary(1) = Summary(1) + R![CatTot]
```

(continued)

(continued)

```
            Case "DSU"
                Summary(2) = Summary(2) + R![CatTot]
            Case "Server"
                Summary(3) = Summary(3) + R![CatTot]
            Case "Hub"
                Summary(4) = Summary(4) + R![CatTot]
            Case Else
                Summary(5) = Summary(5) + R![CatTot]
        End Select
        R.MoveNext
    Loop
End Sub
```

The following aspects of this procedure make it a bit different from some of the other procedures that I discuss elsewhere in this book:

✔ QueryDef. A QueryDef object is the VBA equivalent of a query form. The advantage of using this type of object is that QueryDef supports the Parameters feature. A *parameter* is a value that you can insert into a query without needing to alter the SQL statement. In this case, you use a Key value to determine the order number for the records to summarize. By using an empty string, "", as the QueryDef name, you tell Access 97 to create a temporary QueryDef. The program removes the QueryDef object after the procedure concludes. The OpenRecordset method that you apply to the QueryDef object, Q, creates a Recordset from the QueryDef object. The result is that R contains the summary information you need for the report. The following code shows how a query definition can be used to generate a recordset.

```
Set Q = CurrentDb.CreateQueryDef("")
Q.SQL = SQLText
Q.Parameters(0) = OrderNumber
Set R = Q.OpenRecordset()
```

✔ Summary(). Another unusual element in this procedure is its use of an array variable, Summary(), as one of its arguments. You use the array to solve the problem of passing multiple values between the calling object — in this case, a report that needs the summary information — and the AnalyzeOrder procedure. The next example shows an argument being defined as an array variable:

```
Sub AnalyzeOrder(OrderNumber, Summary())
```

An *array* is a collection of variables that you can reference by their index numbers. In this example, Summary() contains five elements: Summary(1), Summary(2), and so on. The following statement assigns a value to one of the elements in the Summary() array:

```
Summary(1) = Summary(1) + R![CatTot]
```

Access must return five summary values, one for each product type, to the calling procedure. The Select Case structure assigns the element values based on specific product types as shown in the following code fragment:

```
Case "Hub"
    Summary(4) = Summary(4) + R![CatTot]
```

Keep in mind that you can use AnalyzeOrder in many different places to perform the category-based calculation. In this example, a report uses the procedure to add that information to the report's footer section. The procedure inserts totals in a set of controls that print at the end of the report, as shown in Figure 9-8.

Figure 9-8:
A set of controls that you add to the report footer section to display the product categories.

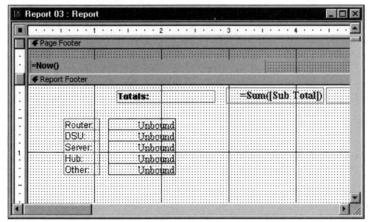

In the report's module, you define an array with five elements in the declarations section. This makes SalesCats a module-level variable that any procedure in the report can access.

```
Option Compare Database
Option Explicit
Dim SalesCats(5)
```

In the `Detail_Print` procedure, `AnalyzeOrder` executes to calculate the summary values for each order. Access 97 stores those values in a *local array* called `OrderCats`. After that array fills with the summary values for this order, the data is copied to the *module-level array* `SalesCats`. As this procedure repeats for each record, the total for all the orders accumulates in `SalesCats`. The accumulated totals remain in this array until the report is ready to print the report footer section because it is a module-level variable. Because `OrderCats` is a local variable, it is reinitialized each time the `Detail_Print` procedure is executed.

```
Private Sub Detail_Print(Cancel As Integer, PrintCount As
            Integer)
   Static RCount As Integer
   Dim OrderCats(5), Pointer
   RCount = RCount + 1
   Me![RNum].Caption = RCount & "."
   AnalyzeOrder Me![Order Number], OrderCats()
   For Pointer = 1 To 5
      SalesCats(Pointer) = _
          SalesCats(Pointer) + OrderCats(Pointer)
   Next
End Sub
```

The final operation takes place during the `Print` event for the report footer. The `ReportFooter_Print` procedure copies each of the values that accumulate in the `SalesCats` array into a control in the report footer. This control corresponds to each product type. A `For` loop performs this copying process. The loop is set for 1 to 5, the number of elements in the array. One trick that I use here is to name the text box controls `SalesCat1`, `SalesCat2`, and so on. Although this is technically not an array, you can refer to the controls by putting `"SalesCat"` with the `Pointer` value to produce the names of the controls that correspond to the elements in the array.

```
Private Sub ReportFooter_Print(Cancel As Integer,
            PrintCount As Integer)
   Dim Pointer
   For Pointer = 1 To 5
      Me("Salescat" & Pointer) = SalesCats(Pointer)
   Next
End Sub
```

> **Form: Report Dialog 03**
> **Report: Report 03**
> **Module: Report Functions**
> **Procedure: AnalyzeOrder**

Multiple Selections

Besides their appearance, one of the differences between combo boxes and list boxes is that list boxes make possible multiple selections. The form shown in Figure 9-9 displays in a list box the names of customers. Notice that I selected more than one of the names in the list. The purpose of the form is to enable you to select one or more customers whose data will be included in the report. You can use VBA to automatically print all these reports by clicking a single button.

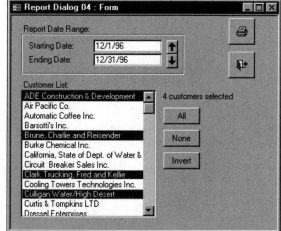

Figure 9-9:
A form that enables you to make multiple selections of names from one list.

The list box shown in Figure 9-9 is called `Customer`. To create a multiple-selection list box, you must set the `Multi Select` property, which is on the Other tab in the property sheet of the list box control. You have the following two options for the `Multi Select` property:

- ✔ **Simple.** Each mouse click toggles the item between selected and unselected status.
- ✔ **Extended.** This method of selecting items is similar to what you use in Window 95 lists; in making extended selections, you use the Shift and Ctrl keys in combination with the mouse to select items.

In a multiple-selection list box, the items in the list form a collection of items. The `ItemData` property enables you to refer to the items in the list by index number, starting with zero. The following statement prints the text of the first item in the list:

```
? forms![report dialog 04]![customer].ItemData(0)
```

The `ListCount` property returns the number of items in the list, as follows:

```
? forms![report dialog 04]![customer].ListCount
```

The `ItemsSelected` collection is a subcollection of the control that consists of only currently selected items. The following statement returns the total number of items selected in the control:

```
? forms![report dialog 04]![customer].ItemsSelected.count
```

The `Selected` property enables you to determine the current status of any item in the list that is `True`, for selected, or `False`, for unselected. The following statement returns a `True` or a `False` value, depending on the selected status of the first item in the list:

```
? forms![report dialog 04]![customer].selected(0)
```

You can use these collections and properties to perform a variety of operations on and with the list box. The form includes a label, `HowMany`, that displays a count of the total number of items you select by including the `ItemsSelected.Count` property in its caption. The `Customer_Click` procedure ensures that this label updates after every selection. This event also triggers if the user uses the spacebar to make a selection in the list box.

```
Private Sub Customer_Click()
    Me![HowMany].Caption = _
    Me![Customer].ItemsSelected.Count _
    & " customers selected"
End Sub
```

As Figure 9-9 shows, you use three buttons to change the selections in the list box. All three automatically update the `HowMany` control to maintain an accurate count of the selected items, as follows:

✔ **All.** This button selects all the items in the list by using the `Command19_Click` procedure shown in the following example. This procedure uses the `ListCount` property to loop through all the items in the list box. The `Selected` property for each item is set to `True`. After the procedure is complete, all the items in the list are highlighted.

```
Private Sub Command19_Click()
    Dim C As Control, Pointer, CustName
    Set C = Me![Customer]
    For Pointer = 0 To C.ListCount - 1
```

```
        C.Selected(1Row:=Pointer) = True
    Next
    Me![HowMany].Caption = _
    Me![Customer].ItemsSelected.Count _
    & " customers selected"
End Sub
```

✔ **None.** This button executes a procedure, shown in the following
example, that sets the selected property of all the items in the list to
False. The highlight disappears from all the items in the list.

```
Private Sub Command20_Click()
    Dim C As Control, Pointer, CustName
    Set C = Me![Customer]
    For Pointer = 0 To C.ListCount - 1
        C.Selected(1Row:=Pointer) = False
    Next
    Me![HowMany].Caption = _
    Me![Customer].ItemsSelected.Count _
    & " customers selected"
End Sub
```

✔ **Invert.** This button inverts the selection, making the selected items
unselected and the unselected items selected.

```
Private Sub Command21_Click()
    Dim C As Control, Pointer, CustName
    Set C = Me![Customer]
    For Pointer = 0 To C.ListCount - 1
        C.Selected(1Row:=Pointer) = _
        C.Selected(1Row:=Pointer) + 1
    Next
    Me![HowMany].Caption = _
    Me![Customer].ItemsSelected.Count _
    & " customers selected"
End Sub
```

The key button on the form is the Print button. In this case, the procedure associated with that button needs to evaluate the `ItemsSelected` collection for the `Customer` list box. The procedure combines the selections so that one report prints for each name you select from the list. The simplest way to work through this collection is by using a `For Each` statement. The following example assigns the names of the selected customers to the variable `CustName`:

```
For Each CustName In Me![Customer].ItemsSelected
```

The entire `PrintButton_Click` procedure revolves around this statement. The following procedure executes one `OpenReport` method for each item in the `ItemsSelected` collection:

```
Private Sub PrintButton_Click()
    Const RName = "Multiple Selection"
    Dim CustName, WClause
    For Each CustName In Me![Customer].ItemsSelected
        Me![NowPrinting].Caption = CustName
        WClause = "[Date] Between #" & _
            Me![Start] & "# AND #" & _
            Me![End] & "# AND [Customer] = '" & _
            CustName & "'"
        DoCmd.OpenReport _
            Reportname:=RName, _
            WhereCondition:=WClause
    Next
    For CustName = 0 To Me![Customer].ListCount - 1
        Me![Customer].Selected(lRow:=CustName) = False
    Next
End Sub
```

The result is a series of reports that a single click of the Print button generates. Keep in mind that this technique works only if you send the reports directly to the printer. If you display the report in the Preview window, only the first report appears on-screen. If you close that report, none of the others appears.

> **Form: Report Dialog 04**
> **Report: Multiple Selection**

Fast Form Letters

The primary purpose of Access 97 reports is to output information in row and column reports. If you want to send form letters — a document that uses paragraph-oriented text — you typically use a paragraph-oriented application, such as Microsoft Word, to take advantage of its merge functions to interact with Access 97 data.

You can, however, also use VBA to automatically generate simple paragraph-style form letters directly from an Access 97 form. This process is a lot faster than that of merging with Word, and the results print much faster.

The basic idea behind this technique is shown in Figure 9-10. The figure shows an Access 97 report form that contains a single, large label control. If you enter large amounts of text into a label control, Access 97 automatically wraps the text to the next line, just as a text editor or word processing program does. You can even start new lines by pressing the Shift+Enter combination as you're typing within the control.

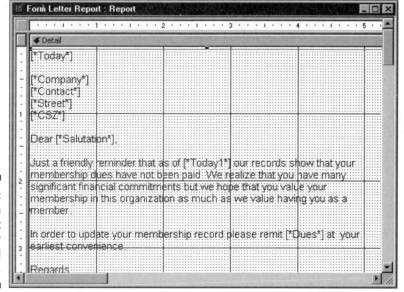

Figure 9-10:
A form letter that you enter as a label on a form.

In addition to the text, the control contains some special text items that you insert where you want to enter information from a table or a form. You enter these special items, called *tokens*, by using a distinct format, as shown in the following example. The token is simply a word or phrase that you later replace with data from a form or a record. In this case, you enclose the tokens in [**] to differentiate them from the normal text. The [**] have no special meaning. This pattern simply is unlikely to appear in normal text.

```
[*name*]
```

The tokens shown in Figure 9-10 represent items that you need to fill in with data from some other source, such as a form similar to the one shown in Figure 9-11. The goal is to print a form letter for the record that appears in the form after you click the form's Send Dues Letter button.

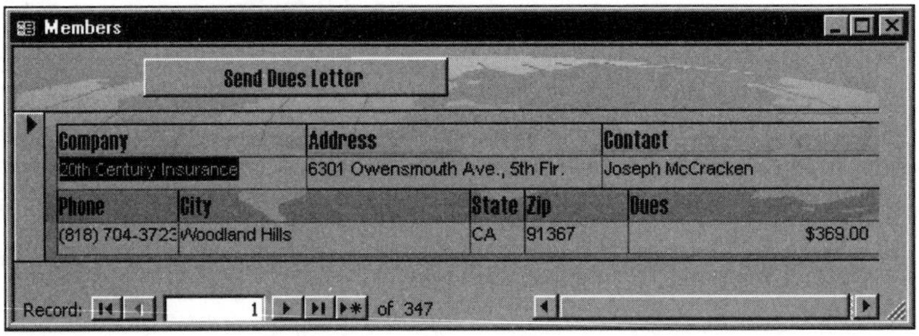

Figure 9-11:
A form for which you can print a form letter.

Why use a Label control? Isn't a text box just as good . . . or better? In this case, a text box doesn't work because an unbound text box can't retain the form letter after you close the form. A Label control, on the other hand, stores the text that you enter into it as its Label property, which the control then retains, along with all the other properties of the form, so that the form letter is still there every time you open the report.

The Replace Function

The key to this form letter technique is an Access 97 Basic function called Replace(). The purpose of this function is to locate a token within a block of text and replace the token with some other text.

The first line in the procedure for the Replace() function lists three arguments, as shown in the following example and described in the following list:

```
Function Replace (Block, Token, ReplaceText)
```

✔ Block. The Block argument is the overall block of text that you're modifying. In the current example, the block is all the text within a Label control on a report. You can reference this text by using the Caption property.

> ✔ Token. This argument is a text value that indicates the portion of the block that you're changing. In the example in Figure 9-10, the tokens are items such as [*Name*] or [*Dues*]. The text of the tokens doesn't matter. The only function of these tokens is to mark the locations in the text where you intend to insert various replacement values.

> ✔ ReplaceText. This argument is the information you intend to insert into the block. In the current example, the form letter report obtains this information from the Access form that is displayed before you print the form letter.

How does this procedure accomplish the goal of inserting text into some location within the block of text? The technique is fairly simple. First, you divide the block of text into the following two parts:

> ✔ Front. This part contains all the text from the beginning to the location of the token.

> ✔ Back. This part contains all the text starting after the token and continuing to the end of the block.

The two parts, Front and Back, combine with ReplaceText in between to create the new block of text.

The first step in the process is to calculate the locations of the token within the text. You accomplish this task with the aid of the InStr function. This function locates the first occurrence of one item (Token) with another (Block). Notice that you must subtract 1 from the InStr() value so that the value doesn't include the first character in the token itself, as follows:

```
StartToken = InStr(Block, Token) - 1
```

You then use StartToken to calculate where the end section of the text begins by adding the length of the token, Len (Token), plus 1, as follows:

```
EndToken = StartToken + Len(Token) + 1
```

After you calculate these two values, you can break the text into the two parts — the text before and the text after the token — by using the Left() and Mid() functions, as shown in the following example. Left() starts with the first character in the block and ends at the character indicated by the StartToken value. Mid() begins at EndToken and includes the remainder of the block.

```
Front = Left(Block, StartToken)
Back = Mid(Block, EndToken)
```

You reassemble the pieces in the final statement, as shown in the following example. You insert the `ReplaceText` between the two parts. Notice that setting the reassembled text to the variable `Replace` (the name of the function) causes the function to return the modified text as its value.

```
Replace = Front & ReplaceText & Back
```

The entire `Replace` procedure is shown in the following example:

```
Function Replace (Block, Token, ReplaceText)
    StartToken = InStr(Block, Token) - 1
    EndToken = StartToken + Len(Token) + 1
    Front = Left(Block, StartToken)
    Back = Mid(Block, EndToken)
    Replace = Front & ReplaceText & Back
End Function
```

You can put the `Replace` function to work in a procedure that specifies how to replace tokens in the `Label` control in Figure 9-10 with actual text from the form in Figure 9-11.

In this example, a function called `FillInForm()` links together the tokens in the report and the data in the form. The following procedure uses two objects: `FillIn` is the form that contains the information you need to fill out the form letter, and `Template` is the label control on the report that contains the form letter that includes the tokens you need to replace.

```
Sub FillInForm(FillIn As Form, Template As Control)
```

The rest of the procedure is simply a matter of executing one `Replace()` function for each token. To insert the correct date into the letter, for example, you replace the `[*Today*]` token with the value of the `Date` function as illustrated by the following code fragment:

```
With Template
    .Caption = Replace( _
    Block:=Template.Caption, _
    Token:="[*Today*]", _
    ReplaceText:=Format(Date, "mmmm dd, yyyy"))
```

In some cases, you replace the token with an expression. You replace the `[*CSZ*]` token, for example, with an expression that combines the city, state, and zip code fields as illustrated in the code following:

```
.Caption = Replace( _
   Block:=Template.Caption, _
   Token:="[*CSZ*]", _
   ReplaceText:=FillIn![City] & "," _
   & FillIn![State] & " " & FillIn!Zip)
```

The [*Salutation*] token doesn't correspond to a field because you enter the contact's first and last names into a single field. For this token, you use an expression that picks out the portion of the contact name from the first part of the contact field, as follows:

```
.Caption = Replace( _
   Block:=Template.Caption, _
   Token:="[*Salutation*]", _
   ReplaceText:=Left(FillIn![Contact], _
   InStr(FillIn![Contact], " ") - 1))
```

The following example shows the entire procedure:

```
Sub FillInForm(FillIn As Form, Template As Control)
   With Template
   .Caption = Replace( _
      Block:=Template.Caption, _
      Token:="[*Today*]", _
      ReplaceText:=Format(Date, "mmmm dd, yyyy"))
   .Caption = Replace( _
      Block:=Template.Caption, _
      Token:="[*Today1*]", _
      ReplaceText:=Format(Date, "m/d/yy"))
   .Caption = Replace( _
      Block:=Template.Caption, _
      Token:="[*Company*]", _
      ReplaceText:=FillIn![Company])
   .Caption = Replace( _
      Block:=Template.Caption, _
      Token:="[*Contact*]", _
      ReplaceText:=FillIn![Contact])
   .Caption = Replace( _
      Block:=Template.Caption, _
      Token:="[*Street*]", _
      ReplaceText:=FillIn![Address])
   .Caption = Replace( _
      Block:=Template.Caption, _
```

(continued)

(continued)

```
      Token:="[*CSZ*]", _
      ReplaceText:=FillIn![City] & "," _
        & FillIn![State] & " " & FillIn!Zip)
    .Caption = Replace( _
      Block:=Template.Caption, _
      Token:="[*Salutation*]", _
      ReplaceText:=Left(FillIn![Contact], _
      InStr(FillIn![Contact], " ") - 1))
    .Caption = Replace( _
      Block:=Template.Caption, _
      Token:="[*Dues*]", _
      ReplaceText:=Format(FillIn![Dues], "currency"))
    End With
End Sub
```

You connect this procedure to the form letter by entering a call to the
FillInForm procedure. The call is made from the Detail_Format event
procedure of the Form Letter Report report form, shown next. The
procedure specifies the source of the data — in this case, the Members
form — and the control to format (the FormLetter label control).

```
Private Sub Detail_Format(Cancel As Integer,_
FormatCount As Integer)
    FillInForm Forms![Members], Me![FormLetter]
End Sub
```

In the form, you assign the following procedure to the Send Dues Letter
button, which opens the form letter. The FillInForm procedure fills the
form letter with the data appearing on the form.

```
Private Sub Command16_Click()
    Docmd.OpenReport ReportName:= "Form Letter Report", _
    view:=acViewPreview
End Sub
```

The result is that you can print a simple form letter, including data that
Access 97 inserts into paragraph text, simply by clicking the Send Dues
Letter button in the form. You have no recordset to manipulate in this case,
because the procedures are what fill in the report, which isn't bound to any
recordset. Because you don't save as part of the report any changes that the
VBA procedures make to the control, you can use the same form over and
over again to print any number of reminder letters. Printing the form letter
doesn't destroy the tokens.

> *Form: Members*
> *Report: Form Letter Report*
> *Module: Report Functions*
> *Procedure: Replace, FillInForm*

E-mail, HTML, and Other Output

In general, you either display reports and other Access 97 objects on-screen or send them to a printer. Two other methods, however, provide additional ways in which you can output information:

- ✔ `Output To`. This method enables you to output a table, a query, a form or a report to a file that's created in a non-Access 97 file format. This method supports the following formats:

    - *HTML*. This option creates an HTML document from the specified object. Tables and queries generate a single HTML page that contains the full output text in a cell/table format. For forms and reports, you output the data in pages that correspond to the pages that you'd send to a printer.

    - *RTF*. The object converts to Rich Text Format. Many applications read RTF files. This format retains many document formatting characteristics but without binary codes. You can send RTF documents without conversion over the Internet.

    - *TXT*. The document converts to a standard DOS text document. You lose all formatting, retaining only the character information. The format stores tables and queries as comma-separated value-format files. Forms and reports print as unstructured text.

    - XLS. The object converts to an Excel 97 XLS spreadsheet format.

- ✔ `SendObject`. This method is similar to the `Output To` method, except that Access 97 inserts the output document as an attachment to an e-mail message (if you use an e-mail system compatible with Microsoft Office, such as MS-Mail or Exchange). If your e-mail program is not running, this statement automatically starts the e-mail program and generates a new mail message. You have the same document format options as you do with the `Output To method`.

Figure 9-12 shows a format with a set of check boxes for printing, creating the output as a HTML Web document, or sending the output as an e-mail message.

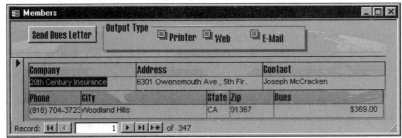

Figure 9-12:
Output
options
added to
the form's
design.

The following procedure activates after you click the Send Dues Letter button. Depending on which check box you select, the procedure sends the output to the printer, stores the output in an HTML document format, or converts the output to text and embeds it as an attachment to an e-mail message.

```
Private Sub Command16_Click()
Select Case Me![OutputType]
   Case 1
   DoCmd.OpenReport ReportName:="Form Letter Report", _
       view:=acViewPreview
   Case 2
      DoCmd.OutputTo ObjectType:=acOutputReport, _
          Objectname:="Form Letter Report", _
          OutputFormat:=acFormatHTML, _
          OutputFile:="C:\FLtr.Htm"
   Case 3
      DoCmd.SendObject ObjectType:=acSendReport, _
          Objectname:="Form Letter Report", _
          OutputFormat:=acFormatTXT, _
          To:="bruce krumm", CC:="walter lafish", _
          Subject:="Dues Notice", _
          EditMessage:=False
End Select
End Sub
```

If the user selects the e-mail option, for example, Access 97 inserts a text version of the format letter report as an attachment to an e-mail message.

> *Form: Members 01*
> *Report: Form Letter Report*
> *Module: Report Functions*
> *Procedure: Replace, FillInForm*

Part IV

Active Controls and Objects

The 5th Wave
By Rich Tennant

Arthur inadvertently replaces his mouse pad with a Ouija board. For the rest of the day, he receives messages from the spectral world.

YOU WILL FORGET YOUR PASSWORD. YOUR HARD DISK WILL CRASH AAAHAHAHAHA

In this part . . .

As great as Access 97 is, many people who use Access don't buy just Access. Instead they buy the whole Microsoft Office package, a package that is getting bigger and more complex with each new issue.

But the components of the Microsoft Office have more in common than the fact that they come in the same box. Microsoft has invested heavily in a technology that ties together all of the components in the Office suite not only with each other, but with other Windows 95 and Internet applications as well as with the Back Office suite of network products.

This technology used to be called OLE (object linking and embedding) but is now called ActiveX (sounds like something they spray on corn flakes to make them more nutritious). Whatever you call it, the chapters in Part IV explain how you can take advantage of the ActiveX features in Access 97.

Chapter 10

Controls and ActiveX

● ●

In This Chapter

▶ What's in a name?

▶ Working with object fields

▶ Using an OLE object field

▶ Using Word 97 as an ActiveX component

● ●

*I*s *ActiveX* something new? The answer is . . . both yes and no. This ambiguous response results from the turmoil in the computer industry that the rapid emergence of Internet technologies has caused. Although applications such as word processing or spreadsheets don't directly concern the Internet itself, the Net can provide a common method of communication among users of different types of computers and software.

Having a common means of communication doesn't do much good if the stuff you're communicating comes in a variety of incompatible formats. (The concept's a bit like being able to place a phone call to any country in the world but not necessarily being able to understand the language of the person on the other end.) You have the communications link but no meaningful communication. ActiveX is the key.

> **Database Folder: Chapter 10**
> **Database File: ACTX.MDB**

To begin, load the database for Chapter 10, ACTX.MDB. Click the Forms tab to display a list of the forms that I discuss in this chapter.

What's in a Name?

World Wide Web users get around the incompatibility problem by limiting all Web communication to a special document format called *HTML*. (Take a look at Chapter 12 for the straight skinny on HTML.) But what about the type of information you store in Office 97 applications such as Word 97,

Excel 97, or Access 97? One solution is to convert Office 97 data to HTML (more on that in Chapter 12). The other solution is to somehow embed sophisticated objects such as spreadsheets inside other objects, such as HTML Web documents.

And here is where you encounter a technology that Microsoft has been working on since the first release of Microsoft Office. This new technology, *OLE*, stands for Object Linking and Embedding. (You pronounce it *O-lay*.) The idea behind OLE is that an application can play two roles: You can use the application to create *native objects* — for example, Word 97 creates documents and Excel 97 creates spreadsheets — or the application can function as a container for other objects — for example, Word 97 may contain a spreadsheet or a chart that you created in Excel 97, *embedded* into a Word 97 document.

This concept sounds a lot like the idea of embedding those same types of sophisticated objects in HTML Web documents. Microsoft put all the old OLE technologies and new Internet technologies together and gave the combined concept a new name: *ActiveX*. Thus, ActiveX is both new and old, depending on what part you work with. The older OLE terminology is built right into Access 97. To embed an ActiveX object in an Access 97 database, for example, you place the object into an OLE Object-type field. Both OLE and ActiveX refer to the same thing, but the older terminology — for example, *OLE object* — appears in the Access 97 table property sheet.

Unfortunately, you'll find no easy way to stay consistent in the use of the terms OLE and ActiveX. If you stick with OLE, some folks may accuse you of using an obsolete technology. If you refer to ActiveX, other people may wonder why you store ActiveX stuff in OLE fields and controls. In this book, I use *ActiveX* and *OLE* interchangeably. I use *OLE* only if the term appears in a property sheet or a VBA statement.

Working with ActiveX

Most of the Access 97 programming techniques you read about in this book involve the use of VBA to manipulate the methods and properties that the various objects in the Access 97 model support.

But Microsoft designed its object model to encompass more than a single application and the set of objects that application supports. The goal of the object model is to break down the barriers between applications so that objects from different applications can interact to form integrated applications. VBA is designed to work not only with Access 97 objects but also with objects that other applications provide, including those in the Office 97 suite (such as Excel 97, PowerPoint 97, and Word 97), plus other network applications such as Exchange, SQL Server, and Internet Server II.

Microsoft uses the name *ActiveX* to represent a set of technologies that enable objects of different types to interact in a common structure. Access 97 can integrate objects that you create in other applications with its set of database objects. This integration takes three forms:

- ✔ **Object fields and controls.** In addition to the text-, number-, and date-type fields that you can store in Access 97 database tables, you can also add OLE Object fields to store and display ActiveX objects that you create in other applications.

- ✔ **ActiveX components.** An ActiveX component is a program that can function as either a stand-alone application or an ActiveX object server. You can use Word 97, for example, as a stand-alone word processing program or to provide word processing services to another application, such as Access 97, that can function as an ActiveX controller. If you use Word 97 as an ActiveX server, your Access 97 VBA program sends commands directly to Word 97 as if Word 97 were a part of the Access 97 system. All Microsoft Office 97 applications are ActiveX components.

- ✔ **ActiveX controls.** An ActiveX control is similar to an ActiveX component in that the control is a separate application that provides Access 97 with special objects that would not normally be part of the Access 97 object model. Controls, however, can't function as stand-alone programs. You can use them only within the context of some other Access 97 object, such as a form. Microsoft supplies Access 97 with an ActiveX `Calendar` control, for example, that builds in a calendar display you can use in Access 97 forms to provide a perpetual calendar.

This chapter looks at examples of all three types of ActiveX features.

Working with Object Fields

The OLE Object field enables you to store objects in your database that you create in other applications. Examples of the type of information that you can store in an OLE Object field include Word 97 documents and templates, Excel 97 workbooks, worksheets, and charts, and PowerPoint 97 slides and slide shows.

An important point to keep in mind is that any stored OLE object is the equivalent of a file you store on a drive. If you store a Word 97 document as an object, for example, you store all the information you would store if you saved the document as a disk file.

The OLE Object field becomes an alternative storage location for blocks of data that you create in any application that supports ActiveX. Why bother? Because, after a while, keeping track of a whole bunch of files gets tedious.

Suppose, for example, that you want to create a historical database of all the U.S. presidents and include PowerPoint 97 slides with portraits of each one. Storing the data itself is easy, because you make one record for each president. But each picture is a separate PowerPoint 97 file. By loading the pictures into an OLE Object field, you can store the picture right along with the name, dates, and other information about the president. This capability greatly simplifies the job of locating, printing, or copying information because you can combine both text and graphics in a single record.

Using an OLE Object field

The simplest use of ActiveX is seen in storing non-Access 97 data in OLE Object fields. You can store a wide variety of objects in this type of field. For a list of the object types or servers available on your screen, choose Insert⇨Object. An *object server* is a program that creates objects such as charts, pictures, or spreadsheets, that you can insert into an OLE Object-type field.

Figure 10-1 shows a simple form into which you can insert an OLE object. Notice that you can't insert an object into an OLE Object field while editing a table, a query, or a form in the Datasheet view. To insert, view, or edit the contents of the OLE Object field, you must create and display a form that contains an OLE bound frame control that you bind to the OLE Object field. In the following example, the control is called Picture.

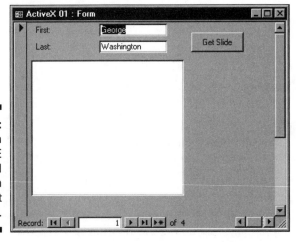

Figure 10-1:
A form with an OLE Object field bound to an OLE Object control.

You can use a VBA procedure to load an object into an OLE frame control. The first step is to set the Class property of the control. You must register each unique type of ActiveX object with Windows 95 as a specific class. A PowerPoint 97 slide, for example, has the class name PowerPoint.Show.8. The following statement sets the class of the object to insert:

```
Me![Picture].Class = "PowerPoint.Show.8"
```

Registration of object classes is a key component of the ActiveX technology. The entries in the system's registry connect an ActiveX object with the application in which you create the object. After you double-click an ActiveX object, Windows 95 loads the application in which you created the object, using information that Windows stores about that object in the system registry.

The next step is to set the type of OLE operation permitted in this control. You can limit the control to linking only, embedding only, or either, as shown in the following statement:

```
Me![Picture].OLETypeAllowed = acOLEEither
```

A linked object simply stores the object's filename. You need the disk file to edit or modify the object. An embedded object is a copy of the original file. After you embed an object, you can delete the original file, because you've copied all the information into the database field.

The third step connects the field to a file on the disk. The SourceDoc property tells Access where to find the original object. The following statement assigns the document name GW.PPT as the source document of the Picture control:

```
Me![Picture].SourceDoc = "gw.ppt"
```

After you specify the SourceDoc, Access 97 doesn't create the object until you use the Action property. After the Action property is set to acOLE CreateEmbed, Access uses the information in the SourceDoc and Class properties to create the embedded ActiveX object. The following statement embeds an object into the Picture control:

```
Me![Picture].Action = acOLECreateEmbed
```

The following procedure enables you to insert a PowerPoint 97 slide into the OLE Object field. Notice that the SizeMode property of the control determines how the picture appears within the control. acOLESizeStretch sets the size mode to stretch so that the image fills the entire control.

```
Private Sub Command3_Click()
    Const HomeDrive = "Q"
    Const HomePath = "Q:\Access Prog Dummies\Chapter 11\"
    ChDrive HomeDrive
    ChDir HomePath
    Dim PixName
```

(continued)

(continued)

```
    PixName = InputBox("Enter Slide File Name:")
    Me![Picture].Class = "PowerPoint.Show.8"
    Me![Picture].OLETypeAllowed = acOLEEither
    Me![Picture].SourceDoc = HomePath & PixName & ".ppt"
    Me![Picture].Action = acOLECreateEmbed
    Me![Picture].SizeMode = acOLESizeStretch
End Sub
```

The procedure prompts the user to enter the name of the file that corresponds to the president's name in the record (in this example, GW, JA, TJ, or JM). Access 97 then inserts the PowerPoint 97 slide into the field and the control displays the slide, as shown in Figure 10-2. Keep in mind that the procedure inserts the picture into the field, not simply the control. You can display the slide in any form that binds a control to the OLE Object field.

Figure 10-2: A form with an OLE Object field bound to an OLE Object control.

ON THE CD

Form: ActiveX 01

Determining the OLE class name

A critical piece of information in dealing with ActiveX objects is the class names of the objects. Most class names follow a logical pattern based on the application name and the object type. Table 10-1 lists object classes that the Microsoft Office 97 suite most commonly uses. By convention, the class names of Microsoft objects begin with the name of the source application, followed by the object name and the version number. The elements are linked by periods. Nothing, however, requires that class names follow this pattern.

Table 10-1   Some Class Names for Office 97 ActiveX Components

Object Type	Class Name
Access 97	Access.Application.8
Access 97 blank database	Access.BlankDatabaseTemplate
Access 97 database	Access.Database
Excel 97	Excel.Application.8
Excel 97 worksheet	Excel.Sheet.8
Excel 97 chart	Excel.Chart.8
Word 97	Word.Application.8
Word 97 document	Word.Document.8
Word 97 template	Word.Template.8
PowerPoint 97	PowerPoint.Application.8
PowerPoint 97 slide	PowerPoint.Slide.8
PowerPoint 97 slide show	PowerPoint.SlideShow.8

If you don't know the class name of the object with which you want to work, you can find it in a few ways. The first is a trial-and-error approach:

1. **Open a new blank Access 97 form.**

2. **Choose Insert⇨Object from the menu to open the Object dialog box.**

3. **In the Object Type list, select the type of object with which you want to work.**

4. **Click Create New, and then click OK.**

   Depending on the type of OLE object you select, what happens after you make the selection varies. Typically, a program of some kind opens a window with a new blank document; for example, Excel opens a new workbook. The program that executes after you create a new OLE Object is called the *object server application*.

5. **Press Alt+F4 to terminate the object server application that your object selection activated.**

6. **Open the control's property sheet (if it's not already open) by choosing View⇨Properties from the menu bar.**

7. **Click the Data tab of the property sheet.**

   The class name appears in the Class property box.

8. **After you have the name you need, delete the unneeded control.**

This approach is okay if you don't need to figure out too many class names. The other approach is to open the Windows registry and read from the list of class names. To do so, follow these steps:

1. **Click the Windows 95 Start button, and choose Run from the Start menu.**

2. **Type** regedit **and then press Enter.**

3. **Double-click HKEY_CLASSES_ROOT in the list of folders that appears.**

4. **If you want to find a class name based on the file extension that the native application uses, scroll down the list of extensions and click the extension name — for example, .doc.**

   The right side of the screen shows the class name — for example, {Default} "Word.Document.8".

5. **To see a list of classes, scroll down the list of extensions past the last one (for example,** .zip**), as shown in Figure 10-3.**

Figure 10-3:
The Windows registration database lists the class names.

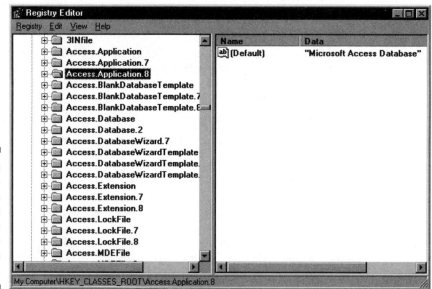

As you close the Regedit program, never save changes you made unless you're a *very* experienced programmer who knows *exactly* how the registry works. Accidentally changing a registry entry can result in programs failing to run correctly — or even run at all.

Changing objects

A remarkable feature of ActiveX involves its capability to use the program that stores the object to manipulate the contents of that object. The object shown in Figure 10-2, for example, is a PowerPoint 97 slide. You can manipulate the contents and the appearance of that slide by writing a VBA procedure that executes methods or changes the properties of the slide object.

PowerPoint 97 objects, for example, consist of one or more slides. From an object point of view, all the slides in a PowerPoint 97 file are a collection. In VBA, all collections have a Count property that returns the number of objects in the collection. (Take a look at Chapter 1 for more information about the Count property.) In theory, you can use VBA to determine the number of slides in the embedded PowerPoint 97 object by requesting the Count property of the Slides collection, as follows:

```
MsgBox ????.Slides.Count
```

Missing from this statement, where the ???? appears, is the name of the object. The trick in using an OLE Object field is to keep in mind the difference between the control that contains the OLE Object (which belongs to Access 97) and the object inside the control (which, in this case, belongs to PowerPoint 97). Me![Picture] is the name of the OLE frame control. To refer to objects inside the control, you must use the Object property:

```
Me![Picture].Object
```

The following statement displays the Slides.Count property of the PowerPoint 97 slide inside the [Picture] control:

```
MsgBox Me![Picture].Object.Slides.Count
```

The following procedure executes from a button on the form shown in Figure 10-4 and displays the value in a message box. In this case, the PowerPoint 97 object consists of one slide.

```
Private Sub Command11_Click()
    Dim Pix As Object
    Set Pix = Me![Picture].Object
    MsgBox Pix.Slides.Count
End Sub
```

Figure 10-4:
VBA
extracts
information
from the
object
within an
OLE frame
control.

You can simplify the code in the procedure by creating object variables. With object variables, you write a statement that looks similar to this:

```
MsgBox Me![Picture].Object.Slides.Count
```

The procedure creates a variable by using the `Object` type. You can use an `Object` type variable to hold any type of ActiveX or Access 97 object. This enables you to refer to the ActiveX object simply as `Pix`. The following code fragment defines an object variable:

```
Dim Pix As Object
Set Pix = Me![Picture].Object
```

This technique is helpful if you use the object name in several different statements. Suppose, for example, that you want to change the color of the background of a slide. You can do so through VBA. In the PowerPoint 97 object model, the color of the background is set by the following two properties:

```
Background.Fill.ForeColor.RGB
Background.Fill.BackColor.RGB
```

The following procedure displays the current background and foreground colors in hex format — `FFFFFF` for white or `000000` for black:

```
Private Sub Command12_Click()
   Dim Pix As Object
   Set Pix = Me![Picture].Object
```

```
    MsgBox Hex(Pix.Slides(1).Background.Fill.ForeColor.RGB)
    MsgBox Hex(Pix.Slides(1).Background.Fill.BackColor.RGB)
End Sub
```

The form is shown in Figure 10-5. The procedure adds a control to the form that enables you to select a background color.

Figure 10-5:
You add a color picker control to the form.

To make the options more realistic, the Form_Load procedure sets the colors of the labels in the option group to correspond to the color name that appears in the label. The label that contains the text *Yellow,* for example, has its background color set to yellow. The procedure also sets the value of the check box controls to the value for that color — that is, the procedure assigns the check box for yellow, PickYellow, the value of yellow, RGB(255, 255, 0), as its option value. Whenever the user makes a color selection, therefore, the value of the frame control is the RGB color value that creates that color. This setup enables you to use the control's value to directly set the background color of the object inside the frame.

```
Private Sub Form_Load()
    Dim White, Black, Yellow, Blue, Red, Cyan, Green
    White = RGB(255, 255, 255)
    Black = RGB(0, 0, 0)
    Yellow = RGB(255, 255, 0)
    Green = RGB(0, 255, 0)
    Red = RGB(255, 0, 0)
    Cyan = RGB(0, 255, 255)
```

(continued)

(continued)

```
    Blue = RGB(0, 0, 255)
    With Me("White")
       .BackStyle = 1
       .BackColor = White
    End With
    With Me("Black")
       .BackStyle = 1
       .BackColor = Black
       .ForeColor = White
    End With
    With Me("Yellow")
       .BackStyle = 1
       .BackColor = Yellow
    End With
    With Me("Green")
       .BackStyle = 1
       .BackColor = Green
    End With
    With Me("Red")
       .BackStyle = 1
       .BackColor = Red
    End With
    With Me("Cyan")
       .BackStyle = 1
       .BackColor = Cyan
    End With
    With Me("Blue")
       .BackStyle = 1
       .BackColor = Blue
    End With
    Me![Pickwhite].OptionValue = White
    Me![PickBlack].OptionValue = Black
    Me![PickYellow].OptionValue = Yellow
    Me![PickGreen].OptionValue = Green
    Me![PickRed].OptionValue = Red
    Me![PickBlue].OptionValue = Blue
    Me![PickCyan].OptionValue = Cyan
End Sub
```

The background of the object links to the selected color by means of the
`SetBackColor` procedure, which uses the value of the option group
control, `SelectedColor`, as the argument for the ActiveX object's background color property:

```
Sub SetBackColor()
    Dim Pix As Object
    Set Pix = Me![Picture].Object
    Pix.Slides(1).Background.Fill.ForeColor.RGB _
        = Me![SelectedColor]
End Sub
```

The SetBackColor procedure executes each time you display a record and whenever you make a change to the selected color. The SelectedColor_- AfterUpdate and Form_Current procedures also call SetBackColor after the user's interaction with the form triggers their corresponding events.

```
Private Sub SelectedColor_AfterUpdate()
    SetBackColor
End Sub
```

```
Private Sub Form_Current()
    SetBackColor
End Sub
```

The form can convert the image of a president (see Figure 10-5) into a silhouette by setting the background color of the slide object to black.

Form: ActiveX 02

The technique that I discuss in this section applies to a wide variety of ActiveX objects, including the Microsoft Graph program that comes with Office 97 to implement the graphing feature in Access 97. Any control that contains a chart in an Access 97 form is really an ActiveX container.

Look at the chart contained in the form in Figure 10-6. This layout is the type that you can create in Access 97 without any programming. The Chart automatically adjusts its contents based on the Recordset specified in the RowSource property of the graph control.

Although the contents of the chart adjust to a change in the values in the Recordset, the same is not true of the settings for the characters that format characteristics. The chart title and the layout of the labels on the axis, for example, are set at the time you insert or manually edit the chart control (by using the default values).

What's interesting in Figure 10-6 is that the title and the axis labels adjust dynamically to reflect any changes in the Recordset of the chart. The chart heading contains the number of years that the values in the chart represent. You can't set the chart title to match the actual range of years in advance, because that range changes each time you display the chart with a different range of values.

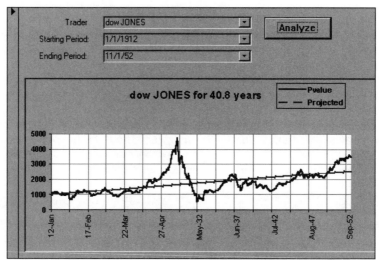

Figure 10-6:
A chart in
Access 97
that you
modify by
using
ActiveX
object
processing.

The solution is to use ActiveX processing on the chart, which is actually an ActiveX object that you insert as a control on the form. In this case, you need to modify two objects: the chart title and the category axis. You assign the object within the control to the variable Chart. Then you define the title and axis objects as elements within the Chart object.

```
Dim Chart As Object, t As Object, Ax As Object
Set Chart = Me![ValueChart].Object
Set t = Chart.ChartTitle
Set Ax = Chart.Axes(xlCategory)
```

The following procedure, which a change in the Recordset for the chart triggers, modifies the title and the category axis to fit the data. The category axis reconfigures to prevent the labels from running together.

```
Private Sub Button2_Click()Dim Duration
    Duration = DateDiff("m", Me![StartingPeriod],
            Me![EndingPeriod])
    Dim Chart As Object, t As Object, Ax As Object
    Set Chart = Me![ValueChart].Object
    Set t = Chart.ChartTitle
    t.Text = Me![Trader] & " for " & Format(Duration / 12,
            "#.0") & " years"
    t.Font.Size = 12

    'Adjust Axis labels
    Set Ax = Chart.Axes(xlCategory)
    'Ax.ReversePlotOrder = False
```

```
    Dim fqLabel, fqMark
    fqLabel = Int(Duration / 8)
    fqMark = Int(Duration / 16)
    Ax.TickLabelSpacing = fqLabel
    Ax.TickMarkSpacing = fqMark
End Sub
```

Using Word 97 as an ActiveX Component

You can also use ActiveX operations to manipulate operations in another program, even if you don't store the object as a permanent part of any Access 97 table. In Chapter 9, for example, you use an Access 97 report to generate form letters on demand from an open form. Another way to generate form letters or other documents directly from Access is to call Word 97 as an ActiveX server. An *ActiveX server* is an ActiveX program that you use as though the program were a component of the current application rather than a stand-alone program.

In effect, using Word 97 as an ActiveX server extends the features in Access 97 to include Word 97 document creation and formatting. In this case, the goal is to create and print an order form by using the information you store in the Access 97 tables. This information enables you to fill in and print a Word 97 document template by clicking a button on an Access 97 form.

You initiate the process by making a selection from a form, such as the one shown in Figure 10-7, which lists the orders you store in the database tables. Notice that the only value bound to the form from the list box is the order number. This number passes to all procedures creating the document. You use the number as the basis of generating temporary `Recordsets` to fill the document template.

Figure 10-7: You use a form to select an order number.

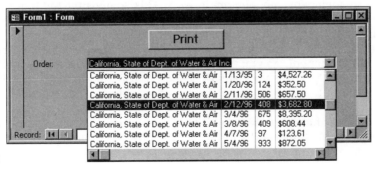

Although you can generate a document in Word 97 from a new, blank document, starting with a template document, such as the one shown in Figure 10-8, is probably more efficient. You do have some practical reasons for using a template: First, more people know how to use a word processing program than other type of application. Second, very few people can prepare the layout of an Access 97 report form. Third, in many cases, you find that someone has already created a document template that you can use as the basic outline of the document you want to generate. Using this template is often simpler than creating a report form from scratch.

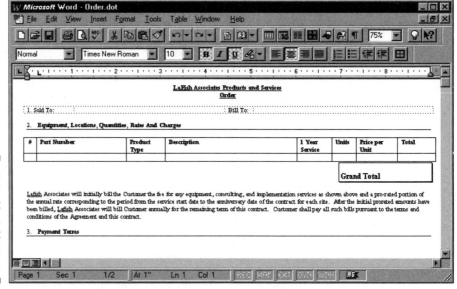

Figure 10-8:
A Word 97 document template, DOT, that you prepare in advance.

The key feature that you need to add to any Word 97 document that you want to fill with Access 97 data is a set of bookmarks to mark key locations in the document. A *bookmark* in Word 97 is an invisible tag that you can insert anywhere in the document. You create bookmarks by placing the cursor at the desired location within the template and pressing Ctrl+Shift+F5. To create the bookmark, you must enter a name that's unique to the document. As you prepare a Word document for use as an ActiveX component, create a bookmark called SoldTo that marks where in the document to insert the customer's address block.

Do not confuse bookmarks in Word 97 documents with the Bookmark property of an Access 97 Recordset. In this chapter, I use the word *bookmark* to refer only to Word 97 bookmarks.

After you establish a bookmark in a Word 97 document, you can move the cursor to that location by using the EditGoto statement, as follows:

```
EditGoto "SoldTo"
```

To perform the same task from Access 97 VBA, you first create an object variable that connects to Word 97 by using ActiveX processing. The CreateObject function assigns Word 97 to the variable (using the class name Word.Basic). After the function assigns the ActiveX component to the variable, all the commands in Word Basic, such as Editgoto, become methods of the ActiveX object, as shown in the following example:

```
Dim Doc as Object
Set Doc = CreateObject("Word.Basic")
Doc.Editgoto "SoldTo"
```

The procedure that triggers after you choose the Print button in the order-selection form, shown in Figure 10-7, includes calls to five procedures designed to work with Word 97 as an ActiveX server. The first creates a new document based on the specified template. The next three procedures fill in the three sections of the document. The final procedure, Command2_Click, prints the document and closes the ActiveX session.

```
Private Sub Command2_Click()
    DoCmd.Hourglass True
    StartNewDoc
    WriteOrderNumber OrdNum:=Me![SelectedOrder]
    WriteAddressBlocks OrdNum:=Me![SelectedOrder]
    WriteTableDetails OrdNum:=Me![SelectedOrder]
    PrintDocument
    DoCmd.Hourglass False
End Sub
```

You use the HourGlass method to turn the mouse pointer hourglass on and off. Because the ActiveX operations take place outside Access 97, the hourglass does not automatically appear while the program processes the form. The HourGlass method manually turns the display on and off at the beginning and end of the procedures.

Because a number of different procedures need to interact with the same ActiveX server object, the declarations section of the module that contains the procedures declares the object variable that you use for Word 97 as a module-level variable.

Chapter 7 states that a module-level variable has two important distinctions from normal local variables: First, the variable is available to all the procedures in the same module. (In this case, that availability enables all five procedures to utilize the same ActiveX object variable.) Second, the variable is static — that is, it retains whatever value you assign it in one procedure even after the next one begins. (In this example, that retention capability enables you to assign Word 97 to the variable in the first procedure and then continue to use the same object variable with the rest of the procedures.) In addition, you define three constants to specify the location of the template. Placing these values at the top of the module helps you adjust the locations to fit whatever system the program runs on.

```
Option Compare Database
Option Explicit
Dim Doc As Object
Const HomeDrive = "Q"
Const HomePath = "Q:\Access Prog Dummies\Chapter 11\"
Const Template = "Order.dot"
```

The first of the five procedures that produce the document is the Start-NewDoc procedure. This procedure actually defines the variable Doc as an ActiveX server object by using the CreateObject function. After the procedure creates the object, you can apply Word.Basic methods to the object. In this case, you use FileNew to generate a new document based on the specified template. StartofDocument positions the cursor to the beginning of the document.

```
Sub StartNewDoc()
    ChDrive HomeDrive
    ChDir HomePath
    Set Doc = CreateObject("Word.Basic")
    Doc.FileNew HomePath & Template
    Doc.StartofDocument
End Sub
```

The following procedure actually begins to fill in the document, using the Editgoto method to move the cursor to the desired location and then inserting the order number into the document. Notice that, in Word 97, the Insert method can operate only on text. If the data in Access 97 is a number, the procedure must convert the number to text before the value passes to Word 97. In this case, the Str() function changes the number to a string (text) before inserting it into the document.

```
Sub WriteOrderNumber(OrdNum)
    Doc.Editgoto "OrderNumbers"
    Doc.Insert Str(OrdNum)
End Sub
```

The following procedure writes the address blocks into the document. The first step is to use the order number to generate a Recordset that contains the desired information. The method you use here creates a query definition that uses a parameter for the order number, which makes specifying the order to use for defining the Recordset easy. Notice that the SQL statement

is quite complicated, because the statement must link two tables, Orders
and Customers, to arrive at the required set of values. Remember that you
need not manually compose complex statements such as the one that
follows. You can create the query in a query grid, switch to the SQL display,
and then copy and paste the statement into your code with only some minor
editing. (This book breaks up long SQL statements so that the text fits on the
printed page. After you copy and paste a SQL statement, the entire statement should fit onto a single line in your module text.)

```
Sub WriteAddressBlocks(OrdNum)
    Dim Q As QueryDef, R As Recordset, SQLText
    Dim CSZ
    Set Q = CurrentDb.CreateQueryDef("")
    SQLText = _
    "PARAMETERS OrdNum Long;SELECT Customers.Name,"_
    & "Customers.Street,Customers.City,Customers.State, " _
    & "Customers.Zip,Customers.Contact,Customers.Fax, " _
    & "Customers.Phone FROM Orders INNER JOIN Customers " _
    & "ON Orders.[Customer ID] = Customers.ID WHERE (((" _
    & "Orders.[Order Number])=[OrdNum]));"
    Q.SQL = SQLText
    Q.Parameters(0) = OrdNum
    Set R = Q.OpenRecordset()
```

After you establish the Recordset, the cursor is at the SoldTo bookmark
where you want to insert the address block. Notice that, in Word.Basic, the
InsertPara method inserts a paragraph ending. In the following example,
you use the same address for both the bill-to and ship-to addresses. At this
point in the program, the top section of the document fills in with Sold To
and Bill To data, as shown in Figure 10-9.

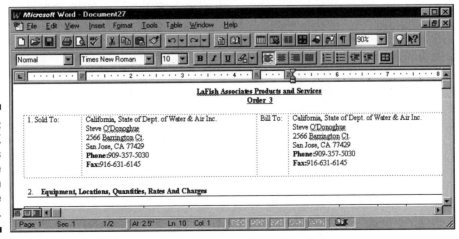

Figure 10-9:
ActiveX
operations
fill in the
top section
of the
document.

```
Doc.Editgoto "SoldTo"
   Doc.Insert R![Name]: Doc.InsertPara
   Doc.Insert R![Contact]: Doc.InsertPara
   Doc.Insert R![Street]: Doc.InsertPara
   CSZ = R![City] & ", " & R![State] & " " & R![Zip]
   Doc.Insert CSZ: Doc.InsertPara
   Doc.Bold 1: Doc.Insert "Phone:": Doc.Bold 0
   Doc.Insert Format(R![Phone], "###-###-####")
   Doc.InsertPara
   Doc.Bold 1: Doc.Insert "Fax:": Doc.Bold 0
   Doc.Insert Format(R![Fax], "###-###-####")
   Doc.InsertPara
   Doc.Editgoto "BillTo"
   Doc.Insert R![Name]: Doc.InsertPara
   Doc.Insert R![Contact]: Doc.InsertPara
   Doc.Insert R![Street]: Doc.InsertPara
   CSZ = R![City] & ", " & R![State] & " " & R![Zip]
   Doc.Insert CSZ: Doc.InsertPara
   Doc.Bold 1: Doc.Insert "Phone:": Doc.Bold 0
   Doc.Insert Format(R![Phone], "###-###-####")
   Doc.InsertPara
   Doc.Bold 1: Doc.Insert "Fax:": Doc.Bold 0
   Doc.Insert Format(R![Fax], "###-###-####")
   Doc.InsertPara
End Sub
```

The WriteTableDetails procedure performs the next part of the job. Again, you define a Recordset by using a QueryDef object with a parameter. The SQL statement performs a join on two tables so that Orders, Order Details, and Parts all link to the same order number. The seven columns in the Recordset arrange to correspond to the columns in the table.

```
Sub WriteTableDetails(OrdNum)
   Dim Q As QueryDef, R As Recordset, SQLText
   Dim TableTotal, Kount, Col, TotalLines
   Set Q = CurrentDb.CreateQueryDef("")
   SQLText = _
   "PARAMETERS OrdNum Long;SELECT [Order Details]" _
   & ".[Part No],Parts.Type,Order Details].Description," _
   & "Parts.[1 Year Maintain],[Order Details].Quantity," _
   & " [Order Details].[Unit Price], [Order Details]." _
   & "[Extended Price]FROM (Orders INNER JOIN " _
   & "[Order Details] ON Orders.[Order Number] = " _
   & "[Order Details].[Order Number]) INNER JOIN " _
```

```
& "Parts ON [Order Details].[Part No] = Parts." _
& "[Part No]WHERE((Orders.[Order Number])=[OrdNum]));"
Q.SQL = SQLText
Q.Parameters(0) = OrdNum
Set R = Q.OpenRecordset()
R.MoveLast
R.MoveFirst
```

Notice that I use the variable name Kount for the counter to differentiate it from the Count method.

The following procedure must insert data into an existing table. Instead of using paragraph endings at the end of each item, you use the NextCell method. Notice that, if you use this method in the last column of the table, the method automatically generates a new column. You must take special care to prevent a NextCell method from performing after you enter the last item; otherwise, an extra blank line appears at the end of the table.

```
Doc.Editgoto "LineItems"
   Kount = 1
   Do Until R.EOF
      TableTotal = TableTotal + R![Extended Price]
      Doc.Insert Str(Kount) & "."
      For Col = 0 To 2
         Doc.NextCell
         Doc.Insert R(Col).Value
      Next
      Doc.NextCell
      For Col = 3 To 4
         If Not IsNull(R(Col)) Then
            Doc.Insert Format(R(Col), "###,###")
         End If
         Doc.NextCell
      Next
      For Col = 5 To 6
         If Not IsNull(R(Col)) Then
            Doc.Insert Format(R(Col), "currency")
         End If
         If Not(R.AbsolutePosition=R.RecordCount - 1 _
            And Col = 6) Then
            Doc.NextCell
         End If
      Next
      Kount = Kount + 1
```

(continued)

(continued)

```
        R.MoveNext
    Loop
    Doc.Editgoto "GrandTotal"
    Doc.Insert Format(TableTotal, "Currency")
End Sub
```

The final procedure, `PrintDocument`, prints the document and closes the Word 97 session. Notice that the argument you use with the `FileClose` method closes the document without saving it.

```
Sub PrintDocument()
    Doc.FilePrint
    Doc.FileClose 2
    Set Doc = Nothing
End Sub
```

The completed document is shown in Figure 10-10.

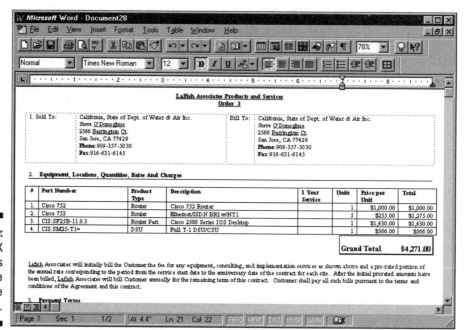

Figure 10-10:
ActiveX operations complete the document.

> **Form: ActiveX 03**
> **Module: Word ActiveX**

Chapter 11

Controls and Objects

• •

In This Chapter

▶ Synchronizing two forms

▶ Finding out about ActiveX controls

▶ Selecting records with the calendar

▶ Adding error handling

• •

*T*he best part of programming, as far as I'm concerned, is that there is no one right way to do things. Starting with a set of tools, such as the Access object model and the VBA language, you are free to create the most interesting solutions for the needs and problems you and other users encounter. In this chapter, I show you some of the techniques I like to use that you might not see too often. They involve some unusual ways to combine object programming with the various types of controls available in Access 97.

> **Database Folder: Chapter 11**
> **Database File: CTRLS.MDB**

To begin this chapter, load the database for Chapter 11, TRLS.MDB. Click on the Forms tab to display the list of forms I discuss in this chapter.

Synchronizing Forms

Subforms are among the most useful features in Access 97 because they enable you to combine two or more related sets of data into a single form. Figure 11-1 shows a typical form/subform display in which the main form has a one-to-many relationship to the data in the subform.

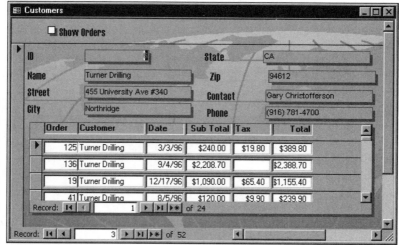

Figure 11-1:
A form with
a subform
control that
you can use
to display
related
records.

Form: Customers

Although subforms are effective, they have one limitation — subforms take up a fixed amount of space within the form. An alternate approach is to use two separate forms, each of which you display in its own window. You see this approach illustrated by the forms shown in Figure 11-2. If you display the data in separate forms, users can arrange the forms to view the data in the way that's most convenient for them at the time. If you use forms in separate windows, you can also take advantage of window stacking to enable the two windows to share the same area of the screen; this isn't possible if you use a form with a subform.

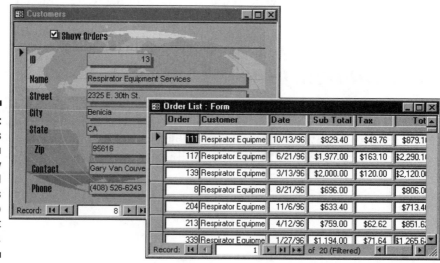

Figure 11-2:
Access
allows you
to display
related
records
in two
different
forms.

| *Form: Customers 01* |

To use a pair of forms that have a one-to-many relationship, you need to write some VBA procedures that ensure that the two forms really show related records. Keep in mind that Access 97 has no built-in facility for linking forms that you open in separate windows.

You need a function that can determine whether a specific form is open. The FormIsOpen function fills that bill. The FormIsOpen function scans through the Forms collection to check whether a specific form is open. Forms that the database window lists but that aren't currently open aren't part of this collection.

```
Function FormIsOpen(FName As String) _
   As Boolean
   Dim Pointer
   For Pointer = 0 To Forms.Count - 1
      If Forms(Pointer).Name = FName Then
         FormIsOpen = True
         Exit Function
      End If
   Next
   FormIsOpen = False
End Function
```

In the code module for the main form, you need two procedures. The first you use to open the secondary form — here, the form displaying the orders that relate to the current customer. The form shown in Figure 11-2 contains a check box. After you select this box (add a check mark), the Orders form opens and its Recordset filters the data so that the form displays only orders for the customer in the Customers form. You accomplish this task by using the WhereCondition argument of the OpenForm method. If you deselect the box (remove the check mark), then the Orders form — if currently open — closes by the Close method.

```
Option Compare Database
Option Explicit
Const LinkedForm = "Order List"

Private Sub Check18_AfterUpdate()
   If Check18 Then
      If Not FormIsOpen(LinkedForm) Then
         DoCmd.OpenForm FormName:=LinkedForm, _
         WhereCondition:="[Customer ID]= " & Me![ID]
         Me.SetFocus
      End If
```

(continued)

(continued)

```
    Else
      If FormIsOpen(LinkedForm) Then
         DoCmd.Close ObjectType:=acForm, _
            ObjectName:=LinkedForm
      End If
   End If
End Sub
```

Notice the use of the SetFocus method in the preceding procedure. You need this method to return the focus to the main window after the Orders window opens. After Access 97 executes the OpenForm method, the program automatically gives the focus to the newly opened form. To keep the focus on the Customers window, you must specifically switch the focus back to that window.

After the Orders form opens, you have nothing to keep the two forms synchronized. Normally, Access 97 enables you to navigate through the records in the Customers form without changing the Recordset in the Orders form. To keep the two forms linked, you must use the OnCurrent event to resynchronize the Recordset in the Orders form to match the new record that appears in the Customer form. The procedure repeats the OpenForm method. In effect, this repetition causes the Orders form to close and then reopen with a new Recordset. Because the form reopens, the form once again gets the focus, that is, it becomes the active form. Switching back and forth between forms each time the recordsets need to be synchronized creates an unpleasant screen display because the windows appear to jump around for no reason. To keep the focus on the main form, and avoid the unpleasant effects of switching focus, the procedure needs to execute another SetFocus method as shown in the following modified version of Form_Current.

```
Private Sub Form_Current()
   If Check18 Then
      DoCmd.OpenForm FormName:=LinkedForm, _
      WhereCondition:="[Customer ID]= " & Me![ID]
      Me.SetFocus
   End If
End Sub
```

You also want a procedure that closes the secondary form whenever you close the primary form. You can accomplish this task by adding a Form_Close procedure, which triggers as the main form closes. In this case, the procedure makes sure that the Orders form also closes when the Customer form closes. The Form_Close event procedure ensures that both forms close at the same time.

```
Private Sub Form_Close()
   If FormIsOpen(LinkedForm) Then
      DoCmd.Close ObjectType:=acForm, _
      ObjectName:=LinkedForm
End Sub
```

> **Form: Customers 01**
> **Module:Form Functions**
> **Procedure: FormIsOpen**

Using the RecordSource property

The preceding example seems okay in theory. But if you actually use the code, you find that constantly closing and reopening the Orders form and then shifting the focus results in a very annoying screen display. A better approach to keeping the forms in sync is to use VBA to manipulate the RecordSource property of the Orders form.

Although most forms use a table or query name as the record source, Access 97 enables you to set a form's RecordSource property to any valid SQL statement. You can set this property in the Design mode or dynamically change the property as you display the form.

The following procedure, which you use with the On Current event, illustrates this approach. In this example, you change the RecordSource property to a SQL statement that uses the current value of the ID field to restrict the records in the Orders form. Notice that the content of the Orders form doesn't change automatically after you alter the Record-Source property. To synchronize the Recordsets, you must apply the Requery method to the Orders form.

```
Private Sub Form_Current()
   If Check18 Then
      Dim F As Form
      Set F = Forms![Order List]
      F.RecordSource = "Select * from orders" _
      & " where [customer id] = " & Me![ID] & ";"
      F.Requery
      End If
End Sub
```

This approach keeps the forms in sync but avoids the jerky screen display that the OpenForm method causes.

> **Form: Customers 02**
> **Module:Form Functions**
> **Procedure: FormIsOpen**

Dealing with long lists

One of the themes of this book is that good interface design calls for you to present users with lists of information instead of requiring them to make manual entries. Figure 11-3 shows one of the techniques for locating a record within a set appearing in a form. At the top of the form, you place a combo box that lists the key value the user needs to locate additional records — for example, a company name. After the user makes a selection from the list, the selected name becomes the active record in the form. As the number of records in the form grows large, however, a single, long list of items, such as the one shown in Figure 11-3, becomes awkward and slow to work with.

One alternative to using long lists is to create a dialog box form that enables you to divide a long list into simple segments. A good way to create such a form is to use a button panel, similar to the one shown in Figure 11-4, that displays a button for each letter in the alphabet.

Figure 11-3:
A single,
long list
becomes
hard to
work with.

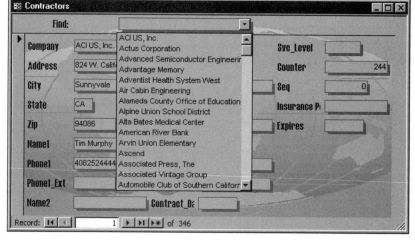

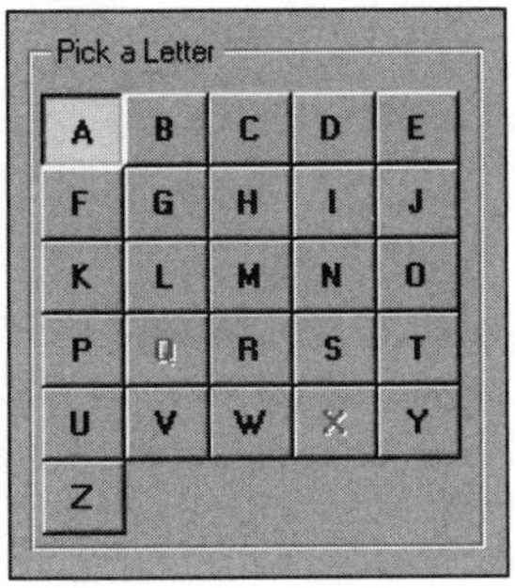

Figure 11-4:
A button panel provides a button for each letter in the alphabet.

To create a button panel perform the following steps:

1. **Create a group frame control that's large enough to hold all the buttons (about 2" by 2").**

2. **Add a toggle button to the group.**

   You need to size the button to a width of about 0.33 inches and a height of 0.29 inches. Keep note of the name that Access 97 automatically assigns to this button — for example, `Toggle2` or `Toggle4`. The number is significant because it becomes the base value you use to calculate the captions and values for the buttons. Manually entering the captions and option values for each button, however, is too time-consuming and tedious. You can handle these tasks by using a procedure.

3. **Use the Copy and Paste commands to make four copies of the button, and then arrange the buttons in a horizontal row as shown in Figure 11-5 in the center image.**

   Make sure that you order the buttons in the row by name — for example, `Toggle2`, `Toggle3`, `Toggle4`, and so on.

4. **Copy all five buttons and then paste four more groups of five; move the groups into place as shown in Figure 11-5 in the right-hand image.**

5. **Select one button and copy and paste that button to make the 26th button.**

You now have a layout like the one shown in Figure 11-5. More importantly, the buttons have consecutive numbers in their names — for example, `Toggle2` through `Toggle27`. The fact that you number the buttons consecutively is important, because you can treat all the buttons as if they were a special collection of objects. You can refer to any of the buttons by using the name `Toggle` with a numeric tail, as shown in the following example of code:

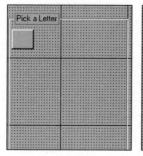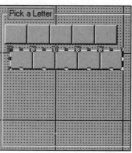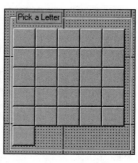

Figure 11-5:
You add
buttons by
copying and
pasting the
original
button.

```
Me("Toggle" & Number)
```

This approach enables you to set the captions for the buttons as A to Z
without manually editing the property sheet for each control. The trick is to
use the Chr() function to insert the desired letters as a caption, as in the
following example. (In ASCII, 65 is the code for *A*.)

```
Chr(65) = "A"
```

If, for example, the first button is Toggle2, the following code labels each of
the buttons as A through Z by adding 64 to the value of the loop counter
Button:

```
For Button = 1 To 26
   With Me("Toggle" & Button + 1)
      .Caption = Chr(Button + 64)
   End With
Next
```

The Form_Load procedure that follows automatically sets the captions
for the toggle buttons as the form loads. In addition, the option value that
you assign to each button is the ASCII code for the letter on the button
caption — that is, button A has a value of 65, button B = 66, and so on.

```
Private Sub Form_Load()
   For Button = 1 To 26
      With Me("Toggle" & Button + 1)
         .Caption = Chr(Button + 64)
         .OptionValue = Button + 64
      End With
   Next
   Me![ButtonFrame] = 65
   SetListContents
End Sub
```

The trick is to use the value of the selected button to restrict the items appearing in a list box to only those items that begin with that letter. You accomplish this task by setting the RowSource property of the list box to a SQL statement similar to the one that follows, which uses the LIKE operator to select records by their first letter:

```
SELECT company FROM contractors WHERE company LIKE "A*"
```

You use the SetListContents procedure to set the RowSource property to match the currently selected button. Recall that the option value of each button is the ASCII equivalent of the letter that appears in the button's caption. The control must then update its display.

```
Sub SetListContents()
    Dim SQLText
    SQLText = "SELECT company FROM contractors " _
        &"WHERE company LIKE '" & Chr(Me![ButtonFrame]) _
        & "*';"
    Me![Names].RowSource = SQLText
    Me![Names].Requery
End Sub
```

The program calls this procedure once as the form loads to set the initial list to *A*'s. The ButtonFrame_AfterUpdate procedure then calls SetList-Contents each time the option frame control updates.

```
Private Sub ButtonFrame_AfterUpdate()
    SetListContents
End Sub
```

Another useful feature is that Access 97 enables you to disable any buttons for which you have no records in the table — typically, those beginning with the letters *Q* and *X*. The following example is a modified version of the Form_Load procedure. The procedure begins by generating a Recordset that contains a list of each unique first letter in the list of company names in the table. The program uses this Recordset to check whether each button has any records that match the button's caption letter. The procedure determines this match (or lack thereof) by searching the Recordset each time you configure a new button. If Access 97 finds no match, the program disables the button so that the user cannot select that particular button. If the search fails to locate any names that start with *Q*, for example, then the button that displays the letter *Q* is disabled.

```
Private Sub Form_Load()
    Dim Button
    Dim R As Recordset, SQLText
    SQLText = "SELECT Distinct Left(company,1) " _
        & "From contractors;"
    Set R = CurrentDb.OpenRecordset(SQLText)
    For Button = 1 To 26
        With Me("Toggle" & Button + 1)
            .Caption = Chr(Button + 64)
            .OptionValue = Button + 64
        End With
        R.FindFirst R(0).Name & "= '" _
            & Chr(Button + 64) & "'"
        If R.NoMatch Then
            'Me("Toggle" & Button + 1).Enabled = False
        End If
    Next
    Me![ButtonFrame] = 65
    SetListContents
End Sub
```

You can put the Letter Buttons form to use by adding a routine that synchronizes the name a user selects in the list box with the record that appears in the related form. You assign the following procedure to the Names_DblClick event. The procedure uses the RecordsetClone/Bookmark method to synchronize the two forms each time the user double-clicks the name in the list box (see Figure 11-6).

```
Private Sub Names_DblClick(Cancel As Integer)
    Dim R As Recordset
    Set R = Forms![Long List 02].RecordsetClone
    R.FindFirst "Company = '" & Me![Names]& _
        "'"
    Forms![Long List 02].Bookmark = R.Bookmark
End Sub
```

Form: Long List 02
Form: Letter Buttons

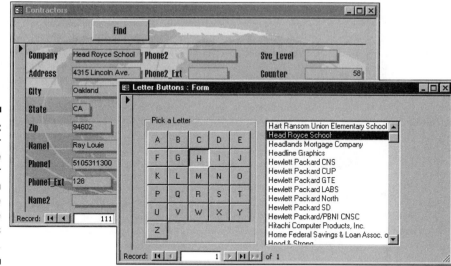

Figure 11-6:
The user
can use the
Letter
Button form
to navigate
through the
Contractors
table.

ActiveX Controls

In Access 97, *controls* are objects that you place on a form to provide a way to display information as well as a way for the user to enter information. Access 97 provides a set of 11 native controls that are part of the standard set of objects in Access 97: check box, combo box, command button, frame, image, label, list box, option button, tab strip, text box, and toggle button.

In addition to the native controls, which appear in the Design mode toolbox, Access 97 enables you to insert ActiveX controls into a form. An *ActiveX control* is a type of plug-in control that adds a new way for users to view or enter information. Keep in mind that you're not limited to using ActiveX controls with Access 97. Other applications that support ActiveX can also use these controls, including Visual Basic, Excel 97, or Internet Explorer.

One example is an ActiveX *calendar control* that comes with Access 97 and as part of the Microsoft Office 97 Professional package, as shown in Figure 11-7. The calendar control provides users with an easy-to-recognize way of displaying or entering date information.

To insert a calendar control into a form, follow these steps:

1. Open a new or existing form in the Design mode.

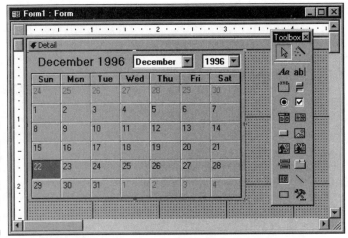

Figure 11-7:
The ActiveX
calendar
control that
comes with
Access 97.

2. Choose Insert⇨ActiveX Control from the menu bar.

This action opens the Insert ActiveX Control dialog box. This dialog box lists the names of each ActiveX control you have installed on your system. Because ActiveX controls work with more than one application, you may find that your system lists controls installed by other applications (such as Visual Basic).

ActiveX controls (formerly called *OLE custom controls*) were first added to Microsoft products in version 3.0 of Visual Basic. Older versions of many of these controls, however, don't always work correctly in all applications. Most of the controls created for Visual Basic, for example, don't work with Access 97 forms, even though these controls appear in the Insert ActiveX Control dialog box. Be aware, therefore, that some of the controls listed in this dialog box may not work correctly with Access 97.

3. Select a control from the dialog box and click OK.

Access 97 inserts the control into the form.

An important point to keep in mind is that ActiveX controls are *not* part of Access 97 but are actually plug-in modules that you add to the Windows system and that forms can access. The MDB files don't store these controls; they reside in the Windows System folder. If you create an application in Access 97 that requires an ActiveX control, any user who doesn't have that control installed can't use those forms. In most cases, the manufacturer of the control provides for the distribution of the controls along with Access 97 applications. (Appendix A discusses the use of the Setup Wizard to create such customized install packages.)

ActiveX control properties

Native Access 97 controls, such as a combo box or command button controls, display all their properties in the tabs of the property sheet window. ActiveX controls, however, have the following two levels of properties:

🗸 **ActiveX container properties.** These properties represent the standard set of Access 97 properties that appear in the property sheet window of every ActiveX control, such as Name, Height, Width, Visible, and Enabled.

🗸 **ActiveX control specific properties.** These are properties that relate specifically to the ActiveX control. The calendar control, for example, has a property called FirstDay that determines which day of the week appears in the leftmost column of the calendar. By default, this property is set to Sunday.

You can access the control-specific properties of ActiveX controls in the following two ways:

🗸 If the control is a new-style ActiveX control (in contrast to an older-style OLE control), the properties of the control are integrated into the controls property sheet, as shown in Figure 11-8. The example in the figure shows the properties that appear for the calendar control.

🗸 You can also access the property list for an ActiveX control by right-clicking the control and choosing the name of the control from the shortcut menu that appears. Then choose Properties to open a dialog box containing settings for the control's properties, as shown in Figure 11-9. In addition to the properties they list, most dialog boxes include a Help button. This Help button is important, because the Help files that come with the control store information about the methods and use of the control. Clicking the Help button opens the Help file for the control. Typically, you discover how to integrate the control into your form from this Help file.

Figure 11-8: ActiveX control properties appear on the Other tab of the control's property sheet.

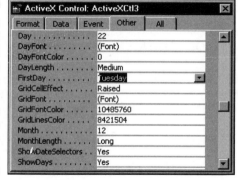

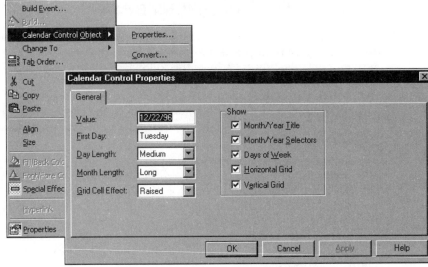

Figure 11-9:
Control-
specific
properties
appear in a
custom
dialog box.

Reading and setting the date from the calendar control

Using an ActiveX control is essentially the same as using any other control, except that the methods and properties are specific to that particular ActiveX control. Figure 11-10 shows a form that includes an ActiveX calendar control called CtrlCal. To set a property on the control, you use the same style of object syntax as you do for any ActiveX object (discussed in Chapter 10). The following statement turns off the display of the month and year boxes within the calendar control:

```
Me.CtrlCal.Object.ShowDateSelectors = False
```

In Access 97, using the Object property for an ActiveX control is optional. The following statement produces the same results as does the preceding example:

```
Me.CtrlCal.ShowDateSelectors = False
```

The value of the control is a date value that is equal to the selected date on the calendar form. The following statement uses the value of the ActiveX control to set the caption of a label control called Top3d:

```
Me![Top3d].Caption = Format(Me![CtrlCal].Object.Value, _
    "long date")
```

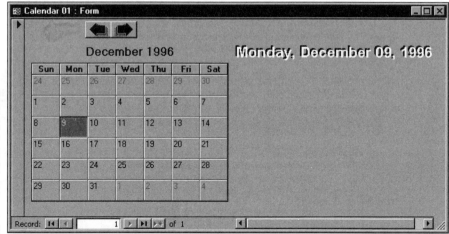

Figure 11-10:
The ActiveX
calendar
control
integrated
into an
Access 97
form.

Because the `Value` property is the default property of the calendar control (and almost all ActiveX controls that return a value), you can drop both the `Object` and `Value` keywords and use the following statement instead:

```
Me![Top3d].Caption = Format(Me![CtrlCal],"long date")
```

You can set the calendar to display a specific day within any given month by setting the value of the control equal to a specific date, as follows:

```
Me![CtrlCal] = #12/25/96#
```

The form shown in Figure 11-10 performs the following two operations that relate to the calendar control:

✔ The form uses the selected date on the calendar control to set the text of a pair of labels, `Top3d` and `Bottom3d`. These labels create the date appearing on the right side of the form. The following `SyncControls` procedure sets the labels:

```
Sub SyncControls()
   Me![Top3d].Caption = _
      Format(Me![CtrlCal].Object.Value,"long date")
   Me![Bottom3d].Caption = _
      Format(Me![CtrlCal], "long date")
End Sub
```

Two events invoke `SyncControls`. The first event occurs at the time the form loads (the form load event) and sets the initial text to match the default date on the calendar control. By default, the calendar always shows the current system date.

```
Private Sub Form_Load()
    Me.CtrlCal.Object.ShowDateSelectors = _
        False
    SyncControls
End Sub
```

The second event occurs whenever the user selects a new date by clicking the calendar control. The `CtrlCal_Updated` calls `SyncControls` whenever this event occurs.

```
Private Sub CtrlCal_Updated(Code As Integer)
    SyncControls
End Sub
```

✔ The form also provides two command buttons, displaying arrow icons, that you can use to change the calendar to the next or previous months. You can change the calendar date, relative to the current date, by using one of the following methods.

NextDay	Move date one day forward
NextMonth	Move date one month forward
NextWeek	Move date one week forward
NextYear	Move date one year forward
PreviousDay	Move date one day backward
PreviousMonth	Move date one month backward
PreviousWeek	Move date one week backward
PreviousYear	Move date one year backward

The following two event procedures change the month of the calendar control, forward or backward, each time you click the buttons.

```
Private Sub Command5_Click()
    Me.CtrlCal.PreviousMonth
End Sub
```

```
Private Sub Command6_Click()
    Me.CtrlCal.NextMonth
End Sub
```

Notice that, in this case, the calendar control events automatically cascade. In other words, if you use the `PreviousMonth` or `NextMonth` procedure to change the current date of the calendar control, the control automatically triggers its own `Updated` event. This event causes the code in the `CtrlCal_Updated` procedure to execute. Clicking the arrow buttons, therefore, updates both the calendar and the label controls.

> **Form: Calendar 01**

Using the Calendar to Select Records

The value of the calendar control is that it presents users with an interface that they immediately understand and can intuitively manipulate. Clicking a date on the calendar to indicate the selection of that date seems only natural.

Figure 11-11 shows a form that contains two main controls: a calendar control and a list box control. In this example, the idea is first to use the calendar control to select a date. You then use that date as a criterion for filling the list box with data for the selected date — in this case, order information.

You can accomplish this task by using the Calendar control with a modified form of the `SyncControls` procedure, as shown in the following example. In this example, you compose a SQL statement that uses the date that the calendar control furnishes to limit the `Recordset` to only those orders from that specific date. You assign the SQL statement to the `RowSource` property of the list box. The `Requery` method then updates the list to match the selected date.

Figure 11-11: Use the calendar control to select records in a subform based on the selected date.

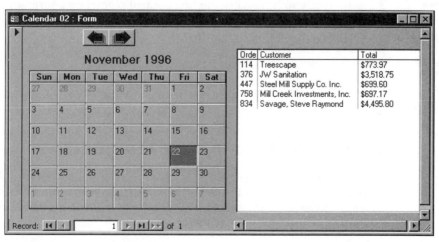

```
Sub SyncControls()
   Dim SQLText
   SQLText = _
   "SELECT Orders.[Order Number], Orders.Customer, " _
   & "Orders.Total, Orders.[Order Date] FROM Orders " _
   & "WHERE (((Orders.[Order Date])=#" _
   & Me![CtrlCal] & "#)) " _
   & "ORDER BY Orders.[Order Number], Orders.Customer;"
   With Me![CtrlList]
      .RowSource = SQLText
      .Requery
   End With
End Sub
```

Notice that the calendar control cascades events. A cascaded event results from a user's indirect action, in contrast to a standard event that a user's action triggers directly.

For example, suppose that the user clicks one of the buttons on the form used to change the month that the calendar control displays. The direct event triggered by that action is the OnClick event of the button control. The event procedures defined for these buttons change the month of the calendar control. However, you will find that the list box (which lists the order information) updates automatically even though the users didn't directly interact with the calendar. Changing the date by using the NextMonth and PreviousMonth buttons triggers the Updated event of the calendar control because the date was changed indirectly. This eliminates the need to specifically call SyncControls each time you use a method to alter the value of the calendar control.

The form controls included with Access 97 do not cascade update events. Suppose that you have a combo box control placed on a form for which you have defined an AfterUpdate event procedure. The event will trigger if the user changes the contents of the control. If you use a procedure to change the value of the control, however, the AfterUpdate event procedure is not triggered. This is an example of a non-cascaded event.

> **Form: Calendar 02**

Using forms as ActiveX objects

Access 97 itself is an ActiveX application that contains ActiveX elements. In Access 97, you can treat forms and reports (that you view in Preview mode) as if they were ActiveX objects. This means you have alternatives to the OpenForm method for displaying forms.

As an example, look at the forms shown in Figure 11-12. These forms are set up to work together so that the smaller form shows the details of the order in the main form. The goal is to synchronize the data that appears in the smaller form (the order details) with the currently selected sales order in the main form.

One way to synchronize this data is to refer to the form you want to open as an object and to set the form's Visible property to True. You can insert the following statement into any procedure in which you want to open the Order form. Notice that the name of the form object is the name of the form, Order, preceded by Form.

```
Form_Order.Visible = True
```

If the form name contains one or more spaces, you must enclose the form object name in brackets. The following example opens the form Line Items 01 by using its object name, [Form_Line Items 01], to set its Visible property to True:

```
[Form_Line Items 01].Visible = True
```

In this book, you typically use the OpenForm method with the Where-Condition argument to restrict the contents of the form's Recordset. Using the object approach, you accomplish the same thing by setting the form's RowSource property to an appropriate SQL statement. (Take a look at Chapter 1 for details about the object approach.) The following example uses a With structure to set the Visible and RecordSource properties of the form object. After you execute it, the statement opens the form (if it's not already open) and sets its Recordset to match the order selected in the main form.

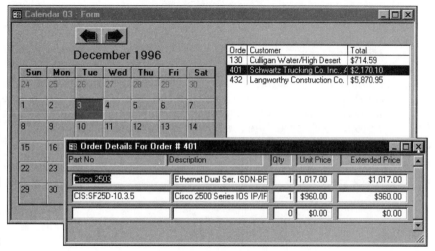

Figure 11-12:
Order details appear in a form that you open as an ActiveX object.

```
With [Form_Line Items 01]
   .Visible = True
   .RecordSource = "Select * from [Order Details]" _
      & " Where [Order Number] = " _
      & Me![CtrlList] & ";"
End With
```

You apply this technique to the forms shown in Figure 11-12 by using the `CtrlList_DblClick` procedure. Double-clicking an item in the list box control triggers the `CtrlList_DblClick` procedure. The procedure uses the form object style of reference to open the form and set a number of properties. You can set the `Caption` property to some text that identifies the contents of the window as the details of the currently selected sales order in the main form.

After the form is open, repeating the `CtrlList_DblClick` procedure simply sets the properties of the already open form. To make the details form active, the procedure uses the `SetFocus` property to activate the details form each time the user double-clicks a sales order in the main form.

```
Private Sub CtrlList_DblClick(Cancel As Integer)
   With [Form_Line Items 01]
      .NavigationButtons = False
      .RecordSelectors = False
      .Visible = True
      .RecordSource = "Select * from [Order Details]" _
         & " Where [Order Number] = " _
         & Me![CtrlList] & ";"
      .Caption = "Order Details For Order # " _
         & Me![CtrlList]
      .Requery
      .SetFocus
   End With
End Sub
```

Although the effect of this technique is similar to the one you can achieve by using the `OpenForm` method, the structure of the code is simpler and easier to understand and modify. It enables a single structure to set a variety of properties that define the form's appearance and contents.

Form: Calendar 03

Using a form as an object variable

In the example in the preceding section, you load a form by referring to that form as an object. The form opens after you set the Visible property to True. But what about closing the form? Because the purpose of the Line Items 01 form is to display details about the order you select in the main form, a logical conclusion is that if you close the main form, the detail form also closes. In the preceding example, however, the form object remains open until either the user closes it or you explicitly close the form by using a statement that sets its Visible property to False.

Access 97 supports another method for dealing with forms as objects that logically tie together the details form with the main form from which you open it. In this technique, you don't reference the form itself as an object. Instead, you assign the form object to an object variable by using the New keyword. New creates a new instance of a form. An *instance of a form* is a sort of form clone. Each instance has all the same properties, methods, and controls as the original, but you can manipulate each instance separately so that each instance displays a different record. Using an instance to open a number of forms is similar to using a single QueryDef object to create a variety of different Recordsets.

The following statement displays an instance of the Line Items 01 form. You create an instance by using the New keyword with the Dim statement. The new instance of the form becomes visible after you set the Visible property of the variable to True.

```
Sub ShowDetails()
    Dim F As New Form_Line Items 01
    F.Visible = True
End Sub
```

This form object takes on the characteristics of a variable, such as duration (that is, how long a variable remains in memory) because you assign the object to a variable. If you create a variable by using the Dim statement inside a procedure, for example, the VBA destroys the variable after the procedure ends. If you look at the preceding code and apply this logic, you see that, after the procedure runs, the form opens for an instant and then disappears from the screen. Why? Because the object variable F (like any local variable) is destroyed after the procedure reaches End Sub.

How can you keep the form visible after you open it by using this technique? You find the answer by asking how you can maintain a variable after the procedure ends. Chapter 8 describes how you can maintain a variable in the following two ways:

✔ **Static.** If you create the variable as a static variable, Access 97 preserves the variable for as long as the module in which you create it remains active. The form that opens in the following example remains open, because a static variable stores the form object:

```
Sub ShowDetails()
    Static F As New Form_Line Items 01
    F.Visible = True
End Sub
```

✔ **Module level.** If you create the variable by using a Dim statement in the declarations section of the module, the variable becomes a module-level variable, which preserves the variable as long as the module remains active.

```
Option Compare Database
Option Explicit
Dim F As New Form_Line Items 01
Sub ShowDetails()
    F.Visible = True
End Sub
```

If the code module in question is a form module, Access preserves the form object variable until the main form closes — which is exactly how you want the form to behave. What's the difference between the two approaches? Static variables are preserved after the procedure has terminated, but you can access or modify them only from the same procedure in which you create them. If the variable is a module-level variable, however, you can access and manipulate the form object from any procedure in the module.

The following example is a modified version of the CtrlList_DblClick procedure that assigns the form object to a static variable. The form that the procedure opens, therefore, remains open as long as the module that contains the CtrlList_DblClick procedure remains open. Conversely, if you close the main form, the details form automatically closes because Access destroys the object variable to which you assign the form.

```
Private Sub CtrlList_DblClick(Cancel As Integer)
    Static F As New Form_Line Items 01
    With F
        .Visible = True
        .NavigationButtons = False
        .RecordSelectors = False
        .RecordSource = "Select * from [Order Details]" _
            & " Where [Order Number] = " _
```

```
            & Me![CtrlList] & ";"
        .Caption = "Order Details For Order # " _
            & Me![CtrlList]
        .Requery
    End With
End Sub
```

| Form: Calendar 03 a |

Error Handling

Defining the form as an object variable links the display of the form to the duration of the variable. The effect is that any forms you open as object variables from a main form automatically close when the main form closes.

But what happens if the user decides to manually close the details form and then tries to open that form again by double-clicking another order in the list box of the main form? An error occurs because the module can't locate the object that the variable references. In theory, if an object you assign to a variable closes, Access destroys that variable. However, the user manually closes a form that you opened as a VBA object from a procedure, Access 97 does not destroy the variable, and this creates a problem. Access thinks there is an active object variable, but the object to which that variable refers has been closed. If you try to reopen the form by creating another instance of the same object variable, Access 97 generates another error.

To handle this problem without making the user aware that a problem exists, you must create an error handler. The term *error handler* refers to the code you add to a procedure that you design to execute only if an error occurs within that procedure. Error handlers in VBA have the following general form:

```
Sub Example()
    On Error Goto Fixit '(1)
    … statements
    Exit Sub '(2)
Fixit: ' (3)
    … statements
    Resume somewhere
End Sub
```

This code contains the following three key elements:

- ✔ On Error. This statement accomplishes two tasks: First, the statement turns off the normal error handling inside Access 97. Normally, if an error occurs within a VBA module, Access 97 displays a dialog box containing a message about the error and options you can use to debug or end the procedure. The On Error statement temporarily suspends that function while the current procedure is running. The second purpose of this statement is to tell Access 97 where to find the code that needs to execute when an error occurs. The On Error statement gives Access 97 the location of that code in the form of a code *label*. The item you designate as (3) in the preceding code is an example of a label. You write a label at the beginning of a line and end the label with a colon. If an error occurs, Access 97 jumps to the first statement following the label that you specify in the On Error statement.

- ✔ Exit Sub. Normally, a procedure ends after it reaches the End Sub statement. If you include an error handler in the procedure and no error occurs, however, you need another way to end the procedure before it reaches the error handler. The Exit Sub statement immediately ends a procedure whenever the procedure encounters it. Typically, you insert the statement before the label that marks the beginning of the error handler code.

- ✔ **Labels.** You use labels to mark specific locations within a procedure. You can have as many labels in a procedure as you want. Normally, Access 97 ignores labels. Labels become significant only if a statement such as On Error specifically refers to a label. Then Access 97 jumps to the first statement following the label and begins executing the code it finds there. You use the Goto statement to get Access 97 to jump to a label location if no error takes place.

In this example, the diagram shown in Figure 11-13 outlines the strategy for the error handler. You place the error handler right after the label FormClosed. The On Error statement sets FormClosed as the label to jump to if an error occurs. In this case, the error occurs if the procedure attempts to change a property of the variable F after the user has manually closed the form that F represents.

If the form represented by F cannot be found, the program jumps to the FormClosed label. The error handler resolves the problem by specifically destroying the variable F by setting that variable equal to the keyword Nothing. Setting any object equal to Nothing destroys the variable, even if the variable is a module or static variable.

```
Set F = Nothing
```

After the Set statement executes, the procedure returns to its original state. The procedure can be allowed to continue by returning to the beginning (marked by the label TopJ), so that it can create a new instance of the form.

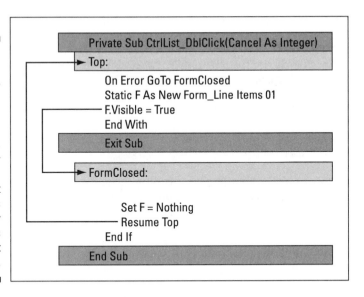

Figure 11-13:
An error-handler routine resolves the problem that occurs if the user closes a form that was originally opened as an object variable.

The following example demonstrates the code that implements the concept shown in Figure 11-13:

```
Private Sub CtrlList_DblClick(Cancel As Integer)
Top:
    On Error GoTo FormClosed
    Static F As New Form_Line Items 01
    With F
        .Visible = True
        .NavigationButtons = False
        .RecordSelectors = False
        .RecordSource = "Select * from [Order Details]" _
            & " Where [Order Number] = " _
            & Me![CtrlList] & ";"
        .Caption = "Order Details For Order # " _
            & Me![CtrlList]
        .Requery
    End With
    Exit Sub
FormClosed:
    If Err = 2467 Then
        Set F = Nothing
        Resume Top
    Else
        Exit Sub
    End If
End Sub
```

One addition to the code is the use of the Err function. Err returns a numerical code that corresponds to the type of error that occurs. In this case, the error code 2467 is the one that occurs if the user causes the problem by closing the form originally opened as an object. Because an error in any procedure may have other possible causes, the statement If Err = 2467 Then ensures that this handler executes only if that specific error takes place. Any other error simply results in the termination of the procedure.

> **Form: Calendar 03 b**

For another example of using forms as objects, see the form Calculator 01 file, which uses a form as a progress meter. The About button on the form opens a box that explains how the form works.

Part V
The Part of Tens

The 5th Wave — By Rich Tennant

"WELL HECK — I THINK THIS COULD BE YOUR PROBLEM!"

In this part . . .

Part V consists of some top ten lists that give you my favorite programming tips, my least favorite programming mistakes, and some good places on the Web to get more information about Access 97 and Access 97 programming.

Chapter 12
Top Ten Access 97 Programming Boo-Boos

- ▶ How to count records
- ▶ When to use brackets
- ▶ Problems caused by punctuation
- ▶ Dim with For...Next
- ▶ MoveNext in Do...Loop

*H*ere are ten of the mistakes that I make most often when writing Access programs.

Counting Records

After you first create a `Recordset` object, the `RecordCount` property does not accurately reflect the actual number of records in the set. The value of `RecordCount` is initially either 0, for an empty `Recordset`, or 1 for a `Recordset` that contains at least one record. To get the correct record count you must use the `MoveLast` method to force Access 97 to read through to the last record in the set. The following example uses `MoveLast` to get an accurate record count and `MoveFirst` to return to the top of the `Recordset`:

```
Dim R as Recordset, SQLText
SQLText = "Select * From Names Where State = 'CA';"
Set R = CurrentDb.OpenRecordset(SQLText)
R.MoveLast    'calculates the actual record count
R.MoveFirst   'returns to the beginning of the recordset
MsgBox "Records = " & R.RecordCount
```

Records Anyone?

If you write a procedure that uses a Recordset generated by a SQL statement, always test the Recordset to see whether it contains any records. If you attempt to apply any method, such as MoveNext or MoveLast, to an empty Recordset, Access 97 generates an error message. The statement If R.RecordCount Then is true if the Recordset contains one or more records. The following example shows how to protect your program from empty Recordsets:

```
Dim R as Recordset, SQLText
SQLText = "Select * From Names Where State = 'CA';"
Set R = CurrentDb.OpenRecordset(SQLText)
If R.RecordCount Then 'are there any records in R
    R.MoveLast
    R.MoveFirst
    statements...
Else  ' No Records
    statements...
Endif
```

Date?

A basic truth of human nature is that you're likely to create a table that has a date type field named Date. This field name is not in itself a problem. Because Access 97 contains a built-in function called Date, however, you may write code that refers to the function instead of the field. Remember to enclose references to a field named Date in brackets ([ ]). Otherwise, Access may treat the reference as a built-in function.

```
MsgBox Date   ' displays the date function value
MsgBox [Date] ' displays the contents of the date field
```

Name?

The problem of using *Name* is similar to that of the *Date* problem described in the preceding section. In this case, the possible conflict involves the Name property, which almost all objects possess. Following are two object references. The first refers to the Name property of the object R. The second is a reference to a field named Name in a Recordset object called R.

```
R.Name
R![Name] = R.Fields("Name")
```

If you want to refer to the Name field, always enclose Name in brackets ([ ]) so that Access 97 doesn't confuse it with the Name property.

Use Brackets in Function Arguments

If you create user-defined functions or use built-in functions such as DSum( ) and DLookup( ) that require table or field names as arguments, remember to enclose the names in brackets ([ ]) if the names include spaces. The first statement that follows results in an error message because the names of the field and table contain spaces; you need to enclose them in brackets. The second example is written correctly.

```
Debug.Print DSum("Total Cost","Sales Orders") 'incorrect
Debug.Print DSum("[Total Cost]","[Sales Orders]")'correct
```

Don't Use Brackets in Method Arguments

If you specify table, query, form, or report names as arguments for methods, such as the methods that the DoCmd object supports, you should not add brackets to the names. The first example that follows is incorrect, because the table name has brackets. The second example shows the correct way to refer to such an object as an argument of a method.

```
DoCmd.OpenTable "[Sales Order]" 'incorrect
DoCmd.OpenTable "Sales Order"   'correct
```

Include Spaces for SQL Statements

SQL statements require spaces after the keywords. If you use an expression to create a SQL statement by combining both literals and variables, make sure that you include spaces as part of the literal text. The first example that follows doesn't include a space inside the quotation marks after the keyword From. This omission results in an error. The second statement produces a valid SQL statement because it includes a space inside the quotation marks.

```
SQLText "Select * From" & Me![TableName]  'incorrect
SQLText "Select * From " & Me![TableName] 'correct
```

Apostrophes in Name

Many of the programs in this book use SQL statements that you store in a text variable. (My favorite name is SQLText.) You then use the variable as an argument for creating query definitions or Recordsets. The following example shows a SQL statement that uses apostrophes inside the text. These apostrophes function as the quotations.

```
SQLText = "Select * From Cust Where Name = '" _
    & Me![Key] & "';"
```

This approach works unless the item inserted by Me![Key] contains an apostrophe — for example, Joe's Plumbing. You can avoid this problem by using Chr(34) to insert the quotations in the text variable, as follows:

```
SQLText = "Select * From Cust Where Name = " & Chr(34) _
    & Me![Key] & Chr(34) & ";"
```

Dim That Counter

By default, all Access 97 modules use the Option Explicit setting (discussed in Chapter 2). Using Option Explicit is a good thing, because it eliminates errors that you may cause by making typos in variable names. Such errors could prove hard to track down during debugging.

You must use the Dim statement to declare any variable that you use in your code. This includes the counter variable you use in For...Next structures, such as the one shown in the following example. If you enter **For k = 1 to 100**, k is a local variable that you must declare by using a Dim statement. Get into the habit of adding a Dim before a For statement so that you don't get caught by an error after you try to run the procedure.

```
Dim k 'declare the counter variable
For k = 1 to 100
    statements...
    statements...
    statements...
Next
```

MoveNext in a Do ... Loop

If you work with Recordsets in your code, you'll find that you use Do...Loop structures frequently. In most cases, however, think of the Do...Loop as consisting of three, not just two, statements. What is the third statement? It is the statement that includes the MoveNext method that advances the Recordset for each cycle of the loop. If you forget this statement your loop spins off into never-never land.

```
Do Until R.Eof '(1)
    statements...
    statements...
    statements...
    statements...
    R.MoveNext(2)
Loop (3)
```

To avoid this mistake, I routinely add the MoveNext method as soon as I enter the Do statement. That way, I don't need to remember later, after the loop is full of other instructions.

Chapter 13

Top Ten Access 97 Programming Tips

*H*ere are ten (plus one) of my favorite ways to improve your Access 97 program.

Opening a Form Automatically

You can set Access 97 to automatically open a specific form after you open a particular database by using the Display Form setting in the Startup dialog box.

Open the Startup dialog box by choosing Tools⇨Startup from the menu bar. In the Display Form list box, select the name of the form you want to automatically open after the database loads.

An alternative is to create a macro that you can call `AutoExec`. You can then use the `AutoExec` macro to open a form by entering an `OpenForm` action as part of the macro.

Stopping a Form from Loading

Even if you select a Startup form or you create an `AutoExec` macro, as described in the preceding section, you can still open the database without having the form appear or having the macro execute.

Choose File⇨Open Database from the menu bar. Press and hold the Shift key and then double-click in the Open dialog box the name of the database that you want to load. Keep holding the Shift key until the database loads. The database opens normally, without any autoform opening or macro running.

Hiding Objects

You can hide specific objects (tables, queries, forms, reports, or modules) so that users can't accidentally delete or change these objects.

To designate an object as hidden, select the object name in the appropriate tab of the database window. Right-click the mouse and select Properties from the shortcut menu that appears. In the Attributes area of the Properties dialog box that appears, click the Hidden check box to place a check mark in the box.

Notice that this action causes the object's icon in the database window to turn gray. To entirely suppress the display of objects marked as hidden, choose Tools⇨Options from the menu bar. Click the View tab and then click the Hidden Objects check box in the Show area to clear the check box.

You can still use the hidden objects, but users can't see their names in the database window.

Generating a Random Number

You can use the `Rnd` function to generate random whole numbers within a specified range by using the expression shown in the following example, which defines the `RandomNumber` variable. The `High` and `Low` values define the range (including the high and low values) for which you generate numbers.

```
Dim High, Low, RandomNumber
High = 100
Low = 50
RandomNumber = Int((High - Low + 1) * Rnd + Low)
```

Generating a Letter

You can also use Rnd to produce a random sequence of letters. The following expression sets the range of random numbers from 65 to 90. These numbers are the ASCII codes for *A* through *Z*, which the Chr() function uses to convert the random numbers to random letters.

```
Dim High, Low, RandomLetter
Low = 65
High = 65 + 25
RandomLetter = Chr(Int((High - Low + 1) * Rnd + Low))
```

Dividing a String

Often a single text item contains two or more items of information with a space or special punctuation separating the items — for example, a full name written in the form *lastname, firstname*. You can use the Mid() and Instr() functions to separate the items into two separate text items by using the expressions shown in the following examples, which define the variables Front and Back. You need to set the variable Key to the character or characters that separate the items.

```
Dim Txt, Key, Front, Back
Txt = "LaFish, Walter"
Key = ", "
Front = Mid$(Txt, 1, InStr(Txt, Key) - 1)
Back = Mid$(Txt, InStr(Txt, Key) + Len(Key))
Txt = "Walter Lafish"
Key = " "
Front = Mid$(Txt, 1, InStr(Txt, Key) - 1)
Back = Mid$(Txt, InStr(Txt, Key) + Len(Key))
```

Using the OpenArgs Property

You can pass a text string to a form if you open the form by using the OpenForm method. The following statement passes the name of the current form and the current control to the form that you're opening:

```
DoCmd.OpenForm FormName:="Popup Calendar", _
    OpenArgs:=Screen.ActiveForm.Name & "/" & _
    Screen.ActiveControl.Name
```

In the open form, you can refer to the text by referring to the Me.OpenArgs object. You can find an example of how you use this object in the Calendar 04 and Popup Calendar forms of the CTRL.MDB database for Chapter 11 (on the CD that comes with this book). These forms show how you can use a popup calendar to insert a date into a field instead of typing the date manually.

Using Optional Arguments

You can provide flexibility in the use of arguments for user-defined functions and subprocedures by using the Optional keyword. The following example requires one argument and makes the second argument optional. You use the IsMissing() function to determine whether the calling procedure passes a second argument to the function. If you have no second argument, you assign the sole argument the value of 1.

```
Function HasOptions(Arg1, Optional Arg2)
    If IsMissing(Arg2) Then
        Arg2 = 1
    End If
End Function
```

See Chapter 13 for specific examples of using optional arguments.

Using With to Apply Multiple Methods to an Object

You can use the With structure to apply a series of methods and properties to an object without repeating the name of the object each time. The properties and methods execute in the order in which you list them. If the object is a `Recordset`, you can assign values to the fields by using the `Fields` method to specify the field names.

```
With R
    .AddNew
    .Fields("Number") = "1"
    .Fields("Txt") = "Hello"
    .Update
    .MoveNext
End With
```

Using LastModified

If you add new records to a `Recordset`, Access 97 doesn't automatically make a newly added record the current record. If you use the `AddNew` and `Update` methods to add a new record, you can then use the `LastModified` property of the `Recordset` to make the new record the current record. `LastModified` is equal to the bookmark of the new record. Setting the `Bookmark` property of the `Recordset` to the `LastModified` property of the same `Recordset` makes the new record the current record.

```
With R
    .AddNew
    .Update
End With
R.Bookmark = R.LastModified
```

Using AutoFormat

Access 97 comes with a set of automatic formatting options, such as Clouds, Flax, and Evergreen. You can add your own automatic formatting styles to this list.

You begin by creating a form with the formatting that you want — the font, size, color, background picture, and so on. With the form open in the Design mode, choose the Format⇨AutoFormat command from the menu bar. Click the Customize button in the dialog box that appears. To create a new format, click Create a New AutoFormat Based on the Current Form. Enter the name for the new automatic format and click OK.

You can now apply this format to existing forms or select the automatic format if you use the Form Wizard to create new forms.

Chapter 14

Top Ten Web Sites and Miscellaneous Tips

*H*ere's a quick hit list of ten (oops, *nine*) tips and online addresses you may need to know to help you along the Access programming path.

Web sites come and go, and their addresses often change with no warning. The following addresses are reliable as of the time of this writing, but are subject to change. If you can't find an address at the location I specify here, use your favorite search engine to try to track it down.

Microsoft's Access Site

What it is: Microsoft's Access site

Where to find it:

```
http://www.microsoft.com/msaccess
```

Microsoft's Office Developers Site

What it is: Microsoft's Access Developers site

Where to find it:

```
http://www.microsoft.com/accessdev/defoff.htm
```

Smart Access

What it is: Newsletters for Access developers

Where to find it:

```
http://www.pinpub.com/access/home.htm
```

Cobb Group Publications

What it is: Newsletters for Access developers

Where to find it:

```
http://www.cobb.com/ima/index.htm
```

List of User Groups

What it is: Duh! A list of Access User groups

Where to find it:

```
http://www.yahoo.com/Computerss_and_Internet/Software/
              Databases/Access/User_Groups/
```

Access User Group San Diego

What it is: The San Diego, California Access user group

Where to find it:

```
http://www.augsd.org/
```

Access User Group of New York

What it is: The New York City Access group

Where to find it:

```
http://204.97.160.61/
```

File Compatibility

Access 2.0, Access 95, and Access 97 all use different file structures. In Access 97, you must convert Access 95 or Access 2.0 databases in order to use them. Older versions of Access cannot use the databases after you convert them.

You can, however, use File⇨Get External Data to import or link to tables stored in Access 2.0 or Access 95 MDB files. This allows you to use the data with an Access 97 application and also allows users with earlier versions to access the data without upgrading their software.

Dot Operator Compatibility

When you convert a database that contains Access Basic code from Access 2.0 to Access 97, most of the code will run in Access 97. One common problem, however, involves the use of the dot operator. In Access 2.0 you can use either a ! or a dot to reference a field in a `Recordset`. Access 95 and Access 97 do not recognize this form.

Unfortunately, Access cannot convert the dot operators when it converts the modules. You must manually search and change your code to get it to run in Access 97. The following items summarize the valid forms of recordset field reference in each version.

Access 2.0:

```
R.Price, R!Price, R("Price")
```

Access 95 or 97:

```
R!Price, R("Price"), R.Fields("Price")
```

Part VI
Appendixes

In this part . . .

Microsoft publishes some special tools designed to help Access programmers develop and distribute their programs. Appendix A looks at the features of the Office Developers Edition which include tools specifically aimed at the Access 97 programmer.

Appendix B tells you all about the helpful CD-ROM included with this book. You can look here for everything from system requirements to setup instructions.

Appendix A

The Microsoft Office 97 Developer Edition Tools

· ·

*M*icrosoft now publishes a set of utility programs that provide help for people who use Access 97 to develop custom database applications. The items in the Office Developer Edition do not affect the way that you develop programs or write Access 97 Visual Basic code. The tools in this kit focus on enhancing your work after you create the actual database application.

Developer Edition Tools

Microsoft sells a product called The Microsoft Office 97 Developer Edition Tools (ODE Tools), which contains programs that help programmers create and distribute Access 97 applications. Here's a look at what's included in the Developer Edition:

- **The Setup Wizard.** This component is an Access 97 program that creates Windows 95-style setup programs that you use to distribute the Access 97 applications you develop.

- **The Microsoft Help Workshop.** Help Workshop is a program that you can use create Windows 95 Help files.

- **The Replication Manager.** The Microsoft Replication Manager helps you create copies (or *replicas*) of a database and disperse the copies to other users. Replication Manager also later synchronizes all the copies to reflect changes that you make to the data and database structure among the copies you distribute.

- **Win32API Viewer.** The Windows 95 and Windows NT operating systems provide programmers the ability to integrate Windows 95/NT functions within VBA applications. The Viewer provides `Declare` statements, constants, and custom data types for all the functions available through the Windows Application Programming Interface (API). You need to be familiar with Windows 95/NT programming concepts to use this feature.

✔ **SourceSafe add-in.** The Microsoft Office 97 Developer Edition Tools provide a software component that integrates various source code control products, including Microsoft Visual SourceSafe, into Access 97. SourceSafe is a program (supplied with Visual Basic and Visual C++ developer editions) that protects and manages complex programming projects.

The ODE also includes two documents, Replication Manager Whitepaper and Source Code Control Whitepaper, that explain the concepts involved in Replication and SourceSafe. (A *whitepaper*, by the way, is a document that explains exactly how terrific a new product really is.)

The Setup Wizard

The Setup Wizard is probably the most useful tool in the ODE. The Setup Wizard provides step-by-step guidance through the process of creating a professional quality Setup program that helps users install your database application on their computers.

Even if you're a beginner at programming, you may find that other users want to use or even purchase the databases you create. The Setup Wizard that comes with the Microsoft Office 97 Developer Edition Tools generates *setup packages*. A setup package contains all the files anyone needs to run a Setup program that installs your application on another computer.

You can distribute the following two types of Access 97 programs by using the Setup Wizard:

✔ **Access 97 MDB applications.** The program you create is an Access 97 MDB file. To use this program, users must have a full version of Access. The Setup Wizard creates a setup program that installs the MDB file and other supporting files on the users' computers. Users can't run the application, however, unless Access 97 is installed on their computers.

✔ **Runtime applications.** If you want to distribute your application to users who don't have Access 97 installed on their systems, you can create a Setup program that installs both your MDB files and a limited version of Access 97 called *Runtime*. Runtime enables other users to run your application, but they cannot make any modifications to the application. Microsoft permits owners of the ODE to distribute the Access 97 Runtime program free of charge as they distribute their Access 97 MDB files.

About the Access 97 Runtime program

Unlike applications created with full programming languages, such as Visual Basic or Visual C++, applications that you create by using Microsoft Access 97 are not stand-alone applications. Others can use Access 97 programs (which you store in MDB files) only if they first install the Access 97 program on their computers.

To enable distribution of the Access 97 programs that you store in MDB files, the ODE contains Runtime, the limited version of Access 97 Runtime enables users to access your programs but does not support all the features of the full Access 97 program.

Unlike the full version of Access 97 that you use to create the application, you can't use the Runtime program by itself. Runtime's only function is to enable users to access the MDB file you distribute along with the Runtime program. Although Access 97 Runtime applications are identical in most respects to applications that run under the full Microsoft Access 97 program, some differences can affect how you design and develop your application. Runtime differs from Access 97 in the following areas:

- The database, macro, and module windows and all design views, including the filter windows, are hidden in Runtime.

- Runtime doesn't include built-in toolbars. You can include your own customized toolbars if you want to add them to your application.

- Access 97 Help is not available in Runtime. If you want to include Help, you must create your own Help file by using the Help Workshop.

- Some windows, menus, shortcut menus, and commands are hidden or disabled in Runtime to prevent users from making changes to your application.

- Access 97 error messages are not available in Runtime. If an error occurs while the application is running under Runtime, the program shuts down the application without warning. For this reason, you need to write a VBA error handler to account for errors that may occur during Runtime execution.

- Certain keystrokes and key combinations are not available in Runtime, such as Ctrl+Break (which halts execution of a VBA procedure), Ctrl+N (which creates a new database), and Ctrl+G (which displays the Debug window).

Using the Setup Wizard

The ODE creates a Start menu icon for the Setup Wizard. After you start the Setup Wizard, the Wizard displays the opening screen. You then have the following two options:

✔ Create a new setup specification.

✔ Load a setup you previously created and saved. If you've run the Setup Wizard before, you can rerun the Wizard to update the Setup files with any changes you may have made to the application.

If you decide to create a new setup, the next screen that appears is the Add File screen. You use this screen to specify the files that you want to include in the setup package. Include at least one MDB file in this list. You are free to include any other file of any type. If, for example, your application creates HTML files (such as the procedures in Chapter 12), you may want to include graphics files that the HTML pages use along with the MDB files. You must designate one of the MDB files as the application's main file. The *main file* is the one that automatically loads after you start the application.

Include also any Help files and custom controls that you want to distribute with your application. You can also specify where on the user's computer to store each of the files that you include with your application. The Setup program supports three general locations:

✔ **AppPath.** The directory where the user chooses to install the application.

✔ **WinPath.** The Windows directory on the user's computer. Notice that the Windows directory is the one from which Windows is running. This directory need not be named Windows.

✔ **WinSysPath.** The system directory in which you store the Windows system files.

You can also specify whether you want to compress the files. Compressed files take up less space than normal files, but creating and installing compressed files takes a bit longer. And after you compress a file, no one can access that file until you decompress the file. If you want to make any last-minute changes to a file (such as a README.TXT file), you can't do so while the file is compressed.

The Setup program decompresses the files as part of the setup process. If you're going to run Setup from floppy disks, you should probably compress the files. If you're using a medium for which space isn't an issue — for example, a Zip disk, a CD, or network shared directories — you many want to save time by not compressing the files.

In addition to the Access 97 MDB files that contain your application, you may want to include some of the following types of files in your setup package:

✔ **ActiveX controls.** Each ActiveX control that you use on a form represents a program you store in a separate file from your database application. The Calendar control that comes with Access 97, for example, resides in the MSCAL.OCX file, which you store in the WINDOWS\ SYSTEM folder, as you do all ActiveX controls. If you want to distribute an application that contains a form containing an ActiveX control, you need to include that control in your Setup package. If you don't include the OCX file, the form can't display the ActiveX control.

How did I know that the Calendar control corresponds to the file MSCAL.OCX? I made a good guess. You have no easy way to figure out which OCX file corresponds to a given ActiveX control other than by the filename. A more cumbersome but surer method is to run the Regedit program and use the Edit➪Find command to search the system registry for a data item that matches the Class property of the control — for example, MSCAL.Calendar.7. You find that data in a key called ProgID. Above that key is another called InprocServer32. Click that key. The default setting in the right window displays the OCX filename.

✔ **README.TXT.** You may want to include a text file that provides users with information about the application.

✔ **Help Files.** If you create custom-designed Help files (HLP) for your application, you need to include those files in the Setup package.

Notice that Access 97 copies any files you add to the list in the Setup Wizard into the Setup package. The original files do not change.

Adding Start menu icons

After you select the files you want to include in the Setup package, you click the Next button of the Setup Wizard to display the panel shown in Figure A-1. You use this panel to specify Start menu shortcuts you want to add to the user's system after the user installs the application. You can add general icons (those that can execute any program) or database shortcuts with special optional settings available only for Access 97 databases — for example, opening a database in shared or exclusive mode. These icons are always added to the Programs submenu of the Start menu.

You use the Setup Wizard's next panel to specify registry keys that you want to add to the user's registry after the user installs the program. This option is for advanced users or developers who are familiar with the Windows 95 registry and how to use it.

Office components

You use the fourth panel in the Setup Wizard to add key Office 97 components to the Setup package, as shown in Figure A-2. Here you can include the Access 97 Runtime program in the package so that users who do not have Access 97 can still run your application. You can also select ISAM drivers that enable your application to connect to non-Access 97 files, such as Excel 97 or dBASE files.

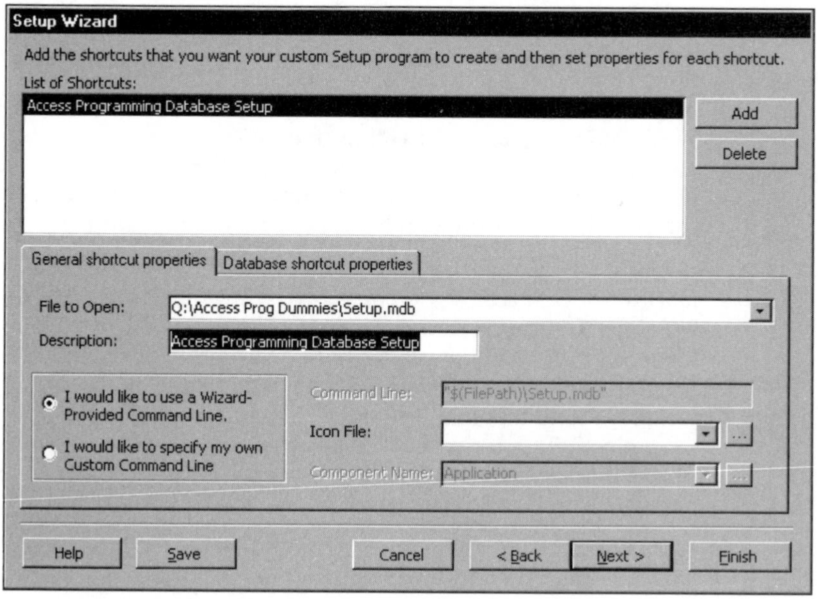

Figure A-1:
Setup can
add icons
to the Start
menu.

You use the fifth panel of the Setup Wizard to give the application a name, set the version number — for example, version 1.0 — and select the default folder into which the application is installed. You can specify a folder name for systems that support long filenames (Windows 95 and Windows NT) and a different folder name for systems that use only short filenames (Windows 3.1 and 3.11).

Run after Setup

You use the sixth panel in the Setup Wizard to specify a program or command that you want to execute after the Setup program finishes running. The Setup program I used to install the sample databases supplied with this book, for example, automatically loads the README.TXT file into the Notepad after the Setup program ends.

This panel displays the following two settings:

✔ **Run the following file.** Use this option to automatically start one of the databases in your Setup package.

✔ **Edit or enter the command line.** This option enables you to enter a command line, such as the line you'd enter in the Start⇨Run dialog box. The following example loads the README.TXT file into the Notepad program following Setup:

```
Notepad.exe "$(AppPath)\Readme.txt"
```

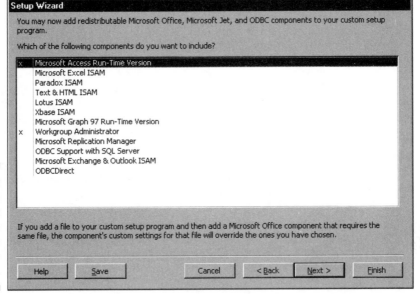

Figure A-2:
Additional
files that
you can
include in
the Setup
package.

The $(AppPath) part of the line is a special placeholder that the Setup program replaces with the pathname of the folder into which the user installs the program. This placeholder ensures that Notepad can find the README.TXT file without regard to which folder the user selects for the application. Setup recognizes other paths, such as $(Winpath) for the Window folder and $(WinSysPath) for the Windows System folder.

Types of packages

The seventh and final panel of the Setup Wizard enables you to select the type of Setup package you want to create and where Access 97 creates the package. You can create any of the following three types of Setup packages:

✔ **Floppy disks.** This option generates a Setup package that Access 97 divides into folders, each of which contains a set of files that fit onto a single 1.44 MB floppy disk. The minimum number of disks is three. Runtime applications use a minimum of five floppy disks. The program stores files for each disk in a separate folder, beginning with the folders Disk1, Disk2, and so on. After Access 97 generates these packages, you can create a set of distribution floppies by copying the contents of each folder to a separate floppy disk. Floppy disk files are always compressed.

✔ **Network (CD).** This Setup generates a single set of files stored in a single folder. You can copy this type of Setup to a high-capacity removable disk (for example, a Zip drive). Another method is to write the Setup to a CD by using a CD-ROM writer, and then run it from a shared drive or a network. These files aren't compressed, so you can access (or copy) the files directly from the Setup package.

> ✔ **Compressed network.** This type of package is similar to the Network
> (CD) package except you compress the files. Compressed files take up
> less space than the original files but you can't use the files directly from
> the Setup package. The files automatically decompress, however, as the
> Setup program installs the files on a new computer.

If you use compression for a floppy or network Setup package, you can have
the Setup Wizard store a copy of the compressed files separately from the
Setup package. This option shortens the time you need to generate a new
package if you decide to make changes to the Setup, such as changing the
name of a Start menu icon or the command to run after Setup finishes. Such
changes do not require the program to recompress the main program files. If
you alter the contents of one of the main files in the package, you must
recompress the entire package.

The Replication Manager

Database replication was one of the key features added to Access 95, and
that feature is further enhanced in Access 97. The ODE contains a utility
program called the *Replication Manager* that provides a graphical interface
to help you create, distribute, and synchronize sets of database replicas.

The Replication Manager's primary advantage is that the utility can coordinate, control, and schedule synchronization among many replicas. In
contrast, Access 97 performs synchronization only between pairs of databases at a time.

What is replication?

The rapid growth of network computing (LANs, WANs, Internet, and intranets,
plus mobile and dial-up networks) makes having a single, centralized database that all users can access at all times increasingly difficult.

Even a modest-sized business, for example, commonly has some users with
laptop computers that they connect to the network when in the office and
disconnect when they leave the office to work in the field or at home. With
applications such as word processors or spreadsheets, the lack of a network
connection is not critical. But what about a database? One solution is to put
a copy of the database (or some portion of it) onto the laptop computers so
that these users can work with the data when they're not connected to the
network.

By using replication, users can have the benefits of a centralized data repository without the limitations that access to a single central database imposes. The following list describes some of replication's key benefits:

- ✔ Coordination of data between users working at different locations and at different times

- ✔ Automatic distribution of fixes, new features, and updates to all users of database copies

- ✔ Improved network performance by enabling users to work with local copies of databases instead of requiring all users to access the same physical database

- ✔ Capability to run backups without needing to take down the system or open the database in an exclusive mode

- ✔ Reduced network traffic (or dial-in time) because you must exchange only changed or new records if you update the copy

Design masters and replicas

Access 97 replication involves the following two types of copies of a given database:

- ✔ **Design master.** The original database. The original becomes a design master after you choose the Tools⇨Replication⇨Create Replica menu command. In the design master, you can change or add to the query, form, report, macro, and module objects. These changes automatically feed to the copies after you synchronize the design master with the copies.

- ✔ **Replicas.** Copies of the design master database. You can add to, change, or delete from the data in the table objects of a replica, but you can't change the designs of the query, form, report, macro, or module objects.

After you synchronize the master and replicas, changes to the query, form, report, macro, and module objects in the master flow out to all the replicas. Changes to the data in the tables flow between all replicas and the master as necessary to ensure that all users see the changes made by any other users.

Replication fields

To implement replication, Access 97 must alter the structure of the tables to include special fields that the replication feature uses to manage the synchronization of the master and its replicas. The program adds three fields (GUID, Lineage, and Generation fields) to the table. (*GUID* stands for Global Unique IDentifier. Some also use the term *UUID*, or Universal Unique IDentifier, to describe these values.) Access 97 uses these values to create *uniqueness* among all the records in all the replicas of the same database master.

The program generates GUID values by using the network node ID number, a date/time value, a value from the system clock, plus a version value. Access 97 uses the GUID values to resolve conflicts (where possible) among the data stored in each of the replicas.

Creating master and replica sets

You can create a design master and replica set from any Access 97 MDB by using the Tools⇨Replication⇨Create Replica menu command. The command converts the original database into a design master database. You can modify all the objects in the master. This operation also makes a copy of the database, called *Replica of database*, which enables you to make changes to the contents of the tables. You cannot, however, make changes to the table design or to the design of other objects, such as queries, forms, reports, macros, or modules.

After you create a master and replica set, you can make additional copies of the replica for distribution to other computers. Make the copies by using the Explorer to copy and paste the MDB files or by using the Tools⇨ Database Utilities⇨Compact Database menu command.

After you open a database that's part of a master and replica set (either the master or a replica), the Tools⇨Replication menu provides a new command, Synchronize Now, that enables you to exchange updates with another database in the replica set. If synchronization takes place between two replicas, they exchange only data updates. If synchronization takes place between a replica and the design master, changes made to the queries, forms, reports, macros, and modules in the design master transfer to the replica in addition to the exchange of data updates.

Using the Replication Manager

The Replication Manager employs a graphical user interface that displays at a glance the relationships among the various replicas.

The following list describes key features of the Replication Manager:

- ✔ Visual setup and maintenance enables you to use the Replication Manager's graphical interface to create or add new replicas to a set, create a design master, and display dialog boxes that contain settings that affect replication sets.

- ✔ You can view in a dialog box a list of objects in any of the databases in the replica set (the same information that appears in the database window in Access 97) without loading the entire Access 97 program.

- ✔ You can schedule exchanges between replicas so that data exchange takes place without user attendance at regular intervals.

✔ You can force immediate synchronization with remote replicas by means of a point-and-shoot command interface — for example, right-click a replica icon and choose the Synchronize Now menu command.

✔ Direct and indirect exchanges accommodate mobile users who rarely connect to the network. Laptop users, for example, can exchange data with another replica on the network. Later, the Replication Manager picks up and exchanges those changes with other replicas and the master.

✔ The Replication Manager supports replication over the Internet.

✔ You can set data exchanges for send only, receive only, or send and receive.

The Synchronizer

The Synchronizer is an *agent* type program that performs data exchanges between replicas in the background with user intervention. The Synchronizer works with the Replication Manager to schedule automatic exchanges between replicas.

Programmers use the term *agent* to describe a program that automatically performs scheduled tasks in the background after requiring the user to initiate the operation. Many e-mail programs, for example, automatically dial your Internet mail server and download any incoming mail on a regular basis.

After you define a synchronization schedule, the Synchronizer can automatically load as part of the Windows Start Up program list. This situation ensures that synchronization takes place automatically.

The Help Workshop

Help refers to the Window Help files (HLP), which are the standard form of hypertext that people use on computers that run Windows 95. Almost all commercially sold programs include some form of HLP file that contains information about the program and how to use it, plus tips and warnings.

After you create an Access 97 application, you may want to create a custom-designed Help file for that program. This is a three-step process:

1. Create the Help text.

You create the actual text that appears on the Help screens in a Word 97 document that you save in the Rich Text Format (RTF). Help documents must follow a specific format. Each Help screen is a separate page. At the top of each page are one or more notes that define various characteristics of the Help screen, such as its title, keywords by which you can locate the screen during a search, and the context ID.

2. Assign Context IDs to each Help screen.

The *Context ID* is a number that an application such as Access 97 uses to call a specific Help screen. You can use the Context ID to associate a specific Access 97 form with a specific Help screen to create context-sensitive Help. To coordinate the Help file with the forms and controls in your Access 97 application, you must develop a plan for using the context IDs.

3. Add Context IDs to the Help Context ID.

Each form and control on a form has a Help Context ID property. Set this property to the Context ID of the Help screen that you want to appear after the user presses the F1 key.

The *Help Workshop* is a program that comes with the ODE to help you create two of the three elements that you need to create a custom-designed Help file (the Help Project and Help Contents files). The following list describes those three elements:

✔ **Help screen text files.** You create the actual screen text that Help displays in a Word 97 document (or in any word processor that supports RTF). Help documents follow a special set of formatting rules that involve the use of special footnotes. The Help Workshop does not provide any tools that aid in the creation of the Help text files.

If you want to purchase a product that helps you automate the process of creating the Help text files as well as the Help Project and Help Contents files, you may want to look at the popular RoboHELP 95, from Blue Sky Software Corp., La Jolla, Calif.

✔ **Help Project file.** The *Help Project file* (HPJ) is a text file that contains specially formatted settings that aid the Help Compiler program (HCW.EXE) in generating Windows Help files (HLP). The Help Project file defines the size, shape, and color of Help windows, the fonts they use, the opening contents screen, the location of graphics files that you include in the Help file, and the level and type of data compression necessary. The Help Workshop enables you to generate an HPJ file by making selections from various dialog boxes instead of typing command lines manually.

✔ **Help Contents file.** In Windows 95, Microsoft added a new feature to Windows Help — the *contents display*, which displays a table-of-contents list that organizes the Help topics as they'd appear in a printed document such as a book. You implement this feature by creating a separate file (CNT) that organizes the topics in the Help file (HLP) in a table-of-contents format. The use of a separate CNT file (instead of integrating the table-of-contents feature into the HLP file) enables Windows 95 to use older-style Windows 3.1 Help files directly. The Help Workshop provides a special dialog box that enables you to create a Help Contents file, as shown in Figure A-3.

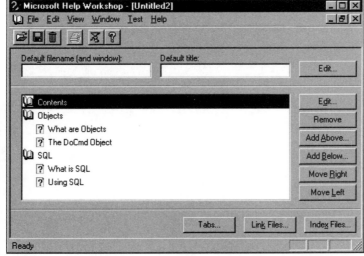

Figure A-3:
The Help
Workshop
dialog box
that you use
to create a
contents
file.

The Help Workshop also contains the following additional Help utility programs:

✔ **Hotspot Editor.** The *Hotspot Editor* program (SHED.EXE) enables you to define portions of a single graphics image as *hotspots* for links to other topics or to execute macro actions, such as printing Help information.

✔ **Multiple Resolution Bitmap Compiler.** You use the *Multiple Resolution Bitmap Compiler* program (MRBC.EXE) to create bitmap images that you can display at different resolutions on different systems. Creating multiple-resolution images ensures that the images display at a high quality on systems that use screen configurations that are different from yours.

Appendix B

About the CD

*F*irst things first: To run the CD included with this book, your system must first meet the following minimum requirements:

- ✔ **Computer:** A 486-based or higher system with a CD-ROM drive
- ✔ **Operating system:** Windows 95 or Windows NT 3.51 (or higher)
- ✔ **Application:** Access 97
- ✔ **Free hard disk space:** 32.3MB
- ✔ **RAM:** 16MB

To help you to understand the Access 97 programming examples in this book, the accompanying CD includes a set of 13 database files — one database file for each of the first 11 chapters of the book and two files that accompany the bonus chapters on the CD. (*Note:* In Access 97, a database file ends with the extension MDB.)

To use these examples, you must copy the files from the CD to another drive. Why do you need to copy the databases to use them? Well, you can load these databases directly from the CD if you want. You can't, however, save onto the CD any changes you make to the databases because CDs are read-only. With almost any other type of file (such as word processing or spreadsheet files), you could get around this problem by using the File⇨Save As command to save any changes to your hard drive. Unfortunately, because Access 97 database files are so complex, you can't use the File⇨Save As approach. Instead, you must copy the entire database file before you open that file if you want to save your changes, additions, and deletions.

I've organized the data on the CD by chapter. Each of the first 11 programming chapters has a folder containing the MDB file that matches the examples in that chapter. Additionally, I've included folders called CD1 and CD2 that correspond to the bonus chapters on the CD. The CD folders contain additional supporting files that relate to the topics of those chapters.

If you're familiar with Access 97 and Windows 95, you can use Windows Explorer to copy the files you need on your own.

A two-step Setup program provides an alternative method for copying the files to your hard disk. The first step runs a standard Windows 95-style setup program that creates a new menu called *Access Programming* on the Programs submenu of your Start menu. The new menu contains a command called Install Databases.

After the Setup program creates the Install Databases command, you can perform the second step by using this command to run an Access 97 database program. This program allows you to select one or more of the supplied databases to be copied to your hard drive. At the same time, the program adds a command to the Access Programming submenu for each database that you install.

You don't need to install all the databases at one time. You can use the Install Databases command as many times as you like to install additional databases.

Using the CD Menu

To use the Install Databases program, you must first run the Setup program on the CD. To do so, follow these steps:

1. **Place the CD in your CD drive.**

2. **Double-click the My Computer icon to open the My Computer window.**

3. **Double-click the icon for your CD drive.**

   The CD displays a menu with five buttons, as shown in Figure B-1.

   • **About this CD.** Use this button to display information about the CD and how to use it.

Figure B-1: The CD's main interface menu.

- **Run Database Setup Program.** Use this button to start the setup program that will install the Install Databases program on your hard drive. This procedure is detailed in the following sections.

- **Install Adobe Acrobat Reader.** In order to read and print the bonus chapters on the CD you need to install a copy of Adobe Acrobat Reader. Use this button to install that program if you don't already have one.

- **View Bonus Folder.** Use this button to open the BONUS folder on the CD that contains the two bonus chapters.

- **Exit.** Exit the CD menu.

If you want to view the two bonus chapters (described above), you have to first install Adobe Acrobat Reader (unless, of course, you already have Adobe Acrobat installed). This program enables you to see the chapter in all its laid-out glory, complete with all the cool icons, fonts, and figures. Feel free to print these chapters out and stick 'em in the back of this book for safekeeping. To install Adobe Acrobat Reader follow these steps:

1. **Click the Install Adobe Acrobat Reader button.**

   The InstallShield dialog box appears.

2. **Click Yes.**

   A Welcome dialog box appears.

3. **Click Next.**

   You see a Software License Agreement dialog box.

4. **After carefully reading the agreement, click yes.**

   The Choose Destination Location dialog box appears.

5. **Click Next to install Adobe Acrobat Reader in the default directory. (You may click Browse if you'd rather install Adobe Acrobat Reader in a different directory.)**

   The Setup Complete dialog box leaps into view.

6. **To view the Readme file and complete the installation, click the Finish button. (If you do not want to view the Readme file, click in the box next to the Display Acrobat Reader 3.0 Readme file option to remove the checkmark.)**

   The Adobe Acrobat Reader 3.0 Readme file appears.

7. **Click the Close button.**

   The Adobe Acrobat 3.0 Setup dialog box appears.

8. **Click OK.**

That's it. You've finished! Adobe Acrobat Reader 3.0 is added to your Start menu.

Running the Database Setup Program

To use the Install Databases program, you must first run the Setup program on the CD. To do so, follow these steps:

1. **Place the CD in your drive.**

2. **Double-click on the My Computer icon.**

3. **Double-click the icon for your CD drive.**

4. **When the CD menu appears, click on the Run Database Setup Program button.**

5. **After the Welcome dialog box appears, click Continue.**

    The next dialog box that appears tells you that the files you're copying are going into the Access Programming folder on drive C.

6. **Click OK to continue.**

    The Setup program then displays the dialog box for installing the Setup database, as shown in Figure B-2.

Figure B-2:
The Setup program dialog box.

7. **Click the Install icon.**

8. **After the files copy to your hard drive, click OK to end the Setup program.**

    After you finish installing the database, the README.TXT file appears. This file contains instructions about using the Setup database, which duplicate the instructions in this section, plus some tips about using the sample databases.

Using the Setup Database

The Setup program that the preceding section discusses installs only a single database called SETUP.MDB. You can install the databases for the chapters by using the program that the SETUP.MDB file contains. You can access this program by using the Start menu command that the Setup program creates. Just follow these steps:

1. **Click the Windows 95 Start button to open the Start menu.**

2. **Click Programs to open the Programs menu.**

3. **Click Access Programming to open the submenu.**

4. **Click Install Databases to run the Setup database program.**

The program displays the Setup database form, as shown in Figure B-3.

If your screen displays the setup database program, then skip the following steps and continue on to the checklist at the end of this appendix.

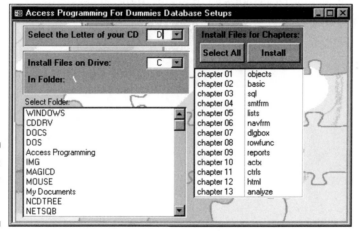

Figure B-3: The Setup database form.

If, after grinding and whirring for a few seconds, your computer protests and spits out an error message, you can manually install the databases from the Access Programming CD by following these steps:

1. **Start Windows Explorer by clicking Start⇨Programs⇨Windows Explorer.**

2. **Click the + sign next to the Acc_prog CD icon.**

3. **Click the + sign next to the APD folder.**

4. Drag the desired chapter folders to the Access Programming folder on your hard disk.

The Setup database form contains the following options:

- ✔ **Select the Letter of your CD.** If your CD drive is not D, select the correct letter designation for your CD drive.

- ✔ **Install Files on Drive.** If you want to store the files on a drive other than C, select the letter of that drive.

- ✔ **Select Folder.** Select from this list the folder in which you want to install the databases. By default, the databases copy to a folder named C:\ACCESS PROGRAMMING.

- ✔ **Install Files for Chapters.** Click in this list the names of the chapters you want to install. Each time you click a chapter name, you toggle the item from selected to unselected. The Select All button selects all 13 databases.

After you select the chapters you want to install, click the Install button. The program automatically terminates after the database installation is complete. The program adds a command to the Access Programming menu for each database that you select to install.

Index

• W •

• Y •

• Z •

IDG BOOKS WORLDWIDE, INC.

END-USER LICENSE AGREEMENT

Read This. You should carefully read these terms and conditions before opening the software packet(s) included with this book ("Book"). This is a license agreement ("Agreement") between you and IDG Books Worldwide, Inc. ("IDGB"). By opening the accompanying software packet(s), you acknowledge that you have read and accept the following terms and conditions. If you do not agree and do not want to be bound by such terms and conditions, promptly return the Book and the unopened software packet(s) to the place you obtained them for a full refund.

1. **License Grant.** IDGB grants to you (either an individual or entity) a nonexclusive license to use one copy of the enclosed software program(s) (collectively, the "Software") solely for your own personal or business purposes on a single computer (whether a standard computer or a workstation component of a multiuser network). The Software is in use on a computer when it is loaded into temporary memory (i.e., RAM) or installed into permanent memory (e.g., hard disk, CD-ROM, or other storage device). IDGB reserves all rights not expressly granted herein.

2. **Ownership.** IDGB is the owner of all right, title, and interest, including copyright, in and to the compilation of the Software recorded on the disk(s)/CD-ROM. Copyright to the individual programs on the disk(s)/CD-ROM is owned by the author or other authorized copyright owner of each program. Ownership of the Software and all proprietary rights relating thereto remain with IDGB and its licensors.

3. **Restrictions on Use and Transfer.**

    (a) You may only (i) make one copy of the Software for backup or archival purposes, or (ii) transfer the Software to a single hard disk, provided that you keep the original for backup or archival purposes. You may not (i) rent or lease the Software, (ii) copy or reproduce the Software through a LAN or other network system or through any computer subscriber system or bulletin-board system, or (iii) modify, adapt, or create derivative works based on the Software.

    (b) You may not reverse engineer, decompile, or disassemble the Software. You may transfer the Software and user documentation on a permanent basis, provided that the transferee agrees to accept the terms and conditions of this Agreement and you retain no copies. If the Software is an update or has been updated, any transfer must include the most recent update and all prior versions.

4. **Restrictions on Use of Individual Programs.** You must follow the individual requirements and restrictions detailed for each individual program in the "About the CD" appendix of this Book. These limitations are contained in the individual license agreements recorded on the disk(s)/CD-ROM. These restrictions may include a requirement that after using the program for the period of time specified in its text, the user must pay a registration fee or discontinue use. By opening the Software packet(s), you will be agreeing to abide by the licenses and restrictions for these individual programs. None of the material on this disk(s) or listed in this Book may ever be distributed, in original or modified form, for commercial purposes.

5. **Limited Warranty.**

    (a) IDGB warrants that the Software and disk(s)/CD-ROM are free from defects in materials and workmanship under normal use for a period of sixty (60) days from the date of purchase of this Book. If IDGB receives notification within the warranty period of defects in materials or workmanship, IDGB will replace the defective disk(s)/CD-ROM.

(b) IDGB AND THE AUTHOR OF THE BOOK DISCLAIM ALL OTHER WARRANTIES, EXPRESS OR IMPLIED, INCLUDING WITHOUT LIMITATION IMPLIED WARRANTIES OF MERCHANTABILITY AND FITNESS FOR A PARTICULAR PURPOSE, WITH RESPECT TO THE SOFTWARE, THE PROGRAMS, THE SOURCE CODE CONTAINED THEREIN, AND/ OR THE TECHNIQUES DESCRIBED IN THIS BOOK. IDGB DOES NOT WARRANT THAT THE FUNCTIONS CONTAINED IN THE SOFTWARE WILL MEET YOUR REQUIREMENTS OR THAT THE OPERATION OF THE SOFTWARE WILL BE ERROR FREE.

(c) This limited warranty gives you specific legal rights, and you may have other rights which vary from jurisdiction to jurisdiction.

6. **Remedies.**

(a) IDGB's entire liability and your exclusive remedy for defects in materials and workmanship shall be limited to replacement of the Software, which may be returned to IDGB with a copy of your receipt at the following address: Disk Fulfillment Department, Attn: Access 97 Programming For Windows For Dummies, IDG Books Worldwide, Inc., 7260 Shadeland Station, Ste. 100, Indianapolis, IN 46256, or call 1-800-762-2974. Please allow 3–4 weeks for delivery. This Limited Warranty is void if failure of the Software has resulted from accident, abuse, or misapplication. Any replacement Software will be warranted for the remainder of the original warranty period or thirty (30) days, whichever is longer.

(b) In no event shall IDGB or the author be liable for any damages whatsoever (including without limitation damages for loss of business profits, business interruption, loss of business information, or any other pecuniary loss) arising from the use of or inability to use the Book or the Software, even if IDGB has been advised of the possibility of such damages.

(c) Because some jurisdictions do not allow the exclusion or limitation of liability for consequential or incidental damages, the above limitation or exclusion may not apply to you.

7. **U.S. Government Restricted Rights.** Use, duplication, or disclosure of the Software by the U.S. Government is subject to restrictions stated in paragraph (c) (1) (ii) of the Rights in Technical Data and Computer Software clause of DFARS 252.227-7013, and in subparagraphs (a) through (d) of the Commercial Computer — Restricted Rights clause at FAR 52.227-19, and in similar clauses in the NASA FAR supplement, when applicable.

8. **General.** This Agreement constitutes the entire understanding of the parties and revokes and supersedes all prior agreements, oral or written, between them and may not be modified or amended except in a writing signed by both parties hereto which specifically refers to this Agreement. This Agreement shall take precedence over any other documents that may be in conflict herewith. If any one or more provisions contained in this Agreement are held by any court or tribunal to be invalid, illegal, or otherwise unenforceable, each and every other provision shall remain in full force and effect.

Notes

Notes

Notes

Notes

Notes

Notes

Notes

Notes

Notes

Notes

Notes

Notes

Notes

Notes

Notes

Notes

Access 97 For Windows For Dummies
CD-ROM Installation Instructions

To use the CD that came with this book, follow these instructions:

1. Place the CD in your CD-ROM drive.

2. Double-click on the My Computer icon.

3. Double-click on the icon for your CD-ROM drive.

4. Click on the menu button of the task you want to perform.

See Appendix B for more information about using this CD.